CONTACT
Customer Service
in the Hospitality
and Tourism Industry

CONTACT
Customer Service in the Hospitality and Tourism Industry

DONALD M. DAVIDOFF

PRENTICE HALL CAREER AND TECHNOLOGY
Upper Saddle River, New Jersey 07458

Library of Congress Catolging-in-Publication Data

Davidoff, Donald M.
    Contact : customer service in the hospitality and tourism industry
  / Donald M. Davidoff
       p.   cm.

    Includes bibliographical references and index.
    ISBN 0-13-808916-7
    1. Hospitality industry—Customer services.   2. Tourist trade-
-Customer services.   I. Title.
TX911.3.C8D38 1994
647.94'068—dc20

Acquisitions editor: Robin Baliszewski
Editorial/production supervision and
    interior design: Maria McColligan
Copyeditor: Barbara Zeiders
Cover design: Laura Ierandi
Production coordinator: Ed O'Dougherty

 Published by Prentice Hall Career and Technology
Prentice-Hall, Inc.

A Pearson Education Company
Upper Saddle River, NJ 07458

Printed in the United States of America
10

ISBN 0-13-808916-7

Prentice-Hall International (UK) Limited,London
Prentice-Hall of Australia Pty. Limited, Sydney
Prentice-Hall Canada Inc., Toronto
Prentice-Hall Hispanoamericana, S.A., Mexico
Prentice-Hall of India Private Limited, New Delhi
Prentice-Hall of Japan, Inc., Tokyo
Pearson Education Asia Pte. Ltd., Singapore
Editora Prentice-Hall do Brasil, Ltda., Rio de Janeiro

**Dedicated to all customer-contact employees
who toil in anonymity everyday to exceed
their customers' expectations**

CONTENTS

3   THE LAWS OF SERVICE   30

PART 2   THE SERVICE ENVIRONMENT: ROLES AND RELATIONSHIPS   39

4   THE PLAYERS   41

5   THE ENVIRONMENT   58

10 PERSONAL DEVELOPMENT   151

PART 4 INTERNAL SERVICE   169

11 INTERNAL CUSTOMERS AND SUPPLIERS   171

12 PRINCIPLES AND PRACTICES OF INTERNAL SERVICE: THE KEY TO QUALITY   180

PREFACE

"Service" has become a buzzword for businesses in the 1990s. This is particularly true for companies whose only real products are services, like those in the hospitality and tourism industries. Hardly a day goes by that managers and executives in these companies don't see an article about service in a newspaper, receive mail about seminars on managing service companies, or read the latest book about how the one thing that separates successful companies from struggling ones is their ability to deliver excellent service.

Universally, these books decry the inability of our education and training systems to teach existing and future workers how to deliver good service. They emphasize the importance of selecting service-oriented employees and then training them how to provide customer service. Yet none of these books actually discuss specifically what employees who come into contact with customers should and should not do.

This book addresses that deficiency. It looks at service from the perspective of those who deliver it—not just those who manage it. Virtually everyone who graduates from a vocational school, a two-year college program, or a four-year college program in hospitality and/or tourism enters the job market in a position that will require them to interact with customers. This book provides them with the basic knowledge and skills necessary to perform well. It also serves as an excellent foundation for them when they move into supervisory and management positions that require them to coach and teach other employees about service.

Writing a book about customer service in the hospitality and tourism industry is no small task. Service as an area worthy of study independent of traditional courses in business, finance, operations, and sales is relatively new. There is no established lexicon. In fact, each segment of the industry has its own term for "customers." Hotels call them "guests," airlines call them "passengers," and travel agents call them "clients." And no one has a consistent term to designate employees who work with customers. This book refers to them as "customer-contact employees." Whether a concierge or front-desk person at a hotel or a guide for a tour operator, the common bond is that all these employees are responsible for making their customers' contact with them and their company successful.

Also, service is a very cultural experience. Service norms and customer expectations vary greatly from one culture to another. This book looks at service in North America in general, and the United States specifically. It assumes that the reader will be providing service to people with a generally "Western" outlook. However, the issue of how the U.S. society deals with an increasingly growing number of foreign visitors and customers is critical to the overall success of many hospitality and tourism companies. In these situations, the basics of service discussed here apply, although the actual implementations may vary slightly. Where possible, the book addresses these situations.

The book follows a simple flow. Part 1 allows students to understand what service is, how it relates to our economy and what is necessary for service organizations to succeed. Having understood the nature of service, students learn in Part 2 about the "players" in the service game: customers, companies, co-workers, and themselves. Once they understand what service is and who does what to whom, they will learn in Part 3 about specific ways that service products can be delivered and what tools are at every customer-contact employee's disposal. Part 4 takes the service concepts developed earlier and applies them to companies' internal systems, giving students an understanding of how companies can operate as a team. Finally, in Part 5 we apply all the knowledge gained in the first four parts, as we examine five specific segments of hospitality and tourism to give students a perspective on real-world applications.

Great care has been taken to give a balanced view of service from all segments of the hospitality and tourism industry. Particular attention has been paid to the lodging and restaurant services of hospitality companies, and the air, cruise, tour and travel agency services of tourism companies. This is not, however, meant to imply that other hospitality and tourism services (car rental companies, theme parks, government tourism organizations, convention and visitor bureaus, etc.) are less important. Hospitality and tourism is a complex and varied industry, and the concepts in this book apply to any organization.

Service will be the deciding factor in any company's success during the 1990s and beyond. This book will hopefully help prepare students for the real-world service encounters they will experience upon getting a job in either hospitality or tourism.

ACKNOWLEDGMENTS

I am deeply indebted to a number of people without whom this book would not have been possible. I thank Jan Carlzon and SAS for giving me my initial interest in service. I will never forget the 8-hour delay I had back in 1982. SAS was so helpful and professional that I still fly them whenever I can *because of that delay*. It was only later that I read Mr. Carlzon's book and realized that such service was the product of design.

I thank Dr. Najdemin Meshkati and Dr. Andrew Imada of the University of Southern California's Institute of Safety and Systems Management for their support in my graduate studies of the subject, as well as Dr. Edgar Schein for the knowledge I gained reading his seminal book, *Organizational Culture and Leadership*. Thanks go out to all the people who made this book possible—the academic reviewers, Prentice-Hall editors and production people, and my cartoonist Derek Barnes. (He made writing this book just a little more fun.)

I also thank my parents, Phil and Doris Davidoff, who introduced me to the hospitality, travel, and tourism industry, gave me my first opportunities to be a customer contact employee and encouraged me to write my ideas down on paper. Finally, I thank my wife, Yvonne, whose tireless support and hours alone enabled me to complete this book.

CONTACT

Customer Service in the Hospitality and Tourism Industry

PART 1

INTRODUCTION

Before we begin to explore service in the hospitality and tourism industry and how customer-contact employees can deliver high-quality service, we must have a basic understanding of what service is. In Chapter 1 we give an historical perspective on how and why service has grown in importance. We also examine some of the common misconceptions about service industries and service jobs.

In Chapter 2 we examine the similarities and differences between manufacturing retail products and producing service products. In addition, we examine many of the reasons that service today is perceived to be delivered poorly, and conclude with some general ideas about what service companies must do to succeed in the highly competitive global business world.

In Chapter 3 we conclude our introduction by discussing three basic laws regarding service. These laws form the cornerstone of our discussions in Part 2 on the roles, relationships, and responsibilities of customers, company management, and customer-contact personnel.

1

WHAT IS SERVICE?

OBJECTIVES

After reading this chapter, you should:

Understand the meaning of service.

Understand the history of service in the United States and its relationship to the manufacturing sector.

Understand the modern concept of customer-oriented service.

Be able to identify and discuss important trends in service.

Understand the importance of service to the American economy.

Understand and be able to refute common myths about service.

KEY TERMS

service

product-oriented

customer-oriented

agricultural age

industrial age

information age

market segmentation

prosumer

high touch

SERVICE

According to *Webster's New 20th Century Dictionary* (second edition), **service** is defined as "Anything useful, such as maintenance, supplies, installation, repairs, etc., provided by a dealer or manufacturer for people who have bought things from him." This may be an acceptable definition for a dictionary but not for anyone operating in today's marketplace. Over the past 40 years there has been a remarkable shift in the outlook and perspective of American industry (Figure 1-1).

As we entered the 1950s, the United States was the world's largest producer country, and American industry enjoyed the advantages of their dominant position. In all facets of manufacturing—development capability, technology, capacity, worker expertise, and productivity—America was unsurpassed. Manufacturing was king, American automobile plants were models of efficiency and the envy of the world, and the quality and quantity of new goods seemed remarkable.

Prior to 1950, business tended to focus on the production of goods. The study of *scientific management* was founded on the premise that businesses needed only to study the efficiency of workers and machines and determine their optimal mix. Scientific management treated people as impersonally as the machine. Consumers were not treated as though they required any flexibility. Henry Ford, noted industrialist and producer of the famous Model A and Model T cars, once said, "You can have any color you want as long as it's black." And people bought black Fords and more black Fords.

By the 1950s, businesses were able to deliver good service just by presenting the public with new or improved products. The television set was invented, and soon there was scarcely a household in the land without one. When the 1960s brought the introduction of color television, manufacturers could sell the product all over again. With only a few notable exceptions, when a major manufacturer introduced a new or improved product, it sold.

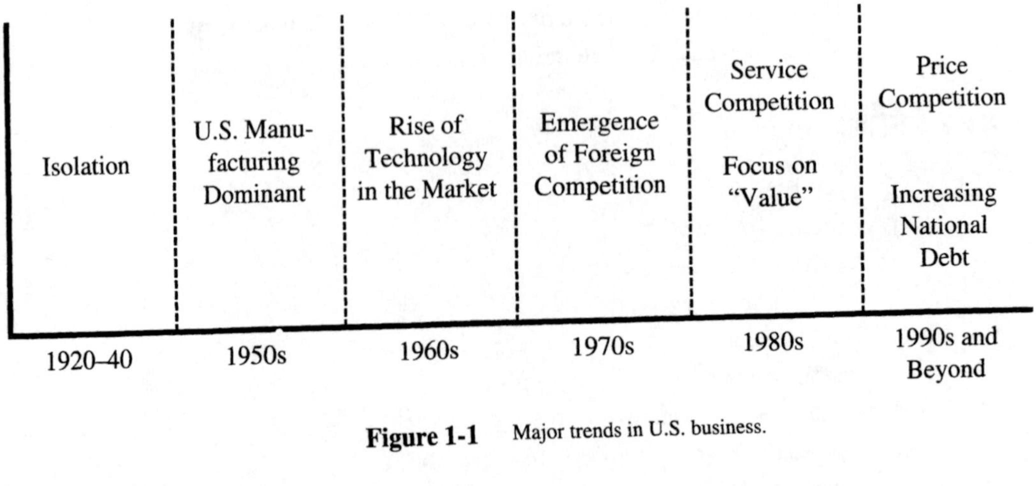

Isolation	U.S. Manu-facturing Dominant	Rise of Technology in the Market	Emergence of Foreign Competition	Service Competition Focus on "Value"	Price Competition Increasing National Debt
1920–40	1950s	1960s	1970s	1980s	1990s and Beyond

Figure 1-1   Major trends in U.S. business.

Service products we now take for granted, such as travel and investment portfolio management, tended to be the exclusive domain of the wealthy. The economic structure was such that mass service product producers (life insurance companies, motels, and amusement parks) could survive without considering many of the principles of service quality. In fact, it was the lack of cleanliness and personal touch that led Walt Disney to develop Disneyland. His quote, "You don't build it for yourself. You know what the people want and you build it for them," became the cornerstone for the development philosophy that still guides the Disney company. As society moved through the 1960s and 1970s, however, a number of things happened that changed the environment drastically (Figure 1-2).

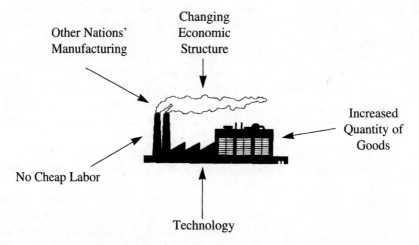

Figure 1-2   Pressures on U.S. manufacturing.

1. Other nations equaled or exceeded American manufacturing capability.   As mentioned earlier, the United States was the single largest producer of goods in the post–World War II world. As other nations (notably Germany, Japan, and now the other Pacific Rim countries) have increased their manufacturing capability exponentially, we can no longer enjoy the advantages of size alone. No longer can manufacturers expect products to be competitive in the international market simply because the "Made in the U.S.A." sign signifies a superior product or the ability to make it in superior numbers.

2. Cheap labor has virtually disappeared in the United States.   The rise in the standard of living in the United States, coupled with the success of unions in winning concessions for their workers, has eliminated most sources of cheap labor. On the other hand, the Pacific Rim countries are often able to get skilled workers at rates well below those for the most unskilled levels in the United States. This means that it is increasingly difficult for U.S. products to be priced competitive. The microchip industry, for example, has suffered greatly from this change.

3. Technical gadgets have lost much of their "gee-whiz" luster. The old saying, "Build a better mousetrap, and the world will beat a path to your door," symbolizes the marketing mentality of the "old school" in the United States. This **product-oriented** view holds that all we need to do is create a superior product and the market will want it. Now, however, customers are increasingly involved in expressing their own needs. Quality is no longer judged by technical capabilities; instead, it is based increasingly on criteria determined by customers. These criteria are based on the usefulness of the product to customers, each of whom is a unique individual—not on the technical wizardry of the gadget.

4. The quantity and types of goods have exploded. The number and types of goods on the marketplace has skyrocketed. Not too long ago Coca-Cola was a radically new product. Now you have to choose between new and old Coke, caffeine or caffeine-free, diet or sugar. Howard Johnson's came out with 28 different flavors of ice cream for their stores, and Baskin Robbins became a household name when they "outnumbered" HoJo's with their offer of 31 varieties. Today we can choose between ice cream, frozen yogurt, and a variety of "nondairy frozen desserts." Even with such low-technology products as bed sheets, towels, paper napkins, and paper towels, there is an almost incredible variety of colors and patterns to choose from. The options available to the consumer today make the marketplace a different environment in which to compete.

5. The economic structure for the consumer has changed. A large sector of our society has a level of discretionary income never before seen. Most people who bought a house in the 1960s or 1970s, for example, currently pay from $1000 to 2000 less per month on their home mortgage than does the typical homebuyer of today. This discretionary income gives them the ability to spend money on conveniences and services that would otherwise not be economical. Among younger people, the economic structure has changed so that in most families, both spouses need to be working. Although they may have more limited discretionary income, these two-income families have an increased desire for service. The adults spend most of the day working, so they don't have as much time for themselves. They often place a premium on services that save time (auto repair, lawn care, food services, etc.) or increase the value of the free time they do have (entertainment, travel, etc.).

The result of all this is a market shift in emphasis from manufacturing to service and a change in the definition of quality and service excellence. The definition in *Webster's* is really no longer sufficient. It is purely a product-oriented view, with the implicit, mistaken assumption that the only services that are useful deal exclusively with goods purchased from a dealer or manufacturer. A much more appropriate definition of **service** is "Anything of value, other than physical goods, which one person or organization provides another person or organization in exchange for something." Implicit in this definition is a **customer-oriented** view. This is because service is anything "of value," as determined by the consumer. What may be of value to one person or organization may not be to another. Also, this definition shows the human interaction necessary for services to be rendered. Service is provided by one person or organization to another. The product we call "service" exists only in this interchange. It is not a tangible good in itself. Finally, because we are talking about the service industry, services are provided in exchange for something. Although this is often money, it does not have to be. Many times, a service may be provided to engender goodwill, or with social services to create some benefit for society.

Many theorists have written about the changing nature and importance of service: what it means for society in general and for service industries in particular. Two of the most famous are Alvin Toffler and John Naisbitt. Toffler, in his book *The Third Wave*, suggests that all of human history is marked by three major "ages": the **agricultural age**, the **industrial age**, and the new **information age** (sometimes referred to as the *service age*; see Figure 1-3). Prior to the First Wave, most human beings lived in small groups that roamed the lands foraging and hunting for food. Roughly 10,000 years ago, the Agricultural Revolution began. With it came villages, farming, cultivated land, and an entirely new way of living.

Starting around the end of the seventeenth century, the Second Wave—the Industrial Revolution—began moving quickly across the continents. Like the First Wave, it introduced a new host of technologies (built around and for use in the factory instead of the farm), it changed the social landscape of society drastically, and it was received enthusiastically by some and rejected violently by others.

Today, in developed countries, the First Wave has spent virtually all of its power. Except for a few tiny tribal populations, everyone on earth has been touched by agriculture. The Second Wave, however, is still running its course. While North America, Europe, and parts of the Pacific Rim have become fully industrialized, many nations are still basically agricultural.

Today, we feel the effect of the subsiding of the Second Wave's force and the emergence of the Third Wave. Sometimes referred to as the "Information Revolution," "Scientific–Technological Revolution," or "Service Revolution," the Third Wave is changing the economic and social patterns of our society as much as the First and Second Waves did. Toffler points to the decade starting about 1955 as a critical period. In that decade, white-collar workers outnumbered blue-collar workers for the first time. Society was introduced to the computer, commercial jet travel, and many other high-impact inno-

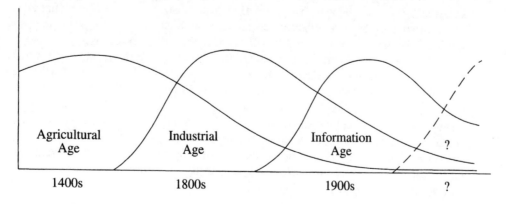

Figure 1-3   "Waves" through history.

THE AGRICULTURAL AGE   THE INDUSTRIAL AGE   THE INFORMATION AGE

© Derek Barnes. Reproduced by permission.

vations. As with the other two waves, some people have embraced the new innovations and others have fought long and hard to reject them.

The Third Wave also describes the dynamics of these change periods. Like waves rolling up on the shore, each age rises in time, reaches its peak, and then recedes as the next wave approaches. It does not, however, disappear completely. If you have stared at waves lapping up on a beach, you can see that one wave interacts with the next. In fact, the time of the most violent interaction often coincides with the time that the newest wave is beginning to reach its peak.

Toffler suggests that we are in one of those periods. The values and systems of the industrial age are ebbing while a new set of values and social systems is evolving to support the rising importance of the service age. The clash is very real, but just like a wave, it is inevitable that the service society will overtake the industrial society.

Whereas Toffler performed an essentially top-down analysis, Naisbitt, in his books *Megatrends* and *Megatrends 2000*, did a bottoms-up analysis (Figure 1-4). Toffler identified the large-scale "waves" of change throughout history. Based on these, he analyzed and evaluated the effects on smaller-scale, sometimes individual, behaviors. Naisbitt, however, began with individual behaviors and made conclusions about trends in society based on the collection of many individual observations. Naisbitt used a process called *content analysis*. By looking at newspapers from across the nation and analyzing how much space was dedicated to what issues, he was able to deduce much about the social changes and trends in society.

Top-Down

⇓

1. Change in how people work together

2. Increase in options for consumers

3. Increase in abilities and importance of consumer

4. Growing corporate identity crisis

5. Backlash of need for high touch

⇑

Bottom-Up

Figure 1-4 Trend analysis.

Used often by the intelligence community for analyzing other cultures, content analysis works because of the principle of *forced choice*. For economic reasons, the total amount of space dedicated to news in a newspaper does not change dramatically over time. Therefore, any time that something new is introduced or coverage is expanded, it must occur at the expense of something else. In other words, content analysis is an excellent tool for discovering what society consistently cares about over time, what causes suddenly become more important, and what causes are forgotten or ignored.

From his content analysis, Naisbitt concludes that what we are witnessing is no less than a revolution in society. Just as the nineteenth century featured a shift from an agricultural to an industrial society, the second half of the twentieth century is characterized by a shift from the industrial to the information society. In his view, we now mass produce information the way we used to mass produce cars.

As Toffler pointed to the decade starting in 1955, Naisbitt points to the years 1956 and 1957 specifically as the critical years marking the start of the information age. The year 1956 was the first that white-collar workers actually outnumbered blue-collar workers in the United States. In 1957, the Soviets launched *Sputnik*, the world's first artificial satellite. The former is significant because for the first time, our government's tax base depended more heavily on the information and service economy than on the manufacturing economy—at a time when America's production might reigned supreme. The latter is significant because it ushered in the global communications explosion.

As Naisbitt points out, "We are drowning in information but starved for knowledge." Raw information is useless; it gains value only when someone processes it into a useful form. Information processing has thus become one of the largest and most critical sectors of the new service economy.

Although they proceeded by drastically different methods, Toffler and Naisbitt came to some remarkably similar conclusions relevant to service industries. Whenever two such dissimilar studies arrive at such similar conclusions, it gives us more confidence in the quality and accuracy of the results.

1. There is change in the way that people work together.   A manufacturing culture requires that all people involved work together in harmony to accomplish the tasks at hand. As a result, there is a high premium on the "ations": standardization, specialization, synchronization, concentration, maximization, and centralization.

A manufacturing culture cannot survive without these; a service culture thrives without them. If everything were standardized, no one would need the services of a travel agent or a variety of restaurant choices. Airlines and hotels often compete as much, or more, on the differences between their services than on a price differential.

Service companies are inherently desynchronized and decentralized. The company cannot control the time when consumers demand the service, nor can top management control the daily and hourly output of the front-line workers—the people who actually create the service product. They cannot live on systems and products conceived and designed at the top and thrust upon the bottom. Rather, they rely heavily on ideas generated from the bottom (either the grass-roots public or the personnel who work with customers), which rise to the top and get organized into a cohesive marketing approach.

Even the federal government, which is the nation's largest provider of services, has begun to realize this. Flextime has been introduced to better meet the needs of employees, and more emphasis has been placed on meeting citizens' needs. Throughout the 1980s there was an effort to decentralize the responsibility and authority for identifying and implementing programs by pushing them down to the state and local government levels. This trend is likely to continue through the 1990s.

Many of today's problems in the service industry come from the fact that many workers were brought up in the manufacturing age and have a culture based on enhancing the "ations." As society follows this trend away from the "ations," the service industry should benefit from a more flexible culture in the workforce (Figure 1-5).

2. There is an increase in options for the consumer.   There has been a virtual explosion of options to the American consumer, and that trend seems likely to continue. The first hotels of the modern world were inns at critical points of stagecoach lines. With the advent of railroads, hotels developed near central-city railroad stations. As Americans embraced travel by car, the industry developed the motel concept to meet these more varied needs. Now, the same hotel company may operate five different types

Past	Future
"ations"	"ilities"
Centralization	Accountability
Concentration	Flexibility
Specialization	Capability
Standardization	Responsibility
Synchronization	

Figure 1-5   From "ations" to "ilities."

CHOICE's (in a) Segmented Market

Market segmentation within the airline and car rental segments of travel and tourism is often difficult to achieve. Aside from a variety of relatively minor peripheral services, the basic product—transportation from point A to point B or a brand-name car—is virtually the same between any two major companies. The hotel industry, however, has been segmented longer than the word has been used to describe that type of marketing practice.

These days, however, segmentation is much more sophisticated. Hotel chains are not only segmented among economy, mass market, and deluxe properties. In fact, one of the world's largest hotel franchise systems, Choice Hotels, is betting its future on creating seven distinct name brands, all within the budget and mass market.

Choice operates over 3000 hotels in seven distinct price categories and service levels under seven different names: Friendship, Sleep, Econo Lodge, Comfort, Rodeway, Quality, and Clarion. At the low end, Friendship Hotels average 49 rooms per hotel and customers pay $20 to $30 per night. These hotels have limited services, although they usually offer cable television and swimming pools. At the high end, Clarion Hotels, Suites, Resorts, and Carriage House Inns offer guests the finest in business and leisure amenities at as much as $100 per night. In between, there is a Choice Hotel option at the price/service trade-off for virtually any mass market customer. Through market segmentation, Choice Hotels is trying to give its customers the option of picking the exact product they prefer among the seven "choices."

---

of properties or more. This approach, often called **market segmentation**, is an attempt by the hotel industry to take a more customer-oriented view. It gives a hotel different service products for different customer needs. In fact, the same person may have different needs at different times. The business traveler who wants a downtown hotel with full business services may want a small, quiet inn-like atmosphere for a vacation.

The same has happened with the airline industry. Even with the failure of no-frills airlines such as People's Express, low-frills airlines such as Southwest still operate successfully. Other airlines, such as MGM Grand and Ultrair, have attempted to operate at the other end of the spectrum. Cruise lines also offer a wide variety of cost versus service options.

The impact of this trend is clear for service industries. Where they used to offer a choice between two options, there is now a choice among many. This means that the employees of service companies who work directly with customers must have more knowledge about a greater variety of products than ever before. These *customer-contact employees* must also be able to deal with a wider variety of customers possessing a broader range of needs and desires. Prior to 1978, most air flights had only two or three fares. Airline reservationists and travel agents had them memorized. Now it is not unusual for there to be as many as 200 or more fares on the flight (often more than the number of seats on the airplane), and these fares can change hourly.

This same level of choice can be seen in the evolution of the press in American society over the years. Throughout the Second Wave, the mass media (major city newspapers and national magazines) grew more and more powerful. But with the rise of the information age, their circulations have dropped. Numerous smaller publications have sprouted—on topics about everything from scuba diving to skateboarding, and from pregnancy and childrearing to retirement. With the advent of desktop publishing, the number of small, private, information-oriented publications has grown exponentially.

There used to be relatively few sources of information. Now, with growingly abundant amounts of information and information "bits," Americans no longer receive a long, related, "string" of ideas organized and synthesized for them. Rather, we now get a multitude of short "blips" of information that we often must synthesize ourselves in order to get any meaning. We are constantly bombarded by such messages through television, newspapers, and movies, which also makes it difficult for anyone to hide information from us. The influence this now has on society cannot be understated. Much of our culture is based on the way in which we get information. Our culture also relies on these methods for transmitting cultural norms from one generation to another. As Marshall McLuhan, a noted modern philosopher, is famous for saying, "The medium is the message."

The impact on service industries cannot be underestimated. Now, more than ever, there is a need for "experts" to help people wade through seemingly endless reams of information. Never before have people such as professional travel agents been a more valued friend to their customers. In a reaction to the information overload, many people prefer the comfort of a known quantity. Airlines and hotels have worked hard to capitalize on this new form of brand loyalty, with frequent-traveler programs and other rewards for loyalty.

3. There is an increase in the abilities and importance of the consumer.

American society has always prided itself on the value it places on each person. Unlike George Orwell's apocryphal predictions in *1984*, the trend is toward increased individualism, not toward society controlling the actions of individuals. George Gilder wrote: "Rather than pushing control to Big Brother at the top, as the pundits predicted, technology by its very nature has pulled power back down to the people. All the world will benefit from the increasing impotence of imperialism, mercantilism and statism. Individuals today possess powers of creation and communication far beyond those of the kings of old."

Not only will the world benefit from this trend, but so will service industries. Wherever the marketplace develops individual needs, companies have a chance to provide value-added services. But at the same time that individualism provides opportunities for service providers, it also presents many challenges. More and more, customers expect to be treated as unique individuals with unique needs. They no longer tolerate the "one product fits all" mentality. Where Henry Ford once envisioned the same black Ford in every driveway, companies like Volvo now offer over 20,000 different option combinations.

Toffler combined the words "producer" and "consumer" to coin a new term, **prosumer**, which describes the growing percentage of the population that is producing and consuming goods and services for themselves that used to be done only by "professionals." Everything from the growing number of do-it-yourself home improvement stores to pregnancy self-tests fit into this category.

This means that what used to be "fenced" businesses are now open to anyone with a product and service approach to meet consumer needs. Bit by bit, routine medical, legal, and similar work need not be done solely by highly paid professionals. Nor, as with tax advice, need it be reserved for the wealthy.

It also means that industries that used to be judged by their products are now going to sink or swim based on their service capabilities. In-store advice and help is the real product of a do-it-yourself home improvement store. Hardware stores of the past were not expected to give such aid.

4. There is a growing corporate identity crisis. The rise of the new age has been accompanied by a rise in entrepreneurialism. In fact, it is entrepreneurial spirit that has driven the change. After all, large, entrenched corporations have a stake in the *status quo*. In a static environment, they are virtually guaranteed profitability without having to invest heavily in new ideas.

Entrepreneurs are perhaps the world's best service people. They usually have broken through the barriers put in place by a product-oriented view. By seeing something the market needs but does not have (new products, cheaper prices, new services, etc.), the entrepreneurs capitalize on their customer-oriented vision. As a result, there are many more smaller companies who make up a large portion of the service industry.

Large corporations have tried to capitalize on this spirit through the concept of intrapreneurialism. Intrapreneurs work within an existing company trying to get the company involved in new projects. They fight the large bureaucracy's tendency to fall into the "ations" very easily. Tom Peters achieved fame and fortune beginning with an examination of intrapreneurial success in his book *In Search of Excellence*.

Manufacturing industries have felt the pressure of change as well as retail and service companies. As customers' needs are diversifying and their expectations of getting these different needs met are rising, the importance of standardized mass production of goods is decreasing. There is a corresponding increase in the need for customized production. With the use of computer-aided manufacturing, it is possible to use the same production line to produce substantially different versions and variations to meet different client needs. The emphasis on mass production of a single design is becoming obsolete. As consumers become more used to these capabilities, they will come to expect this special treatment as a basic required service for everything they buy. Consumers are often not satisfied when their needs are treated as if they are the same as those of everyone else.

Another part of the problem is that businesspeople are finding it increasingly difficult to answer the question, "What kind of business am I in?" Today's leaders grew up in an environment where businesses were easy to categorize and analyze. The Dow Jones Industrial Average has long been held up as the best measure of the "industrial strength" of the nation's economy. Traditionally, that meant companies in manufacturing, power, and transportation. In 1991, the Dow replaced stalwart USX Corporation (formerly U.S. Steel) with Disney. Although Norman Perlstine, editor of the paper, claimed, "We've always thought of 'industrials' as meaning more than manufacturing," the inclusion of this travel and leisure giant at the expense of a steel company sent a clear message to the American public that the "business of America" has changed.

These types of changes continue. Through expansions and acquisitions, almost all of the Fortune 500 companies have diversified their portfolio of activities significantly. In fact, the notion of service industry versus manufacturing industry may itself already be obsolete. Harvard Business School professor Theodore Levitt argues: "There are no such things as service industries. There are only industries whose service components are greater or less than those of other industries. Everybody is in service." This represents a radically different view of the business world than existed 20 or even 10 years ago.

When Naisbitt examined large corporations, he saw the traditional pyramidlike hierarchies of power, a situation almost as true today as it was when *Megatrends* was written in 1982. But while the hierarchies remain, he noticed that our belief in their ability to function well does not. Bit by bit, company by company, there is a trend toward flattening the corporate organizational chart. Rather than forcing communication to flow only up and down a hierarchy, the trend is to allow and encourage lateral communication. By having people communicate and share information and ideas across all company functions, corporations are moving toward a network structure.

This trend is particularly important to service industries. The more a company empowers customer-contact personnel to be able to handle customers, the better the service level. The fewer levels of hierarchy that customers need to deal with to get satisfaction, the more likely that customers will feel good about their interaction with the company.

5. There is a backlash of a need for high touch, corresponding to the increase in high tech.   Over the past decades, much has been written about the growth of technology and the pervasive role the computer has in our world. The often unwritten irony, however, is that the higher the level of technology, the more the need for human balance—**high touch**.

One can still remember the prediction of many futurists that the computer was soon to lead to the "paperless" office. The reality has, in fact, been the opposite. The computer has become a tool for creating more paperwork. While computer technology may be used increasingly for data transfer, there is still nothing as soothing to the human psyche as the ability to hold onto a piece of paper and scan it for the information desired. The computer is an excellent tool for generating the reports, but the high-tech CRT screen is not always a sufficient substitute for the hand-held paper.

Other futurists, Toffler included, have predicted that "cottage industries"—workers at home linked by telephone, fax, and computer modem—will soon dominate industries. Naisbitt contends, though: "The more high technology around us, the more the need for human touch." As such, most people need the human interaction of an office environment. They need to deal face to face with co-workers and/or customers. There is a social function to the workplace that can be more important than pure income production.

This trend is a boon for the service industry. Technology gives us the capability to do more, faster. It allows us to process more information in a shorter amount of time, thus making it more valuable. In essence, it makes the service provider more productive than ever. But at the same time, the definition of service implies an interaction between two people or organizations. More often than not, one or both sides of the interaction want contact. Service is, by definition, a high-touch process. Many service companies have developed to fill the need for high touch created by the advent of high technology.

THE IMPORTANCE OF SERVICE

The single largest trend in business in the United States over the past 40 years or so has been the increased importance of service and service-related industries. The sheer volume of the service industry alone makes it critical to the U. S. economy. As George F. Will once commented: "McDonald's has more employees than U.S. Steel. Golden arches, not blast furnaces, symbolize the American economy." Service is no longer merely a by-product of an industrial society. Rather, it is a major economical force in and of itself.

Ironically, there are major programs throughout the nation to improve the quality of manufacturing and production, yet there is comparatively little effort to improve our services. This does not mean that there is no effort. Throughout society, many companies are engaged in efforts to improve the quality of service to their customers. However, improving service quality has not received the same attention and fervor as has improving manufacturing quality. This is probably true because it is so much harder to quantify and judge service, and service has not traditionally been viewed as being as important as manufacturing.

As the world continues to become more complex, the importance of delivering high-quality service will continue to increase. In today's business world, time and information are critical resources. Many services deal with the ability to transfer information of some form or another between people or organizations in an efficient manner. Without excellence in the service sector, these transfers will take longer, thus reducing overall productivity.

Furthermore, the importance of delivering the service right the first time is increasing. In the hectic pace of the business world, there is precious little time to correct mistakes. There is a saying, "If you can't afford to get it right the first time, can you afford to do it over?" The answer today is a resounding, "No!" In manufacturing, mistakes can be corrected, albeit at some cost. In a service business, mistakes usually result in time and money lost that no longer have value. But aside from being a cost saving, excellence in service can increase revenues. Providing high-quality service can be the competitive edge that more than balances out any marginal increase in costs.

MYTHS ABOUT SERVICE

In the business world, there are many attitudes about service. Traditionally, the service sector has been looked down on by those in manufacturing. The feeling is often that the service sector does not really contribute to the economy in the way that building "things" contributes. Even as we enter what all analysts agree is a new "age of service," and despite all that has been written about service industries, many myths still pervade our understanding of service businesses.

1. A service economy produces services at the expense of other sectors. This argues that the growth of services implies some lessening in importance of other industries, which in turn results in some loss to society.

This makes about as much sense as arguing that the change from an agricultural society to an industrial society lessened the importance of agriculture and hurt the society. In fact, what happened in the United States was that due to massive improvements in productivity, the output of the agricultural industry increased even though the number of agricultural workers declined significantly. From 1910 to 1981, the number of people in agriculture declined from 10 million to 3 million and our production went up 220 percent. Today, the United States is the single greatest agricultural producer in the world, despite using far fewer workers and less land than in the old agricultural society.

The same thing is happening as we transfer from a predominantly industrial society to a predominantly information and service society. The importance of manufacturing and industry is not decreasing. Rather, through the use of information, its demands on society's resources are decreasing. As Russell Ackoff of the Wharton School of Business has argued: "What [the shift from a manufacturing to a service society] does mean is that fewer people will be required to produce manufactured goods."

2. Service jobs are low paying and menial.   This myth is borne from the mistaken belief that the vast majority of service employment opportunities are in essentially nonskilled positions such as clerks and fast-food operators.

This belief is contradicted by the reality of the hospitality and travel industry. Jobs in this industry may not be the highest paid in the country, but they are far from menial. Travel agents must be familiar with literally a world of destinations as well as be competent with complex computer systems. Flight attendants are highly trained, and hotel and restaurant management is a very complex business.

There are also some very high-paying service jobs. Pilots do not normally come to someone's mind when asked about service occupations. However, they are among the highest-paid workers in the service industry. Sales and marketing and accounting and finance positions are known for good pay. Many white-collar computer-oriented jobs are available in the industry as well. As companies become increasingly aware of the importance of customer service, those jobs that deal directly with hotel, restaurant, and other travel customers are being given more authority, responsibility, and higher wages.

3. Service production is primarily labor intensive and low in productivity.   When people consider service industries, they tend to think of the actual act of service being given. This, it is true, is labor intensive. However, many service industries require immense amounts of capital to enable the service provider to perform. For example, the banking industry could not function without expensive, complex computer systems. This is true for the travel agency industry as well. And how could airlines or hotels function without large amounts of capital?

In fact, a study by the U.S. Department of Labor that ranked 145 industries on the basis of capital investment per unit output showed that the majority of service industries rank in the top 20 percent most capitally intensive. None were in the least capital-intensive category.

Similarly, with increased sophistication of information systems, the productivity of the service provider continues to rise. In the early 1970s, for example, the entire air transport industry relied solely on handwritten tickets, a time-consuming and error-prone activity. With today's sophisticated computer reservation and ticketing systems, virtually all tickets are generated by automation. Time that airline personnel and travel agents used to spend writing tickets can now be used to serve other clients. The same computers are used to control the complex yield management fare system, thus optimizing revenue per passenger.

4. Service work is not a worthy pursuit for someone who values individualism.   Since Americans have a healthy respect for individualism and a tendency for a "What's in it for me?" attitude, many think that the service industry is "beneath them." They feel that service tasks amount to menial labor, which is at the very least unrewarding, if not demeaning. Thomas Kelly, an assistant professor at Cornell University's School of Hotel Administration, comments: "In our culture, these jobs are not considered a worthwhile occupation. When workers view giving service as beneath them, it shows." Furthermore, in a society that values upward mobility, these jobs are often viewed as being stagnant.

As with most myths, this couldn't be further from the truth. Service is anything but boring. One of the biggest advantages to the service industry is its variety—both in the number and kinds of jobs and the number and kinds of tasks that each job requires. As for mobility, many corporate vice presidents began their careers giving service as a customer-contact employee. Dick Nunis, the number 3 person in Disney, got his start as a guide on the Jungle River ride in Adventureland. As the importance of quality is increasing, more and more businesses are establishing executive-level positions responsible solely for developing and implementing service improvement programs.

SUMMARY

Over the past 40 years, there has been a remarkable shift in the perspective of American business. To respond to internal economic pressures and external competition from other nations around the world, American businesses have shifted from being the single dominant manufacturer to being just one among many. There has been an accompanying shift from an economy dependent on the manufacture of durable goods to one highly dependent on services. No longer can service be defined as simple value-added features to a manufactured product. Now, service and services are products of their own.

Society moved from an agricultural age to an industrial age approximately 200 years ago. Today, it is changing again, to an information age. In 1956, for example, white-collar workers outnumbered blue-collar workers in the United States for the first time. These changes have had a dramatic effect on society. Businesses are beginning to be much more flexible in approaching how people work together. Consumers are getting a much wider range of options from the marketplace and are getting access to many more do-it-yourself options. There is a clear and growing corporate identity crisis as established businesses wrestle with the changes and feel the pressures of new upstarts in previously protected markets. Also, there is a backlash against technology as the answer to every problem.

Unfortunately, as service continues to grow in importance and power, a number of myths persist. Many people believe that growth in the service sector must be at the expense of manufacturing. They believe that service jobs must be low paying and menial, labor intensive and low in productivity, and not a worthy pursuit for entrepreneurs and those with ambition. The fact is, however, that service grows on its own strength as more people require its products independent of manufacturing. The number of well-paying service jobs is large and growing, many service businesses have high productivity as well as paths for career advancement, and most jobs in today's service sector require people who are highly skilled and trained.

QUESTIONS FOR REVIEW

1. What five trends since World War II have eliminated America's ability to be the single dominant manufacturing power?
2. Define service as it pertains to today's business marketplace.
3. What is a "customer-oriented view"?
4. According to Alvin Toffler, what are the three major "ages" of society? Where is society now?
5. What is a "prosumer"?
6. According to Naisbitt and Toffler, today's customers are looking for high-technology solutions and what else?

QUESTIONS FOR DISCUSSION

1. Can the service industry regain a positive reputation? If so, how? If not, why not?
2. Why do myths about service persist? What can the service sector do to overcome these myths?

REFERENCES

NAISBITT, JOHN. *Megatrends.* New York: Warner Books, 1982.

NAISBITT, JOHN, and ABURDENE, PATRICIA. *Megatrends 2000.* New York: William Morrow, 1990.

ORWELL, GEORGE. *1984.* San Diego: Harcourt Brace Jovanovich, 1982.

PETERS, THOMAS, and WATERMAN, ROBERT, JR. *In Search of Excellence.* New York: Harper & Row, 1982.

TOFFLER, ALVIN. *The Third Wave.* New York: William Morrow & Co., 1980.

WEBSTER, MERRIAM. *Webster's New 20th Century Dictionary.* Springfield, MA: G. & C. Merriam Co.

2

UNDERSTANDING THE SERVICE PRODUCT

OBJECTIVES

After reading this chapter, you should:

Understand the difference between service and retail products.

Understand why there are problems with delivering good service in the American society.

Understand what will be needed in the future for service industries to succeed.

KEY TERMS

intangibility
simultaneity
customer participation
progressive nature
people skills

WHY IS SERVICE DIFFERENT FROM RETAIL?

For many years, businesses treated services and service much the same as they treated any retail good. Hiring and firing, quality control, organizational design, and all other facets of business management and marketing approached service from the manufacturing mentality. In the 1970s, however, a new view emerged—one that understands service is distinctly different from retail.

The basic nature of the service product differs from that of the retail product in three major characteristics (Figure 2-1):

1. Relative intangibility of services
2. Simultaneity of service production and consumption
3. Customer participation in the production of services

As we will see, these three characteristics combine to make the delivery of service a uniquely different task than the selling of retail goods.

Intangibility refers to the fact that the consumer rarely gets a "thing" as the result of a service. The outcome is more often an experience than a possession. For example, even though an airline passenger gets a ticket, the real product is the transportation from one city to another. It is difficult for people to show off their air tickets to friends the way they might show off a new car. Even in service businesses where possessions can be gained, such as a stock brokerage, the real product is intangible. The real product that brokers give is advice. Customers may be able to get tangible goods as a result of the broker's product, but the product itself is still relatively intangible.

Simultaneity refers to the time lapse between the production and consumption of services versus retail products. Unlike the manufacture and sales of a toaster oven, services are usually produced and consumed at the same time. Therefore, service products are highly perishable. Once a hotel room goes unused for the night, it cannot be sold again. Similarly, a travel agent's hour cannot be "saved" in inventory for use during peak periods. Furthermore, there is no time between production and consumption to inspect the product to ensure that there are no defects. Once a customer gets bad service from a bank teller with a surly attitude, there is no way to recall that encounter and replace it in inventory with a friendly teller's service.

Customer participation refers to the fact that customers of service companies participate actively in the production of many of their services. In fact, service organizations could not possibly create their product without substantial input from the consumer. Whether the input is an order to a waiter or the description of symptoms to a doctor, the service does not really begin without the assistance of the customer. No one could imagine themselves going into the Ford or GM plant and watching over every detail of the

Retail	Service
1. Produces and sells "things"	1. Produces and sells "experiences" and "feelings"
2. Produces *then* sells	2. Produces *when* sells
3. Produces away from customers	3. Produces along with customers

Figure 2-1 Differences between service and retail companies.

I don't know...could it be we've discovered service? (© Derek Barnes. Reproduced by permission.)

production of their car, yet many service customers expect that kind of insight and control when they receive products from service companies.

The customer is, in fact, critical to the production of a service. Product choice and quality are highly dependent on the questions that the customer asks. The customer's personality, attitude, and mood also affect it. When a service customer is in a hurry, it changes the service process, but none of these factors directly influence the production of retail goods.

THE FUTURE OF SERVICE

Before we can discuss the future of service, we need a better understanding of what it is today. All one has to do is go into a department store, stop by the local restaurant, or run into a problem with an airline and he or she will experience some of its problems. The doomsayers among business and academic communities say that service in the future is sure to decline even further. The problems are deeply rooted in both the nature of the service product itself and in today's business and education culture. But once we understand these problems, we can examine what it will take for service excellence to be the norm rather than the exception.

WHY IS SERVICE BAD TODAY?

1. Giving good service is a very difficult task. The simple, plain fact is that service is not an easy job. The three major characteristics of service we discussed earlier combine to make it very difficult to control and guarantee. Given the definition that service is "anything that when added to a product, increases its utility or value to the customer," the range of functions that must be mastered to give excellence in service is staggering.

Not only is service excellence difficult to deliver because of its intangibility, simultaneity, and customer participation, but it is also **progressive in nature**. In other words, what customers consider to be excellent today may only be adequate or may even be insufficient tomorrow. Airlines today are better able to provide transportation services than ever before. In the 1950s it took approximately 10 hours for a Constellation to fly from New York to Los Angeles. Today's jets make the same flight in 5 hours. A flight that arrives 2 hours late is still 30 percent better performing than the Constellation. Although this would be amazing service to the 1950s passenger, it would be considered deplorable service by today's passengers. Similarly, a customer may come to a customer-contact employee after receiving poor service from another establishment and thank him or her for the wonderful service. A year later, the same customer may take this service quality level for granted.

2. Our education system does not teach service. From elementary to high school and from undergraduate to postgraduate institutions, not enough emphasis is given to teaching service and service skills. This often reinforces the myth that service work is menial and not a worthy career pursuit.

Good customer-contact people need to have the skills and attitudes that allow them to work well with other people and a good perspective on problem solving, yet early education tends not to emphasize these skills. High schools focus on teaching precollege subjects or technical vocational skills but don't teach students the **people skills** necessary to prepare them for customer-contact service jobs.

Higher education also does not support the burgeoning service economy. There are almost no undergraduate programs that focus on the service industry. They teach liberal arts, business, and engineering, but not how to apply these fields specifically in a service environment. Even business schools often avoid or ignore the specific difficulties associated with a service industry. They often teach as though the only real businesses are retail or manufacturing.

3. Few businesses give enough priority to education and training in service. Once an educated person gets into the workforce, there is little training in service available. The thought of giving employees training dedicated specifically to service is rather new to businesses. Too often, service companies rely on on-the-job (OJT) training. The problem with OJT is that there is little control over the training—just as many bad habits are taught as good habits.

Most of the training that is available concentrates on the technical aspects of the job, thus neglecting the all-important human side of service. Reservationists are taught how to handle the phone, the computer, and pricing structures, but they are not taught how to handle potentially complicated special requests, how to deal with an irate customer, or how to manage their own stress levels so that they don't react poorly to a client.

Often, businesses work hard to design service jobs to be as simple as possible. This allows them to hire the least skilled people and pay the lowest wages. The result is a staff undertrained to deal with the complexities of human business interactions. Take the least skilled workers, design the job around them, pay them low wages, and they act accordingly. As Karl Albrecht, a well-known management consultant and author of *Service America: Doing Business in the New Economy*, exclaims: "Service people can become so robotized in their actions that they greet any customer request with a standardized response."

4. Service providers are often not motivated to give good service.   In many service industries, employees are actually motivated to provide poor service. Anyone who talks with phone operators at reservation or ordering centers probably has felt rushed at some time or another. This is because many of these companies use computers to monitor the workers' performance on phone calls. To maintain production quotas, they expect their employees to take no more than a certain amount of time. Workers are more motivated to get customers off the phone as quickly as possible than they are to deliver excellence in service. Harley Shaiken, professor of work and technology at the University of California at San Diego, observes: "These assembly line methods increase profits [in the short term] by boosting productivity, but there is a long-term hidden cost—the decline in service."

Staffing levels also contribute to a lack of service. Most of us have had the painful experience of calling a "customer service" desk only to get the message, "All of our service agents are busy right now; please hold and the first available agent will be with you." Because many companies try to keep their costs as low as possible, they staff phone operations at minimum levels—levels that may not support even an average call load. At best, many companies staff for the daily average, thus leaving waiting people who call at peak times.

The same phenomenon is seen in the airline industry. Flight attendants used to have time to chat with passengers and try to make the trip a truly enjoyable experience. Now, to save labor costs, crews are cut to minimum standards for safety and forced to deliver food and drink services as quickly as possible. If today's jumbo jets were staffed at the levels of the early 1970s, they would carry 20 flight attendants instead of the 12 to 14 that most carry now.

If that isn't enough, many customer-contact service jobs are low paying, even minimum wage. The result is that the best workers probably will not take the job. Those who do are more often looking for the next opportunity to move up rather than concentrating on delivering quality service today.

5. We suffer from an overreliance on technology.   Many Americans have become so enamored with technology that they see it as the solution to everything. It is true that technology is a great tool for increasing the productivity of people and for providing levels and types of service that could not otherwise be accomplished. After all, without computers, no customer-contact employee could deal with the number of clients that travel agents, hotel front-desk agents, airline ticket agents, and many other travel and tourism companies are expected to handle.

Unfortunately, technology is not a panacea for all service problems. It does not replace human contact—the friendly smile, the personal service of a well-trained waiter, or the right joke at the right time. It is also limited by the old GIGO rule: "Garbage in, garbage out." It cannot replace the judgment of a hospitality and tourism professional trained to meet customers' needs.

Finally, technology can sometimes cause as many problems as it solves. There's an old saying, "To err is human, but to really foul things up takes a computer." We have a tendency to trust something because "The computer said so." But when we rely on the computer to do our thinking for us, more often than not we end up providing poor service. Customers paying for services are paying for human help. If all they needed was a machine, they could do it themselves.

DOES SERVICE HAVE A CHANCE?

With all the myths about service plus all the problems with service today, it may seem as if there is very little chance that the service industry will be able to thrive and excel. Many "experts" promote the belief that service is sure to follow the decline of manufacturing, probably at a more rapid pace. While these naysayers take a cynical view of service, they miss or misrepresent the following basic underlying facts about service industries.

1. Service industries are the largest single sector in the U.S. economy. The economic clout and importance of the service sector is astounding. As long ago as 1986, the U.S. Department of Commerce's Bureau of Economic Analysis reported that it accounts for more than 68 percent of the gross national product and more than 71 percent of employment. The importance of service is sure to continue to rise long before it declines.

Furthermore, our society's entrepreneurial spirit has always been adept at reading the market's needs and finding ways to meet them. As consumers make it more clear that they not only expect but demand good service, companies will be forced to find ways to meet these needs if they are to survive. Those that cannot adapt to the new reality will go out of business and will be replaced by new enterprises founded on the basis of service excellence.

There are also many large companies that have a reputation for service excellence that can be used as models of how to do the job right. Just as Ford was a model for the industrial society's need to learn effective mass production of consumer goods, so is Disney a beacon to those who want to learn how to deliver satisfaction. The same can be said for the Scandinavian Airlines System, British Airways, Federal Express, T.G.I. Fridays, the Ritz-Carlton Hotels, and a whole host of other service organizations. In our capitalist society, wherever there is a market as big as the service sector with as many good ideas to learn from, success is usually not too far behind.

2. Services are in high demand.   Most people who take a cynical view of service voice an implicit belief that service functions are somehow secondary to the "real" job of manufacturing and construction. Like our dictionary definition, they see services as something to provide after the retail product is sold.

The reality, however, is that services are not responses to marginal demands that people satisfy only after they meet their product needs. They desire services for what they are: convenience, comfort, security, and flexibility. Today, when it comes to discretionary income, people are just as likely to spend their money in a nice restaurant as they are to use it for a new appliance, or to decide to put off buying a new car in order to take a nice vacation.

3. Service industries are an excellent business investment.   Service is the growth industry of the 1990s and beyond. All the trends identified by writers such as Toffler, Naisbitt, and Peters suggest that service will continue to grow in scope and importance. The globalization of economies will continue to be a boon to the travel and communication sectors.

Furthermore, service companies today are of a sufficient scale to be sophisticated buyers and sellers. The presence of high technology is pervasive, and the potential for a continued increase in productivity is limited only by one's imagination. From the small "Mom and Pop" restaurant to the largest international airline, there is room for growth well in excess of inflation.

WHAT IT WILL TAKE FOR SERVICE TO SUCCEED

In *Service America: Doing Business in the New Economy*, Karl Albrecht and Ron Zemke lay out what businesses must do to succeed in the future: "The capacity to serve customers effectively and efficiently is an issue every organization must face. No one can evade this challenge: manufacturers and traditional service providers, profit-making and non-profit organizations, private-sector and public enterprises must all face the task of responding effectively and efficiently to customers who expect quality and service as a part of every purchase." They argue that organizations concerned with honing a competitive edge for this new environment must develop two new capabilities. First, they must be able to think strategically about service and build a strong service orientation into their strategic vision of the future. Second, they must learn how to manage effective and efficient design, development, and delivery of service.

Taking Albrecht and Zemke one step further, these new capabilities require that companies do a number of new things:

1. Focus on the customer.   Service begins with the customer. Albrecht and Zemke's assertion that organizations must learn how to think strategically implies that most companies think more about other things than they do about service. Sadly, this is often true.

For companies to change their strategic thinking and build a strong service vision, they must begin with the customer. As Albrecht and Zemke point out, too often the atti-

Of course it doesn't fit you...It's Steve's! (© Derek Barnes. Reproduced by permission.)

tude in American companies has been, "This would be a great business if it weren't for all the damned customers." But in today's competitive environment, businesses are finding it more difficult to succeed unless they provide service to the customer. This is true even in manufacturing, where the only difference between two products is often nothing more than the logos and service reputations of the competing companies.

    Everything about how companies run their business must be analyzed with respect to what the customer wants and needs. Market research activities should focus on identifying these needs. Policies and procedures must be structured to meet these identified needs. Education and training activities must be geared toward preparing customer-contact employees to provide for these needs. In addition, all the follow-up feedback, evaluation, and analysis activities must be used to determine how well these needs were met and to prescribe any required corrective action.

2. Understand the role of the customer-contact employee. Businesses must learn to understand the role of customer-contact employees. It is somewhat ironic that in a nation that values the role of the individual we place such an emphasis on vertical job mobility. We give all the rewards, perks, and prestige to the management echelon. Yet it is the customer-contact employee who is truly responsible for much of the success or failure of any organization. There are libraries of books about management and almost no books about customer-contact employees. Prestigious schools are built to teach the wonders of management theory, yet customer-contact employees are left to learn from haphazard on-the-job experiences. There are many good-quality vocational and technical schools that teach job-oriented skills, but few of them teach enough about how to deliver a service product in a high-quality manner.

Second, businesses must empower customer-contact employees with enough knowledge and authority to meet the awesome responsibility of delivering high-quality service to customers. This particular aspect of what it will take to succeed is discussed in detail throughout Part 2 of this book.

3. Weave a service culture into education and training systems. Two of the major reasons why service is so bad today revolve around the lack of proper education and training. Our nation's education infrastructure is woefully inadequate for the needs of a modern service organization. To make matters worse, most of our businesses are not well prepared to provide the necessary training when a potentially good employee comes out of the education system.

The education problem is not a trivial one. Not only is the school system (from elementary through high school and into college) not geared to teach the requisite skills and knowledge for customer-contact work, but neither is most of our society prepared for the emotional and psychological sacrifice that is often required. Our culture does not champion service providers—in fact, it tends to look down on them. If we are to succeed as a nation in developing and maintaining superior service companies, we must correct the weaknesses of our society and reorganize schools to prepare people.

The second half of the education and training equation can only be solved by American companies themselves. They must remember that a few days and dollars of training will more than pay for itself in the long run. The old saying, "If you think education and training is expensive, try ignorance," applies now more than ever. As more and more companies realize this, the service standard in the nation will rise.

4. The more businesses use "high-tech" systems, the more they need to emphasize "high touch." There is no doubt that service companies will continue to use more and more technology. Anything that will either increase the efficiency of a service transaction (and thus the productivity of the service provider) or that will transport or process information better will find an immediate use in these industries.

The irony, however, is that the more customers are forced to rely on high-technology systems in all facets of their lives, the more they will crave the social interactions and support of face-to-face activities. This does not mean that businesses should avoid the use of newer technologies. Quite the contrary—they should encourage the use of them. But at the same time, they must develop processes and procedures that still provide a high-touch atmosphere in the eyes of the customer.

5. Thrive on change. Albrecht and Zemke say that successful organizations will need to develop a "tolerance for—perhaps even an enjoyment of—sudden and sometimes dramatic change." Tom Peters simply titles one of his books *Thriving on Chaos*.

Both agree that the one constant in service is change. Whether it is the changing customer needs or the changing environment in which those needs are met, things will change. What is good today may not be good tomorrow, and what may be impossible today may be standard procedure in the future. Aggressively and proactively pursuing the new opportunities brought on by change is the only way to get long-term success.

SUMMARY

Service products are distinctly different from retail products in three pivotal ways. First, services are essentially intangible. Customers rarely get a "thing." Second, services are usually produced and consumed at the same time. The product is thus highly perishable, and there is no way to stock up on inventory. Finally, customers often participate in the production of services. In fact, their input is essential to the success of most service transactions.

In the United States today, service does not enjoy a very good reputation. The popular press and academic management analysts routinely decry the lack of good service. These problems have many sources. To begin with, it is difficult to provide good service. Worse, the American education system does not teach service skills, and few businesses give service training enough priority. Most businesses don't motivate workers to provide good service, and people tend to rely too much on technology to make up for the shortcomings of people systems.

These problems are not insurmountable. In fact, the future of service in the United States is quite bright. Service industries are the largest single sector in the U.S. economy; they are in high demand, and that demand is likely to increase; and service businesses are excellent investments. For service to regain a positive reputation and realize its full potential, however, businesses must do a number of things. They must focus on customers. Too many businesses start by focusing on their products and how to sell them to customers rather than asking customers what they want and trying to develop new services to meet those needs. They must understand the critical role that customer-contact employees play in the service game. They must weave a customer-oriented service culture into all their education and training systems. They should emphasize high-touch systems along with technological advancements. Finally, they need to learn to thrive on change. Change is the only constant in business today, and those companies that can identify changing customer needs and meet them are virtually guaranteed long-term success.

QUESTIONS FOR REVIEW

1. What are the three greatest differences between service products and retail products?
2. What are the five biggest reasons that service in the United States is perceived as being poor?
3. What is the single largest business sector in the United States today?
4. What five things must businesses do to excel at service?

QUESTIONS FOR DISCUSSION

1. Given the differences between service products and retail products, how can a service company make sure that its services are consistently of good quality?
2. Is service in the United States really poor? If the critics are correct, why do you support them? If you think that the service industry suffers from a poor reputation that is undeserved, how do you support your feeling?
3. How can the educational system in the United States better prepare its students for careers in service industries?

REFERENCES

ALBRECHT, KARL, and ZEMKE, RONALD. *Service America: Doing Business in the New Economy.* Homewood, IL: Dow Jones-Irwin, 1985.
PETERS, THOMAS. *Thriving in Chaos.* New York: Alfred A. Knopf, 1987.

3

THE LAWS OF SERVICE

OBJECTIVES

After reading this chapter, you should:

Understand the basic laws of service.
Understand the seven basic customer expectations.
Know how to avoid the seven deadly sins.

KEY TERMS

First Law of Service
expectations
    accessibility
    courtesy
    personal attention
    empathy
    job knowledge
    consistency
    teamwork

perceptions
Second Law of Service
halo effect
Third Law of Service
customer's point of view

In Chapters 1 and 2 we reviewed service from a historical perspective, discussed the differences between service and retail products, and drew conclusions about what society must do to make service better. Now we turn our attention to what makes a service encounter good or bad.

FIRST LAW OF SERVICE

We know that service is anything other than physical goods that is valuable to customers. This customer perspective leads to the **First Law of Service**—the most critical relationship in all service work:

Satisfaction equals perception minus expectation.

$$S = P - E$$

The first important point about this law is that both variables, perception and expectation, are psychological phenomena. They are not objective and may have almost no relationship to reality. One of the most common mistakes that service providers make is to judge performance or customer expectations based on what they feel the customer should think—not what the customer actually thinks. The ability to put yourself in someone else's shoes, often called *empathy*, is a critical skill in delivering excellence in service.

This law also says that if customers expect a certain level of service and perceive that an equal or higher level was delivered, they will be satisfied. On the other hand, even when good service (as measured by some objective standard) is delivered, if the expectation was for better service, customers will be dissatisfied.

The result is that service providers have both to manage customer expectations and deliver quality service. An excellent example of the former is that of restaurant maître d's who tell people that the waiting time will be slightly in excess of what it is really expected to be. This guarantees that customers will not experience a longer wait than they expected and will be very happy when the wait is actually shorter than predicted.

Expectations

For customer-contact personnel to deliver service that meets customers' **expectations**, they must first understand what it is that the typical customer expects. These expectations fall into seven basic categories:

- Accessibility
- Courtesy
- Personal attention
- Empathy
- Job knowledge
- Consistency
- Teamwork

1. Accessibility.   Customers expect prompt and efficient service. This means that they must be able to get to someone in the organization who can help them. Whether it is waiting for initial processing or talking to someone about fixing a problem, they do not expect to go through a maze of paperwork and red tape. They want their questions answered and their needs met as soon as possible.

2. Courtesy.   Customers expect to be treated in a professional manner. They react poorly to rudeness. Even in a situation where nothing can really be done to fix a problem, a kind word will go a long way toward soothing ruffled feathers. Customers expect their property to be treated with respect as well. Employees should treat customers' luggage, cars, and so on, as if it were their own. They also expect a neat and clean appearance. Disney, for example, has built a reputation for the way it keeps its theme parks and hotels bright and clean and its personnel under strict dress codes.

3. Personal attention.   Customers want to be treated as unique individuals, not just another name on a long list. They want to know that the company they are dealing with cares about them as individuals. They expect to be told what services will be provided, and they expect someone to care about their problems (and do something about them). They do *not* want to have to find things out for themselves or be surprised.

4. Empathy.   Empathy is a person's ability to see and feel things from someone else's point of view. Customers expect that service employees will understand what they care about. Empathy is the essence of a "customer-oriented" philosophy. Customers do not expect to be treated as though their presence is an imposition on the employee or an interruption to an otherwise pleasant day.

5. Job knowledge.   Customers expect that employees will know the facts about their job and their company. They expect honest answers. On some special requests, they may accept an employee going to a supervisor for an answer, provided that the answer comes quickly. They do not, however, accept this as a regular routine.

6. Consistency.   Customers expect to get the same answer no matter who they talk to. If everyone meets the criteria for job knowledge, there is no reason for two different employees to give conflicting answers. They also expect to get treated the same as they see other customers being treated. There are some instances where a variety of treatment may be acceptable (grocery store express checkout lines are a good example), but only when they see and understand an obvious and compelling reason for a difference in treatment.

7. Teamwork.   The company may be composed of many different departments with different goals and methods of operation, but to customers it is a single entity. They do not expect internal turf battles to affect them nor do they expect to be passed from one department to another for answers to simple questions.

Seven Deadly Sins

Once we understand the expectations of our customers, it is critical that we deliver a service level that causes them to perceive that they have received quality for their dollar. Getting this **perception** requires that all facets of their experience with us meet or exceed the standards they expected. The old saying, "One bad apple spoils the bunch," applies here more than anything else. While good service is often the result of many small things going right, poor service is often the result of just one or two things going wrong. In keeping with that, there are seven particular behaviors, the "seven deadly sins," that can spoil an otherwise excellent service product. All customer contact efforts should ensure that they never occur.

1. Leave someone expecting a reply. Despite being intuitively obvious, this is probably the most often violated of the seven deadly sins. Whenever we tell someone we will call or send something, we must follow through and do it. If the customer calls us first to check on it, we have lost. It may appear that the customer doesn't mind at that time, but the person probably does mind. Over time, the customer will continue to remember that bad impression. Even if we don't have an answer or anything else useful to say to a customer, we can call the customer to say that we have no new information yet and are still working on it. It is important that the person not feel forgotten or ignored. The goodwill we engender will go a long way toward keeping customers satisfied.

2. Argue with a customer. If you remember the old saying, "The customer is always right," you already know about this sin. Even when customers are completely wrong, service providers do not get any points for proving it. Taking an argumentative tone with a customer puts a service person in a poor position from the start. We may get the personal satisfaction of knowing we are right while suffering the consequences of watching valued customers take their business, *and their money*, elsewhere.

3. Present a dirty or unprofessional look. This is one of the best ways to get off to the wrong start with a customer. Dirty facilities or unprofessional-looking employees immediately undermine the overall credibility of any service organization. In the food and beverage sector of the industry, it specifically undermines the appeal of the product (and may violate laws or regulations). We've all been told, "Don't judge a book by its covers," but people do. Many companies require uniforms to enhance the visual appeal of their staff, and most others at least have some form of dress code. Cleanliness will almost never be cited as a particularly good service quality, but the lack of cleanliness will be noticed immediately.

4. Give conflicting or incorrect information. Nothing is more frustrating to a customer than hearing two conflicting pieces of information from two different people in the same organization. We may realize that it is impossible for perfect communication within our organization, but most customers do not. They expect each of us to be perfectly up-to-date and knowledgeable about practically everything to do with our products. When we don't know something, we are much better off tactfully admitting our lack of knowledge and promising to call them back (we must make sure we do call them back lest we violate sin 1 and give the appearance that we really didn't care anyway). It is far better to admit lack of knowledge than to take a guess and give incorrect information.

5. Argue with a fellow worker in front of a customer. Nothing undermines our professionalism more quickly than arguing with a co-worker in front of a customer. As human beings, we will certainly have disagreements with fellow staff members; however, there is a time and a place for working out these differences. It may even

If you talk to Curt you better keep your distance. He's going to be struck down by lightning any day now! (© Derek Barnes. Reproduced by permission.)

take a screaming match to work it out—but not in front of customers. We can almost always wait to discuss it until the customer has left. In those few cases where something must be resolved immediately, we can ask our co-worker to go into a back room where we can discuss the problem, come to an agreement, and then go back to deal with the customer as a team.

6. Imply that a customer's needs are unimportant or trivial.   Under expectations, we talked about how customers want to feel that they are important and that their needs are unique. They may be the fiftieth person that day that we have had to deal with on the same service need, but to them, this is the first time that day they've needed it. The worst thing we can do at that moment is to trivialize their needs or make it seem as if they are an imposition on our otherwise carefree day. If we don't want them to impose on us, they may decide to impose on someone else who wants the business.

7. Pass the buck.   A common practice in service organizations, especially those with large bureaucracies, passing the buck can be very frustrating to customers. This is true especially because it occurs most often when there is a problem. Customers are already tense because something has or may go wrong, and we double that pressure by sending them through a maze of red tape. The best way to avoid this is to be knowledge-able about who in the organization has the authority to help this person. If possible, find out what the specific problem is so that you can help a supervisor before he or she talks to the customer. If a supervisor is not immediately available, offer to have someone call the customer back. Then, the bureaucracy is at least responsible for contacting the cus-tomer rather than making the customer forge his or her own way through the bureaucra-cy. Sometimes company policy may force you to pass the person off, but do so in as friendly and informative a manner as possible.

SECOND LAW OF SERVICE

The importance of perceptions leads us to the **Second Law of Service**:

First impressions are the most important.

Working in a service field is like being on a football team with a great running attack, but no passing game—it's hard to play catch-up ball. Once customer-contact employees make a bad first impression, customers will be in an "Oh no, what's next?" mindset. It will take an awful lot of things going right before they change their attitude.

On the other hand, if just a few things are done right at the beginning or a complex initial problem is handled well, service providers will benefit from a **halo effect**. The customers' initial good encounter will leave them in a frame of mind that is positive. They will allow more leeway on little things in the future because credibility has already been established. They know that the customer-contact employees have their best interests at heart and are committed to meeting their seven expectations.

Most service companies understand this law and go to great lengths to make a good first impression. They concentrate on the look and feel of their physical facilities. They hire and train people to deal with the public in a friendly manner, and they set up systems designed to process newcomers as efficiently and effectively as they can. The objective is to make a great first impression—one that will last a long time, perhaps a lifetime.

The second law does not absolve customer-contact employees of the need to continue to follow through with good service. Just because they make a good first impression does not mean they are guaranteed a satisfied customer. But it does give the advantage of getting customers on their side rather than alienating them.

THIRD LAW OF SERVICE

The first two laws of service tend to get people to focus on the personal interaction between the customer and the customer-contact employee. This is good because it is impossible to deliver service excellence without a customer-oriented philosophy and without considering the importance of the role of the customer-contact personnel. Unfortunately, as the **Third Law of Service** suggests, this is a necessary *but not sufficient* condition:

A service-oriented attitude alone will not assure good service.

An organization filled with customer-contact employees who are motivated to serve customers cannot succeed on the basis of this good attitude alone. They need to be supported by an infrastructure that allows them to succeed. Most important, serviceability must be designed into the product. This means that the product designers must look at the service from the **customer's point of view** and create systems that meet the customer's needs, not internal company needs.

In "The Coming Service Crisis" William Davidow says that an excellent service infrastructure includes "training employees, documentation, spare parts distribution, and most of all, imbuing everyone in the company with an attitude towards quality." The push for quality requires a management force that supports and encourages customer service and a training program which ensures that customer-contact employees have the requisite technical knowledge and skills to go with the service-oriented attitude.

From the Third Law comes an interesting corollary:

Eliminate the need for service, and you are giving good service.

Some manufacturers have made their reputation for quality and service on this corollary alone. We all remember the poor Maytag repairman. He was always so lonely because no one ever called him to repair a Maytag washer—they didn't need to. By eliminating the need for service, Maytag developed a reputation for being good.

This applies equally to the hospitality and tourism industry, particularly in "mass" service products such as air travel, car rental, and hotel services. In these areas, most customers put a premium on receiving a hassle-free experience. Each encounter with an employee is often just an opportunity for the customer to get impatient at the wait or frustrated with the employee. "Services" such as express check-in and checkout are an effort by companies to design out the need for the service encounter. With these, customers can get what they need themselves and deal with customer-contact employees only when there is a problem or a unique need. This increases the employees' productivity for the company, allows them to focus only on those situations where their expertise is

---

The Third Law in Action

In January 1989, The Hertz Corporation launched one of the most innovative service enhancements in car rental history—they practically eliminated the need for service encounters with frequent rental customers. After two years of extensive market research, they realized that customers wanted speed, accuracy, no stopping at counters or waiting for cars, and—no less significant—shelter from the elements.

The result was Hertz #1 Club Gold Service. Customers complete one master enrollment agreement, and Hertz stores that information in a database for future rentals. The information includes car rental size preferences, smoking or nonsmoking preferences, credit card numbers, and other necessary information.

When customers make a reservation and arrive at their destination, they go straight to the Hertz bus and tell the driver that they are a member of Hertz #1 Club Gold. The driver's first stop at the rental site is the #1 Club Gold Plaza. Here, customers walk under a weather-protected canopy where an electronic signboard displays their names and the stall numbers of their preassigned vehicles. The car is ready to go—complete with a preprinted rental record hanging on the rear-view mirror, a map, trunk open, and car running. #1 Club Gold members drive to the gate, show the attendant the rental agreement and driver's license, and away they go.

All of the items necessary for renting a car—rental records, car assignment, the giving of keys, and so on—are now done on Hertz's time, not while the customer is waiting. Hertz, through #1 Club Gold service, now is able to give the fastest personalized service possible, *with virtually no direct customer contact.* By removing the need for service, Hertz is now perceived as providing excellent service.

really needed, and leaves customers with the perception of excellent service even if no one did anything for them—a win/win/win situation.

SUMMARY

Having defined service, it is now important to understand some of the basic laws of customer service. The most critical, the First Law of Service, says that satisfaction is based on whether customers perceive that the service exceeded, equaled, or fell short of their expectations. This judgment is based on their subjective attitudes and opinions, not necessarily on an objective evaluation of facts. Different customers may perceive the same service in different ways, and even the same customer may perceive it differently at different times.

In general, though, customers have seven basic expectations: accessibility, courtesy, personal attention, empathy, job knowledge, consistency, and teamwork. And while many acts may or may not be perceived poorly, there are seven deadly sins that are sure to upset customers: leaving someone expecting a reply, arguing with a customer, presenting an unprofessional look, giving conflicting or incorrect information, arguing with a fellow worker in front of the customer, implying that a customer's needs are unimportant or trivial, and passing the buck. Customers also tend to place an exaggerated importance on first impressions. If the first impression is bad, it is difficult to make up for it. If it is good, service companies can benefit from a halo effect.

Finally, an attitude that cares about service may be necessary, but it is not enough. It must be backed up with the knowledge and training, distribution and service delivery systems, offices and equipment, and everything else necessary to get the service product to customers quickly and effectively. As a corollary, if these systems eliminate the need for any actual service to be delivered, the company will be perceived as delivering good service.

QUESTIONS FOR REVIEW

1. Why is the First Law of Service not based on objective analysis?
2. List the seven basic customer expectations.
3. List the seven deadly sins.
4. Why are first impressions so important?
5. Give three examples of how eliminating a service improves the perception of that service.

QUESTIONS FOR DISCUSSION

1. How can service companies use the Laws of Service to design better service delivery systems?
2. How can understanding these laws help a customer-contact employee deliver better service in an individual service encounter?

REFERENCES

DAVIDOW, WILLIAM. "The Coming Service Crisis." *Field Service Manager* (October, 1986).

PART 2

THE SERVICE ENVIRONMENT: ROLES AND RELATIONSHIPS

Now that we have a basic understanding of the service product—what it is, why it is important, and some of its most basic principles—we turn our attention to the service environment. This includes the people and places involved in delivering the service product.

It is important to understand the roles and relationships of everybody involved in a service encounter. This includes everyone in the company, ourselves, and our customers. We must also understand the environment in which we perform our jobs. This includes not only the setting in which we work but also the trends in our industry that will affect how we continue to function.

In Chapter 4 we look at "the players"—the customer and the company. It answers the question, "Who are customers and what makes them tick?" We also discuss the roles and relationships of everyone in the company, from customer-contact employees all the way up to executive managers. In Chapter 5 we proceed to examine the aspects of the service environment and key trends in the industry. Chapters 6 and 7 return to the players to examine the specific responsibilities of the company and customer-contact employees, respectively.

4

THE PLAYERS

OBJECTIVES

After reading this chapter, you should:

Understand why customers behave as they do.

Understand the complexities of satisfying customer expectations.

Understand the role that personality plays in customer behavior.

Understand how age and family situation affect needs in the hospitality and tourism industry.

Understand the difference between traditional and modern management theories.

Understand the characteristics of a successful modern service organization.

KEY TERMS

customer

Maslow's hierarchy of needs

    physiological

    safety

    social

    self-esteem

    self-actualization

two-factor theory

    satisfiers

    dissatisfiers

expectancy theory

equity theory

attribution theory

allocentric

psychocentric

life stages

traditional management theory

modern, service-oriented organization

span of control

"flattening the pyramid"

The most basic model for the roles and relationships involved in the service industry has only two elements: the customer and the company (Figure 4-1).

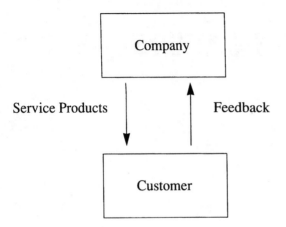

Figure 4-1   Basic roles and relationships.

THE CUSTOMER

In this model it may seem that the customer is the simplest part. After all, the complex part is the company with all its departments, rules and regulations, business and marketing goals, and so on. The customer is simply the person who wants something from the business.

Many companies take this attitude, and therefore so do their customer-contact employees. Needless to say, they couldn't be more incorrect. Each customer is an individual, with all the qualities and quirks that each of us has. If it were true that the customer was a simple part of the model, the entire field of market psychology would not exist.

All customer-contact employees need to be aware of how customers may behave and what their motivations may be. Since customers deal with companies primarily to satisfy needs, it is important to understand some basic theories about individuals' needs. Also, since individuals' underlying motivations often govern their reaction to events and situations, it is necessary to learn a few simple motivation theories as well.

Although an in-depth discussion of the details of human psychology and motivation is obviously beyond the scope of this book, it is imperative that we examine the basic principles behind some of the most important modern theories.

Need Theory

One of the most influential theories was developed by Abraham Maslow in the 1940s. He has suggested that human beings behave in order to satisfy a **hierarchy of needs** (Figure 4-2). Like building a pyramid, they will be motivated to meet a higher-level need only when the lower level has been at least minimally met.

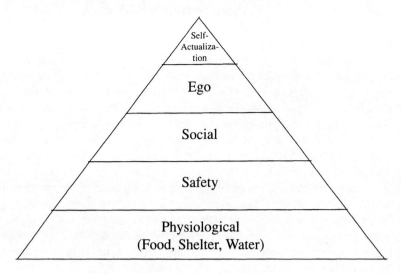

Figure 4-2   Maslow's hierarchy of needs.

Physiological needs, the lowest-order level, include such things as food, shelter, and water. Since most customers of hospitality or travel services are sufficiently well-off to want to purchase such services, it is not likely that we will be dealing with people who are insecure in their ability to meet their physiological needs. However, we have all noticed how much more irritable people can be when they are hungry or tired. Not surprisingly, this is the time when people are likely to be most critical about their perceptions of how they are being treated. Unfortunately, restaurant workers most often have their first encounter when the customer is hungry, and hotel workers have their first encounter when the guest is tired after a long flight or drive. Given the Second Law of Service, which emphasizes the difficulty of making up for poor initial impressions, these service providers must be particularly attentive to the customer's needs at these crucial first "moments of truth."

Safety needs are next. Once basic physiological needs are met, human beings are motivated to gain protection against danger, threat, and deprivation. Although it is also true that there are many legal ramifications if customers are injured in our care, the plain fact is that safety makes good service sense. No one can enjoy the conveniences of any services if they are concerned about their physical and emotional well-being.

The third level in the hierarchy is **social needs**. These include such things as friendship, love, affection, and a sense of belonging and acceptance. There is no doubt that people's attitudes, opinions, and perceptions are heavily shaped by these needs.

Most of the people to whom customer-contact employees in the hospitality and tourism industry provide service have already met their minimal needs on the first two levels. They are looking to meet social needs. In fact, the need for high-touch service systems to go with the increasingly complex, highly technological world we work in is our customers' logical response to meeting social needs. And because most customer-

---

Marketing through Maslow

Maslow's hierarchy of needs may seem like the last place that a person who wants to market services would look for new ideas. After all, it seems like a fairly dry theory that has its place more in the halls of academia than in the planning rooms of major corporate service providers. The theory may also seem to have limited applications for the hospitality and tourism industry because it may seem that customer-contact people usually work with customers who are operating in only two of the five levels of need. Yet a quiet revolution swept the hospitality industry through the 1980s and early 1990s, fueled solely by an application of the safety and security needs level of Maslow's hierarchy.

In those years, the single biggest growth segment of the travel world was the female business traveler. Armed with growing access to economic and job opportunity equality, the numbers of women in middle management and sales positions (and consequently, the number of travelers) grew tremendously. As a group, American women have a different set of needs and desires in travel than the traditional male business traveler. For example, most American men do not mind sitting on a hotel bed with a customer or supplier and opening up their briefcase to do business. Women, however, generally consider their bedroom to be private space and are uncomfortable in this situation. Similarly, men tended not to mind dark, smoke-filled bars in the corner of a hotel; many women are uncomfortable in such settings when they are away from home.

Yet in the 1970s, most hotels offered only bedroom accommodations at a single- or double-occupancy rate, and lobbies often featured low lighting and corner bars. A few forward-looking companies saw the future growth and realized that their future customers would want a more secure feeling in their "home away from home." Many hotels increased lighting levels in hallways, brought home-style furniture into their lobbies and rooms, and put bars in the middle of lobbies where access was open and easy.

They also began to build and market the "all-suite" hotel. These hotels sacrifice some of the space in the bedroom to provide a sitting/work room with a table. Guests can close the bedroom door, leaving it as private space while they conduct business in the other room. Although many of those who began marketing these new styles of hospitality service were motivated to meet the safety and security needs of the increasing number of women travelers, the result has been that many men prefer them as well. Maslow, after all, is not gender specific.

---

contact employees interact with the customer for only a short period of time, there is little opportunity to do anything more than appeal to the customers' needs for friendship, acceptance, and a kind word.

After meeting social needs, people are motivated to satisfy their **self-esteem needs**. These include the need for achievement, status and recognition, freedom, and prestige. VIP customers most often fit the category of people who are seeking self-esteem needs the most. However, the nature of the hospitality, travel, and tourism industry is such that all of its customers are motivated to meet self-esteem needs to some degree.

The fifth and highest level in the hierarchy is the **self-actualization need**. This is the need to realize one's true potential. The best example of this is the need for a musician to continue to compose or a writer to continue to write. If all their other needs are met, they will still be motivated to achieve an inner success independent of money, recognition, or friendship. Only those service providers who deal with the upper end of the service spectrum come into much contact with customers whose motivations are based more on self-actualization than anything else. Even then, it is rare that we do service those kinds of people. When we do, it is often very pleasant, although it can be demanding. People who eat at exotic restaurants or travel because of a need to learn and grow are more forgiving about the petty little things that go wrong. This is because they understand that everything can't be perfect, and they look at these little inconveniences as a natural part of the process—provided, of course, that these inconveniences are not the result of careless service or insensitive workers.

There are a few important points to be made about this theory before we move on. First, the hierarchy is dynamic. This means that it changes with time and situation. What one person's needs are today is not the same as what they may be tomorrow. Second, behavior is often determined by a composite of needs. For example, eating may be needed to meet physiological needs, but using the services of a restaurant may also help satisfy social or self-esteem needs.

Finally, the needs hierarchy should not be looked at as an all-or-nothing proposition. All the needs do not have to be met for someone to be satisfied. For example, Maslow suggested in 1943 that in our American society, 85 percent of the people met their physiological needs, 70 percent their safety needs, 50 percent their social needs, 40 percent their self-esteem needs, and only 10 percent their self-actualization needs. This does not mean that only 10 percent of the American population was happy in 1943. Rather, it means that there were many people content with satisfying lower-level needs and not looking to "self-actualize."

Maslow's need theory may leave the impression that satisfaction and dissatisfaction are simply the endpoints of a single line: in other words, it may suggest that the same criteria that cause dissatisfaction can also be used to achieve satisfaction. Unfortunately, substantial research indicates that the process is much more complex than that.

There actually seem to be two different sets of criteria at play. On the one hand, there are some things that customers expect to be able to take for granted—such as cleanliness and ease of access (Figure 4-3). The absence of these will surely cause dissatisfaction, but the presence does not imply satisfaction. At best, customer-contact employees can meet these expectations, but they cannot exceed them. It is exceedingly rare that a customer will rave about how clean a restaurant, airplane, or office is, but they will certainly complain if it is dirty.

On the other hand, there is an entirely different set of criteria that can cause satisfaction but whose absence will not necessarily cause dissatisfaction (Figure 4-3). For example, when customer-contact employees go out of their way to help a customer, it will be remembered. If employees offered merely routine service, the customer is not

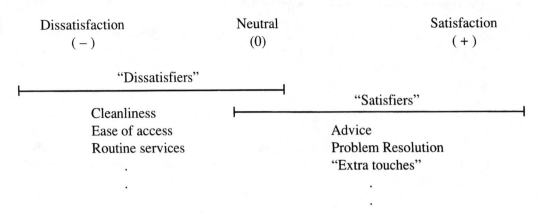

Figure 4-3   Two-factor theory.

likely to complain to friends and family. But when employees exceed the expectation for routine service, they generate extreme satisfaction within the customer. This phenomenon should not surprise us. When we think about it, everyday experience shows that people are attracted to positive things and experiences while attempting specifically to avoid negative ones. To achieve customer satisfaction, then, service providers must hold out the "carrot" of the positive factors, **satisfiers**, while creating an environment devoid of the negative factors, **dissatisfiers**.

This **two-factor theory** can be very useful in understanding what it takes to get customers to perceive that they have received excellent treatment. In general, dissatisfiers deal with the environment, so service providers should design their physical surroundings to be conducive to service encounters. Satisfiers tend to deal with the personal touch involved in the encounter. This means that customer-contact employees are the only people who possess both the capability and the opportunity to create true satisfaction—the kind that generates customer loyalty. The impact of these two ideas cannot be understated.

Three theories about motivation are worth discussing as well. As with the theory discussed above, most research has focused on behaviors in a work environment. However, these theories are broad enough to be applicable to an understanding of the motivations and behaviors of customers as well.

Expectancy Theory

Simply put, **expectancy theory** argues that a person's behavior must be analyzed with respect to the person's perceived likelihood (expectation) that an action will lead to a certain outcome and the value of the outcome to that person. Customers are motivated to work with a service organization because they expect to get something from that organization that is of value to them. Whether it is a quick hamburger, the variety of a bistro-style restaurant, or the sophistication of a gourmet meal, customers have certain expectations about what they will get.

This is critical to the First Law of Service (satisfaction equals perception minus expectation). This theory tells us that the expectation part of the equation is made up of two parts: the probability that the customer expects something to happen and the importance they attach to its happening.

Equity Theory

The evaluation of a situation depends on more than its objective properties. It is often determined by how a customer interprets it in relation to something else. **Equity theory** describes one of the ways in which people make this determination.

All of us, particularly in American society, seek some form and level of social justice: that is, we all have some sense of what is right and wrong and what is fair and unfair. In a given circumstance, this determination is based on an interpretation of the situation as compared to similar situations that have been experienced or heard about. Newspapers and news shows such as "60 Minutes" have been successful by presenting to us situations that seem so clearly unfair that they motivate us to feel particular emotions and perhaps even to take some form of action.

Customers behave and are motivated by the same forces when they work with service organizations. The perception part of the First Law is therefore not an objectively measurable variable. It is often a perception that the customer holds by comparison to something else or to someone else. This explains why customers who pay more for a product expect more for their money. They expect to see some measurable difference that is of value to them to justify the expense. Many companies actually use this to motivate people to alter their plans to increase the total use of their product. Restaurants may offer an "early bird" special, and cruise lines, hotels, and tour operators offer "off-season" rates. By giving better value when their product is not in high demand, they hope to encourage people to change their schedules to take advantage of the perceived benefit. At the same time, they do not offend their other customers, because these customers understand that they are receiving an equitable benefit by getting the product at a "premium" time.

Customers may also compare what they are getting to someone else they see. In the air industry, for example, this causes a number of problems since pricing practices dictate drastically different fares for exactly the same seat depending on purchase date, length of stay, and other non-product-related factors. When business people flying coach coast to coast learn that they are paying three times the fare that the family sitting next to them is paying, they wonder what it is they are getting for their money. The situation violates their basic expectations for consistent treatment.

Attribution Theory

The final motivation theory to examine is referred to as **attribution theory**. Briefly, it suggests that peoples' final analysis about a situation, and thus their satisfaction level, will depend on where and to what they attribute the success or failure of the service. Thus it is possible for good service to go unrewarded and bad service to go unblamed.

It is even possible for relatively good performance to be perceived as bad. A classic example is the case where an airplane is delayed or canceled due to weather. Safety dictates that it is improper for the flight to go, yet among one planeload of people you can get a wide range of reactions. Most travelers, if treated with care and courtesy, understand that it is not the airline's fault. Yet a persistent few will get very worked up, as though the airline could do something about it. These few, who have attributed blame to the airline, need very special care. No matter how ridiculous their behavior may seem, the fact that they are paying customers means that they are still deserving of courteous, individual treatment. Once they look back at the situation in hindsight, they will probably forget that they blamed the airline for the weather, but they will not forget whether or not they were treated well.

Need theory and motivation theory do not sufficiently describe the forces behind customers' behaviors. They, like all people, have differing personalities. Some are leaders, and some are followers. The former are referred to in psychological terms as **allocentric**, the latter as **psychocentric**. Allocentric customers are trend-setters. They are the first in a community to travel to a new place or try a new type of food. They actively seek out new experiences and like to "do" things more than relax. Psychocentrics tend to shy away from anything new until they are sure of what it is like. The psychocentric prefers to return to the same destination rather than trying something new and is more interested in interacting with people of a similar culture than in "doing" things or being adventurous.

Most people, of course, are midcentric, falling somewhere in the middle of this scale. Judging where on the scale each customer falls will help a customer-contact employee determine how to meet that person's needs. Every customer-contact worker will encounter psychocentric, allocentric, and midcentric people. Knowing where their own services and products fit on this curve can help ensure that service encounters with any type of personality meet each customer's expectations.

Customers' needs and motivations also change as they go through a variety of **life stages**. One study done by the United States Travel Service identified nine-different stages of life (Figure 4-4).

Stage 1—bachelor stage: young, single people not living at home

Stage 2—newly married couple: young, no children

Stage 3—full nest I: youngest child under 6

Stage 4—full nest II: youngest child 6 or older

Stage 5—full nest III: older couple with dependent children

Stage 6—empty nest I: older couple, no children living at home. Head in the labor force

1   2   3–5   6, 7   8, 9

Figure 4-4 Life stages.

You think this is something? Dad wanted to put us in the kennel! (© Derek Barnes. Reproduced by permission.)

Stage 7—empty nest II: older couple, no children living at home. Head retired
Stage 8—solitary survivor, in labor force
Stage 9—solitary survivor, retired

With the ongoing changes in our social structure that we discussed in Chapter 1, other stages have become important as well. These include the single-parent household, divorced parent with children visiting occasionally, the no-children household, and the older couple, parents dependent.

Although it has become impossible to identify any single dominant life cycle, each person does go through a progression of stages, each of which has a substantial influence on the person as a customer. People in stages 1 and 2 generally have some amount of discretionary income with relatively few responsibilities. They are therefore able to spend for hospitality and tourism services. In stages 3, 4, and 5 customers have the greatest number of budget items competing for their discretionary dollar. They may be more budget-minded. At the same time, they represent a large portion of the business traveler market.

People in stages 6 and 7 frequently return to the hospitality and tourism market to do the things they had dreamed of doing before. In stages 8 and 9 people may make use of hospitality and tourism services, but generally only if health permits and if they can do so in a comfortable manner. It is also important to distinguish "empty nesters" from "never nesters." The latter is a growing part of our population, and their experience and savvy with hospitality and tourism services is likely to be much greater than those of people who spent their early adult lives raising children.

THE COMPANY

The second half of the seemingly simple model is the company. So much has been written about how to organize and run a company that we will not attempt to cover the entire subject in detail. However, it is important to call attention to some basic ideas about how customer-contact employees fit into the company since this has a direct impact on how they can provide service.

Figure 4-5   Traditional management hierarchy.

In **traditional management theory** and practice, a company is a hierarchy composed of executive managers at the top (the CEO, COO, CFO, and important vice presidents), customer-contact employees at the bottom, and middle managers in between (Figure 4-5). In large corporations, customer-contact employees report to a group of first-line supervisors who have been promoted from customer-contact positions but do not yet qualify as middle management. Salaries, perks, and prestige are all based on this hierarchy. In small businesses, customer-contact employees may report directly to the single manager or owner, thus combining the functions of executive and middle management into a single entity.

In the traditional implementation of this hierarchy, all the power lies at the top,

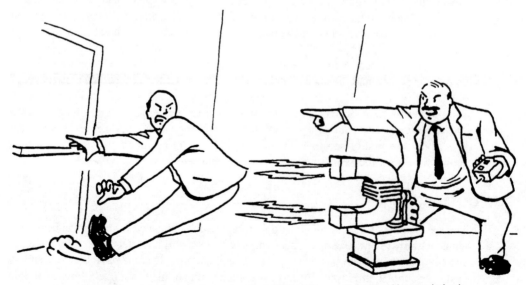

Ah-ha! I knew someone was stealing paper clips! (© Derek Barnes. Reproduced by permission.)

with the executive managers. They set policies and procedures that are expected to be complied with in all circumstances. All deviations from the "norm" require approval and review by middle management at a minimum, and usually through a vice president. Middle management is relegated to the role of supervising customer-contact employees and/or the first-line supervisors to ensure compliance with policy and procedures. Customer-contact employees are expected to conform, often resulting in an environment where compliance to company rules and regulations is more important than the fulfillment of customers' needs.

The problem with this organization style is that the customer is at the bottom. Upper management has isolated itself from the customer so that it can no longer understand or predict customer needs. To make matters worse, this system has a tendency to cut off communication from customer-contact employees up the chain of command. Upper management is not only isolated physically but also prevented from getting useful feedback from their own employees.

Another problem is that this system requires central direction to accomplish anything. Routine functions are handled by policies and procedures and the nonroutine is beyond the scope of authority of the customer-contact personnel. However, the inherent difficulties of providing service and the complex nature of the service product make it impossible for management to set a policy for every conceivable situation. In service encounters, the nonroutine is often the norm. The requirement for centralized direction creates an atmosphere guaranteed to result in negative moments of truth. With the combination of these problems, it is not surprising that this sort of organization struggles over time to keep abreast of, and meet, customers' needs.

To make matters worse, this type of organization breeds a culture that de-values the customer-contact employee—the very person who Jan Carlzon, CEO of Scandinavian Airlines System (SAS) and a noted service proponent, states "is [the company] during those 15 seconds [of encounter with the customer]." By putting the customer-contact employee at the bottom of the totem pole, by creating an environment in which they are absolutely powerless to deal with many of the immediate needs of the customer, and by neglecting their training needs, the traditional hierarchy perpetuates the myths that service work is menial and not a worthy pursuit.

Modern Service Organization

In the past, most organizations thought of themselves as the sum total of their physical facilities, other equipment, and *perhaps* their personnel. The result was a product-oriented culture run by the traditional structure discussed above.

Over the past decade, there has been an increasing trend—perhaps even a revolution—in the approach that many service companies are taking to organizing for service excellence (and thus success). This new approach is best described by one of its earliest, most successful, and best-known proponents, Jan Carlzon: "Last year, each of our 10 million customers came in contact with approximately five SAS employees, and this contact lasted an average of 15 seconds each time. Thus, SAS is "created" in the minds of our customers 50 million times a year, 15 seconds at a time. These 50 million "moments of truth" are the moments that ultimately determine whether SAS will succeed or fail as a company. They are the moments when we must prove to our customers that SAS is their best alternative."

While the number and length of moments of truth vary significantly within the various service industries, this statement is essentially true for all companies in our business. Carlzon has taken the emphasis off the importance of the rank structure within the company and put it on the only reason that the company exists—the customer (Figure 4-6). The result is the **modern, service-oriented organization**, which has some very different characteristics:

1. The customer really comes first.   In the new organization, this is more than mere lip service. Upper management makes decisions about corporate goals and policies using customers and their needs as the criteria for making decisions. Middle management now allocates resources based on what is needed to meet customer requirements, not to satisfy internal desires. Supervisors praise and punish on the basis of employees' ability and willingness to work for the customer, not for the company's rules and regulations.

Furthermore, supervisors are more than willing to jump in and lend a hand when things get too busy—speeding up the delivery of service to the customer is more important to them than the trappings and ego of their "management" positions. In peak periods, when customers are waiting, the restaurant manager pitches in to help bus a table and the hotel front-desk supervisor takes a position to check guests in and out. Customer-contact personnel are selected, trained, and rewarded on the basis of their ability to deliver quality service to the customer.

2. Customer-contact employees are empowered with authority.
Customer-contact personnel have the enormous challenge of meeting the needs of customers in a real-time basis. If they do not have the authority to take the action necessary to deliver service excellence, they cannot wait for approval. By then, the opportunity to

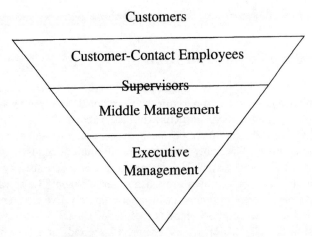

Customers

Customer-Contact Employees

~~Supervisors~~

Middle Management

Executive
Management

Figure 4-6   Modern management hierarchy.

If you'll wait just a moment, one of our customer representatives will be right out to help you, sir.
(© Derek Barnes. Reproduced by permission.)

meet the customer's need is gone. It's much like a soccer game. If a player were to break away toward the open goal and suddenly have to abandon the ball to run back to the bench and ask the coach for the order to kick the ball into the goal, not only would he lose the ball, he would lose the entire game.

The leader of a modern organization passes along to customer-contact employees the authority to respond to the needs and problems of customers. This gives them the ability to fulfill their responsibility to meet those needs. By reapportioning authority and moving it toward customer-contact positions, where customers interact with the company, the modern organization maximizes the probability that the encounter will result in a positive perception of the company in the customer's mind. Instead of being merely an "order-obeyer," the customer-contact person now has the authority to take positive action to improve the service encounter.

3. Customer-contact employees are given respect and status.

Customer-contact work is no longer viewed as being at the bottom of the totem pole nor as merely an entry-level job that one is forced to do before moving on to bigger and better things. Rather, customer-contact people are championed for the critical role they perform. Since customer-contact employees "are the company" in the eyes of the customer, management treats them with the respect they deserve.

4. Education and training is a key part of the employee experience.
One of Carlzon's most famous quotes is, "An individual without information cannot take responsibility; an individual who is given information cannot help but take responsibility." Education and training is an essential part of the modern organization's efforts to support customer-contact personnel. Without general education on customer service, customer-contact representatives cannot possibly be equipped to handle the rigors of regular interchange with customers. Without specific training on the processes involved with a particular company and its products, even the most talented service providers will fall flat on their faces. Job knowledge is one of the seven basic customer expectations, and without education and training, no customer-contact person will be able to meet it.

5. Equal attention is given to touch and technology.   The new organization understands the need to balance high-technology systems with high-touch customer support. It is not afraid to implement new technologies, but it always considers the implementation from the customers' perspective. Customers are never left to wrestle with the uncertainties of a new system—there is always someone available if necessary. Similarly, new customers are not treated as ignorant people just because they are not as familiar with the service delivery systems as regular customers.

To achieve these goals and create a successful service environment, service providers do not have to become 100 percent better at one or two specific things. Rather, if they work within the guidelines above, they need only become 1 percent better at one or two hundred things. Constant attention to detail and performance of the "little things" are what is critical to creating customer perceptions that will meet or exceed their expectations—the definition of good service.

If it seems as though the entire organizational chart from the traditional hierarchy has been turned upside down, it has—and more. The idea is that customers and their needs now drive all decisions and behaviors in the company. Obviously, the ideal is never quite met, but the culture supports and promotes customer-oriented behaviors.

The levels of hierarchy discussed in the traditional structure have not disappeared. Rather, they have been reoriented and given significantly new roles (Figure 4-7). Where upper management used to manage the company, their new role is to lead it. Where they used to set policy and specific procedures, they now set a vision and empower the rest of the organization to achieve this goal. New leaders are no longer decision-making machines. Rather, they are coaches and cheerleaders. Certainly, there are still many deci-

Traditional	Modern
- Authoritative	- Empowering
- Decision-making machine	- Involves others; encourages creativity
- Limits access to information	- Encourages communication
"BOSS"	*"COACH"*

Figure 4-7   Manager traits.

sions to be made. But there is now time to focus decision-making energy on long-term strategies and new marketing opportunities instead of day-to-day "nitpicking."

Middle management is no longer responsible for merely transmitting policy and procedures and then policing the adherence to them. Instead, middle management takes the strategic vision set above and determines operationally how it can be achieved. They now have complete authority to allocate resources within their part of the organization—from personnel to capital equipment to cash to training.

The immediate supervisor's job is no longer part police, part parent. Instead, it is more like that of a teacher. Supervisors train and develop their customer-contact people, sharing the experiences that they have had and taking a hands-on approach when necessary to satisfy customers or teach a skill that someone is having problems with. Certainly, when necessary, they have to have the strength to administer punishment. However, in the new organization, this is delivered in a constructive fashion.

Customer-contact employees can now focus on what their job has really been all the time—servicing the organization's customers. The difference is that where once they had the weight of the entire organization riding on their shoulders (often making it difficult to do their job), they now have the entire strength and structure of the organization serving as a foundation to support their efforts (Figure 4-8). Although it may look like a slight change in form in the organizational chart, it is very substantive in its implementation.

Another important characteristic of the new organization style is that many of the hierarchical tiers of responsibility are eliminated to create an organization that is more flexible and ready to react to customers' needs more quickly. This is done in two ways. First, the ratio of the number of customer-contact employees to the number of vertical

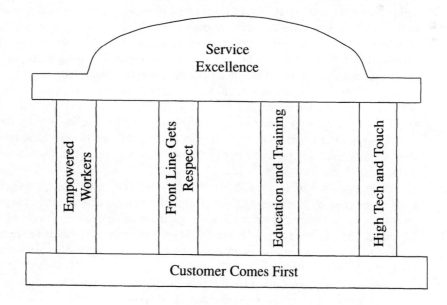

Figure 4-8   Successful service company.

levels of command is increased significantly. This reduces the number of middle managers, thus increasing the **span of control** of the existing ones. With responsibility for more customer-contact employees, they have to restrict their time to critical issues only and delegate more authority and responsibility downward. They cannot afford to waste time in "make work" activities that serve internal interests but do not benefit customers (also, there are fewer managers around to create "busy work").

At the same time, walls are broken down between customer-contact employees in different departments or those with different responsibilities. Instead of each customer-contact person being responsible for a single part of the entire company's service delivery, they are put together in teams, cross-trained, and held accountable for the entire service process—not just their little piece. Where customers once had to wait for a busy employee to provide a portion of the service, they now can get that service from someone else on the team who is trained to cover for the busy employee's area. The variety can make this job more enjoyable and less stressful for each employee.

These thoughts are practically heresy to many who still follow the old school. But **flattening the pyramid** really can work. Carlzon's turnaround at SAS is but one success story based on this principle.

SUMMARY

In its simplest form, there are two players in the service business: the customer and the company. Understanding either player, however, is not so simple.

Customer behavior is so complex that it is impossible to understand exactly why they do what they do. However, their behavior is governed by what motivates them, by their own personalities, and by what stage of life they are in. They are motivated to satisfy a variety of needs—from basic physiological and safety needs to social, self-esteem, and self-actualization needs. They expect equal treatment, and their satisfaction is often based on where they attribute blame for problems or give credit for pleasant experiences. Customers take some things for granted—being dissatisfied with the lack of them but not necessarily satisfied if they are present. Other things will generate satisfaction but their absence does not necessarily mean that customers will be dissatisfied.

Different customers will react to similar service products in different ways. Some of this can be attributed to whether they are trend-setters (allocentric), whether they prefer to stay within a known comfort zone (psychocentric), or whether they are somewhere in the middle (midcentric). They will also react quite differently depending on where in their life they are: bachelor stage, newly married, full nest, empty nest, solitary survivor, and so on.

Companies act in an equally complex fashion. They may follow traditional management theories by implementing the philosophy that executives make the decisions, employees in customer-contact positions implement these decisions, and middle managers make sure that the decisions are followed. Unfortunately, this tends to stifle creativity and leaves customer-contact employees with little authority to meet customer needs at the critical moment of truth.

More modern companies follow a philosophy that considers the customer to be the most important player in the service business, empowers customer-contact employees with authority to meet these needs, gives these workers respect and status, educates and trains them, and gives the need for high touch equal attention with the need to stay current in technology. Executives are responsible for setting a vision of where an organization should go and act more like coaches than like authoritarian bosses. Customer-contact employees can focus on serving the customer, and middle management and supervisors determine how to allocate resources and training to meet the executives' vision of the future. Also, by reducing the number of levels of management and thus flattening the traditional corporate structure, they get everyone in the organization closer to the customer. The result is a much more flexible and responsive company.

QUESTIONS FOR REVIEW

1. List the five needs that motivate customers according to Maslow's hierarchy.
2. Explain the difference between satisfiers and dissatisfiers.
3. Explain the difference between allocentric and psychocentric customers. Give an example of a service product that is good for each type of customer and one that is not.
4. List and explain the nine generic life stages.
5. What are the roles of executive management, middle management, supervisors, and customer-contact employees in a traditional management theory company? In a modern management theory company?

QUESTIONS FOR DISCUSSION

1. Why are some things dissatisfiers and others satisfiers?
2. What are the shortcomings of the life stages model for describing customer behavior? What are its strengths, and how can a service company use this information to improve its service?
3. How can a company change from traditional management to modern service management?

5

THE ENVIRONMENT

OBJECTIVES

After reading this chapter, you should:

Understand the forces that shape, mold, and change the hospitality and tourism industry.

Be able to explain how technology has caused rapid change.

Be able to explain the impact of economic and competitive pressures.

Understand the role that social and cultural forces play in society and in an organization and be able to explain the trends in modern American culture that affect service industries.

Be able to explain the increased importance that political and legal forces play in the business community.

KEY TERMS

automation	nuclear family
communication technology	DINKs
buildings and equipment	consumer sociology
direct competition	organizational culture
indirect competition	protection
sociology	redress
demographics	consumerism
organizational culture	caveat emptor

Understanding the roles of the various "players" is the most important step in understanding how service is delivered in the hospitality and tourism industry. However, all human behavior is highly situational. Therefore, we need to understand the situation, or "environment," in which service encounters occur. Like physical geography, the hospitality and tourism environment is the result of numerous forces that make an impact on how business is done. Just as geological forces can be categorized (erosion, eruption, etc.), the forces at work in the hospitality and tourism environment can be categorized to understand them better. In general, there are four basic categories: (1) technological, (2) economic and competitive, (3) social and cultural, and (4) political and legal.

TECHNOLOGICAL FORCES

Nothing has had a more profound effect on the way that business operates today than the rapid advancement and expansion of technology. Although it is true for all industries, it is particularly strong in hospitality and tourism. This is because all hospitality and tourism industries depend heavily on the processing and flow of information and/or the transportation of packages or people.

Even in the hotel sector, which existed long before the Industrial Revolution, we see the impact everywhere. The growth of technology-linked transportation systems such as trains and airplanes has made long-distance travel possible for the average person. This, in turn, has fueled growth in the number, size, and variability of hotel chains and individual properties. Computers and telephones have made it possible for travel agencies and individuals to make quick, reliable, and relatively simple reservations. Other technologies have allowed some properties to develop service systems for express checkout, business needs, and meeting and convention support. If technology has had such a tremendous impact on something as inherently "low tech" as a night's lodging, we can imagine the impact it has had on the facets of the hospitality and tourism industry that depend on technology for their very existence.

The most obvious impact from technological forces is the increase in the availability, capability, and importance of **automation**. Automation includes anything that can be done in the absence of human interaction. This includes everything from a computer search for the lowest airfare, to a cruise or tour operator printing a run of passenger documents overnight instead of handwriting them, to a restaurant getting a credit card approval without the need to talk with anyone over the phone.

Computers and automation have practically taken over the industry. It was only a few short years ago that computers were the private domain of high-tech or very large companies. With the onset of the personal computer revolution, people can now get that same processing power right at their desks for a fraction of the cost. Today's software explosion, which shows no signs of slowing down, gives everyone a wide range of "application programs," ranging from spreadsheets to databases to word processing to desktop publishing. There is hardly anything today in the industry that is not touched in some way or other by an automated system.

An equally important technological force is the increasing capability and scope of **communication technology**. Without communication technology, the automation advances would be close to useless. Communication lines are needed to link computers

A mainframe computer that can do 6,000,000 operations a second is very impressive, son, but do you think we really need one for the newsstand? (© Derek Barnes. Reproduced by permission.)

through modems so that they can talk to each other. Communication is needed so that customers and companies can talk to each other and so that people within a company can exchange information necessary to meet customer needs. In Part 3 we discuss the variety of communication technology in detail. There is no doubt, however, that phones, telefaxes, reproduction machines, and a host of other information retrieval, processing, and transfer technology has had a major impact on hospitality and tourism companies and their ability to meet and exceed customer expectations.

A third area greatly affected by technological forces is **buildings and equipment**. In some cases the impact is obvious; in others, it may be more subtle. The air transportation sector has always been tied to technological advancements. In its early days, each advancement brought new capabilities for size, distance, and comfort. Advancements for safety and size continued, culminating in the development of wide-body aircraft such as the 747, DC-10 and L-1011. Recent developments have focused on economic and environmental factors such as fuel efficiency and noise abatement as well as continued safety improvements. The future is likely to focus on customer comfort and service as much as anything else. As technology reaches its limits on efficiency and reliability, aircraft manufacturers and suppliers of peripheral equipment are likely to look toward service-oriented features. This is already happening. Boeing has put into service the 767, which was specifically designed to have a seat configuration with fewer middle seats and more storage space than those of any other plane. GTE has marketed the AirFone to allow business travelers to make phone calls anywhere while flying. These trends are likely to continue.

Airlines are not the only hospitality and tourism companies heavily dependent on technology for their equipment. Although most people don't think about it, cruise lines are also very dependent on technology. When they began, they were limited by the ships available. These were mostly transatlantic passenger ships and converted freighters. As cruising grew in popularity, new ships began to be built with the passenger and the cruise experience in mind. Continued advances in naval architecture, engineering, propulsion, and electronics have led to a whole new generation of "superliners" and "megaliners" that are larger, more comfortable, and more stable in the water than anything thought possible a few decades ago.

Technological forces are not limited to sectors that are heavily dependent on equipment. Hotels and restaurants, which utilize buildings rather than large vehicles, have also been benefactors of technology. Improvements in architecture, civil engineering, and construction technology affect the buildings themselves. Climate control, insulation, and lighting technology make it possible for large inside areas to be kept comfortable for people at an affordable cost. Furthermore, improvements in human factors—the study of how human beings interact with their surroundings—have crept into all facets of architecture and interior design.

No matter where one looks today within the hospitality and tourism industry, technological forces have worked to mold the environment in which service is provided to customers. Whether we pine for "the good old days" of supposed simplicity, or whether we look aggressively toward the challenges of a new and different tomorrow, the fact is that technology will continue to advance. Its pace will continue to quicken, and service providers will continue to need to learn and adapt to optimize its use. The days are gone when care and concern alone would satisfy customers. Service providers need to make use of technology to meet customers' needs for efficiency and knowledge while continuing to give the personal attention and individual concern that customers crave.

ECONOMIC AND COMPETITIVE FORCES

Economic and competitive forces are those parts of the environment that deal with the cost/price structure of the service products that companies offer. Economic forces affect the cost of doing business. This includes the human resources costs (salaries, training, time involved to give the service, back office expenses such as marketing and accounting, pension plans, etc.), facilities costs (buildings, rent, utilities, etc.), financing and risk costs (interest on loans, cost of money, insurance, etc.), consumables (office supplies, etc.), advertising, and anything else that is an expense. Like the cost of living, these costs may vary from one geographical area to another.

Competitive forces come from other companies. They may be in our line of business or not. It is obvious that American Airlines is in **direct competition** with United Airlines and that McDonald's is in direct competition with Burger King. Less obvious, but equally true, is that a travel agency is in **indirect competition** with a car dealership, a jewelry store, and a carpeting shop. This is because all of these businesses compete for consumers' discretionary income. When an agency markets to the public general reasons why travel is the best value for their money, it is often doing as much to help its profitability as when the effort is to convince the consumer of the agency's superiority. As a result, even in a location that has only one agency, that agency feels the pressures of competition.

Competitive forces can work to promote or inhibit service excellence. In general, the trend is moving toward encouraging good service. Many companies are beginning to realize that service excellence is required to keep current customers and is often the only way to distinguish themselves from the competition in the marketing battle to get new customers.

Competition fosters service improvement in several ways. In a reactive way, a company may add services or renew a focus on service quality to match something the competition has introduced. An excellent example of this is the credit card industry, where American Express is feeling the pinch from VISA and MasterCard, both of whom have matched the vast majority of American Express's member benefits.

In a proactive way, a truly service-oriented company will seek new ideas and create new systems to make its own products obsolete and stay ahead of the competition. This also directly addresses the dynamic nature of the First Law of Service. Those services which exceed customer expectations today are likely to become expectations tomorrow. Therefore, competitive pressures of the environment force us to improve our service systems continually.

Unfortunately, competition occasionally discourages service excellence. As we'll discuss later in this chapter, much of the consumer public is looking for a "deal." Some companies respond to this pressure by searching for cost-cutting ideas. Since services and service are "soft" products, they become the first to suffer. The result is a staff that is either too small or unable to perform its job effectively due to lack of support. Ultimately, morale is damaged—sometimes beyond repair. There is a legitimate (and large) place in the market for servicing "budget-minded" customers, but there is a fine line between providing the appropriate service level for that market and cutting corners. We would all be wise to remember the John Ruskin quote highlighted in Baskin Robbins ice cream stores: "There is hardly anything in the world that some man cannot make a little worse and sell a little cheaper, and the people who consider price only are this man's lawful prey." Budget-oriented customers are part of the environment, and competitive pressures will always give rise to no-frills and low-frills operations. Some, like Motel 6, are very successful within their niche. Others, like People Express, rise and fall quickly. Either way, the effects of the competitive forces they created can be felt throughout their respective industries.

One other effect from economic and competitive forces comes in the form of company and shareholder goals. For all of our desires to provide unparalleled service excellence, the economic reality is that all organizations rely on money for their existence. They cannot continue to function if the cost of services continually exceeds revenues. Furthermore, companies are not in business to break even. They, and their shareholders, expect a profit.

These economic constraints often affect the service delivery system. Gourmet restaurants may desire to set a particular ambience in their environment. Unlike a cafeteria or fast-food restaurant, they are unable to crowd tables too close together. They are also unable to get the same number of new customers per hour at each table. All of this affects the prices they must charge to be profitable—and the higher the price, the better the service they must provide to get customers to be willing to pay for these added-value items. Similarly, one mark of an upscale cruise package over a standard one is a ship that has single-seating dining. This allows guests to spend much more time in the dining room, but it is much more costly to the cruise company. The fact is that service company leaders must balance the type and style of service delivered with the associated costs.

Companies also need to maintain a sufficient cash flow to be able to cover expenses. These needs often govern policies regarding accounts receivable. For example, while most manufacturing or retail companies will allow their accounts 30 days to pay a bill, most travel agencies cannot afford to. Travel agencies keep only about 10 percent of the money the customer pays. The other 90 percent gets sent to the supplier in a matter of days. They often cannot afford to "float" 90 percent of the money for the client for 25 to 30 days. Cash flow is also a critical part of the economic environment for companies that are highly seasonal. For example, ski resorts, tour operators, and the hotels, restaurants, and shops in those areas can spend only a certain amount of money prior to the season. Each year, many of them need either to borrow money or to set some aside to cover service and other business expenses prior to the next big earnings season. This means that service companies that operate in highly seasonal areas often have to consider cash flow as much as total profitability when they make service quality–related decisions such as upgrading equipment or computers, whether or not to hire new customer-contact employees, and what and how many service-related reference materials they can afford to create and distribute.

SOCIAL AND CULTURAL FORCES

All organizations involve people: customers, workers, management, and stockholders. The normal human interactions between these people thus apply social and cultural forces on the service environment. In a broad sense, there are pressures on the environment from society in general or the large group of people that constitute a company's potential market. Understanding these elements of the environment requires a study of basic **sociology** and **demographics**. The latter is the quantitative statistical study of the population; the former is the qualitative study of the interactions and relationships of people within the society. Closer to home, each company has an environment unique to itself. Study of these "mini-societies" is often referred to as the study of **organizational culture**.

Demographics

A demographic look at the American society in the 1990s reveals some very important trends relevant to the hospitality and tourism industry. Understanding these trends in the environment helps service providers understand better what is necessary to meet customers' needs today and how they will need to adapt to meet them in the future.

By comparing the demographics of society today to society only 20 or 30 years ago, we find some remarkably useful information. First and foremost, Americans tend to be healthier and live longer than ever before. Although there are some exceptions in the poorer elements of society, this holds true in general for the middle class, which constitutes the vast majority of the population. People also tend to be better educated and are shifting in geography. It used to be that the northeast was the center of political and economic power. Over the years, however, there has been a mass exodus to the south and to the west. The result has been the rise in importance and economic clout of such states as Florida, Texas, and California and the decline of traditionally strong states such as New York and Pennsylvania.

There are also some remarkable trends regarding the family. In the 1950s and 1960s, the "American Dream" was to get your own house in the suburbs with a two-car garage and live there with a spouse and 2.5 children. Now, however, there is a greater variety of lifestyles and living situations, and many more people aspire for quite different things. Toffler and Naisbitt both have described the decline of this concept, often referred to as the **nuclear family**. Instead, young people are getting married much later in life, and divorce has become almost a normal phase in life's relationships. When adults do have children, they are having fewer; and many are choosing not to have any. Coupled with the increasing number of professional women, this has given rise to a whole new group of people, referred to as **DINKs** (dual income, no kids). Because DINKs have the extra discretionary income of two workers and do not have the expense of caring for children, they have become a powerful part of the hospitality and tourism environment.

Today's wage-earners work fewer hours and take more vacations than did those of yesteryear. They have more leisure time, yet they feel greater pressures from life. The general perception is that the world is much more complicated than it was and is much more difficult to live in. The perception that everything is so complicated and that, "I never have enough time to do what I want to do," means that people are more appreciative of service than ever before—particularly if the service saves time, simplifies choices, or just makes life a little easier for a few moments. This is why restaurants, travel agencies, and other small businesses in the hospitality and tourism industry have thrived and grown continuously over the past few decades.

Sociology

As we look at the sociological aspect of the environment, we can look at two different aspects. The first is a general discussion of the attitudes and institutions that characterize American society. From this we can get a general understanding of the acceptable cultural "norms" of our environment. The second is an investigation of consumer sociology. This is a much more specific look at the behavior patterns and norms of Americans as buyers and sellers of goods and services. This is very important since all customer-contact employees operate in the consumer environment.

Around the world, each major geographical and cultural area has its own unique style and characteristics. The American society is no exception. Americans tend to be very individualistic in nature. As a rule, they champion the individual over the institution. They come from a wide variety of ethnic and cultural backgrounds. Compared to most of the rest of the world, their history is very short. Native Americans are the only true natives of the land, and their economic, social, and political power is almost insignificant. Years ago, Americans were proud to be a "melting pot" of cultures where each culture added something to the whole. These days, however, social forces have resulted in a different attitude—one that tends to emphasize the differences in culture over the similarities. There is an Afro-American community, a Hispanic community, an Asian community, and so on.

Coupled with this is a strong degree of sensitivity about fairness. People in the United States are quick to perceive a social injustice, sometimes to the point of reading things wrong, and they have a very strong press with a vested interest in publicizing these stories. Americans are also very quick to pick up or drop a new cause. They are very susceptible to "fads." Paradoxically, although their attention span is short, they can be moved to massive action when they become committed to a new idea. It is not our role in this book to comment on merits or problems with these trends. Rather, we point them out because service providers must deal with these characteristics of their customer population.

The early 1990s were marked with a major increase in Americans' concern for better care of themselves and their environment. Society continues to be bombarded with messages about what to eat and what not to eat as well as how to be more environmentally sound as to how we handle our garbage. Major corporations that have violated these "new rules of behavior" are attacked by organizations both to get them to change and to get publicity for their cause. McDonald's, the stalwart of the fast-food restaurant service sector, used to be held up as the example of the worst way to do business. However, they took advantage of the new social forces and created a new marketing advantage for themselves. They introduced the McLean hamburger amid much fanfare, and they trumpeted their change from Styrofoam containers to "biodegradable" paper products. In the process, they gained invaluable public relations coverage and realigned themselves with mainstream social forces.

While these are some of the general characteristics of American society, there are also some specific characteristics that society has as consumers. This **consumer sociology** is an important part of understanding the environment. Over the years the trend has been that American consumers are looking more and more to get "deals." Years ago, the only way to find a significant discount for retail goods was to go to a limited number of factory outlets. Now, there are membership stores, mail-order buyer clubs, discount outlets, and a variety of other ways to find a sale. It has gotten to the point where the "manufacturer's suggested retail price" is almost fictitious. It has become merely a number from which to base the discount. In the air industry, for example, 96 percent of the people who traveled during the spring of 1992 used a "discount" ticket—and the average discount was 60 percent.

This emphasis makes things very difficult for customer-contact employees. They are usually the first to offer a price quote and must be familiar with a much more complicated price structure than ever before. They must also be prepared to use sales skills to leave prospective buyers with the perception that they are getting a good deal. At the same time, because every other business is doing the same thing, the customer has been taught to be fairly cynical about everything in the marketplace.

Customers today do not exhibit the same degree of natural loyalty as before. They are much more likely to change on the basis of price. This is usually because the companies involved have been unable to convince customers of the existence of any value difference in the product and service they offer to compensate for an additional cost. As we discussed in the section on equity theory, customers will not continue to pay a premium unless they perceive that they are purchasing something worth more. At the same time, American consumers are much better educated and sophisticated about the market than ever before. If a service provider has a truly superior product at a reasonable price, they will probably be willing to pay for it.

One final observation is also important to the hospitality and tourism industry. Services and products in these businesses are particularly progressive in nature. Customers are particularly quick to move from "Wow, this is great" to "So what? What have you done for me lately?" All service providers must constantly be on their toes to look for new opportunities to meet new needs.

Organizational Culture

Another major social and cultural force in the environment exists within companies themselves. Just as individual societies have cultures that distinguish their attitudes and behaviors from other societies, companies have internal cultures that distinguish their attitudes and behaviors from other companies. MIT professor Edgar Schein has given perhaps the best definition of this phenomena in *Organizational Culture and Leadership*, where he describes **organizational culture** as "a pattern of basic assumptions—invented, discovered or developed by a given group as it learns to cope with its problems of external adaptation and internal integration that has worked well enough to be taught to new members as the correct way to perceive, think and feel in relation to those problems."

Although the definition is very technical, it points out some very important characteristics of organizational culture. First, and foremost, the assumptions and beliefs are *shared* by members. If two members of an organization disagree about a basic assumption, we are probably witnessing two subcultures in the organization that are running countercurrently. A classic example might be union labor and upper management in a large corporation. If they share a view toward appropriate ways to solve or cope with their differences, this shared assumption about acceptable methods of conflict resolution is a part of the culture.

Second, these basic assumptions operate unconsciously, usually in a "taken for granted" manner. Just as in a society, they do not surface unless they are looked for actively. However, they are at play constantly in every service encounter. If they are not appropriate for meeting customer needs, it may be too late for the company by the time this is discovered. Finally, it is a learned response. This means that it is a dynamic characteristic of the organization—it changes over time. Unfortunately, for a company with a dysfunctional culture, it changes very slowly. Even if the company understands it needs to change, it cannot do so overnight.

Culture is visible in everything done by a company. It can be seen in its logo, its physical surroundings, the uniforms or dress of its people, and the way they act. The beliefs that come from the culture represent the organization's sense of "what ought to be." When the culture emphasizes and teaches the view that the customer is the most important person around, customers will notice it. Conversely, when the culture treats customers as an intrusion on the company's time and space, they will notice that as well.

Most important, because the culture defines basic assumptions about what is right and what is wrong, it is not affected or affirmed by mere slogans. Simply stating, "The customer is number one," does not make it so. Culture is taught more by role modeling than by words or direct training. Just like the parent who tries to teach a child about honesty, yet brags about how they are getting away with cheating on taxes, supervisors who try to teach a service attitude yet act as though customers are unnecessary pests undermine their attempt to promote a service culture. Their actions are more powerful than their words, and customer-contact employees usually notice those actions.

POLITICAL AND LEGAL FORCES

No discussion of the environment would be complete without considering political and legal forces. These are the forces brought to bear on our activities by laws, legislatures, executives, and judicial officials of local, state, and federal governments. *Legal forces* refer to the power of existing laws to require or prohibit various activities. *Political forces* come from those people in a position to either make or enforce the laws. Sometimes the threat of a new law or the lax enforcement of an existing law can be just as powerful or even more powerful than the force of the law itself.

In general, political and legal forces exist for two purposes, **protection** and **redress**. Laws and regulations that require truth in advertising, disclosure of terms and conditions, and give consumers certain rights and privileges are designed to protect them from unfair practices. Laws and regulations that allow a consumer to receive some compensation for being wronged by a company are designed to give them redress.

Two trends in the political and legal area are worth noting as well. The 1990s are likely to be remembered as a decade of rapid international commerce growth. Throughout this decade, Europe has worked toward unification in at least an economic sense. Although it will take a while for political unification to match the symbolism, it is nevertheless clear that Europe is trying to become a truly single economy in the same sense that the United States is a single economy. This, coupled with the advances in communication and automation discussed earlier in the chapter, represents a deep and significant change in the hospitality and tourism environment.

Service, including hospitality and tourism, is one of the few industries in the United States that generates a trade surplus. The growing ease of international travel and commerce may encourage more Americans to seek the opportunity to experience the hospitality and tourism of other nations. But at the same time, the United States has a lot to offer other nations' citizens. As Europe becomes stronger economically and the Japanese look to increase their vacation time, the United States is poised for a major influx of tourists. The problem is that we are not really prepared for the difficulties and pressures of dealing with foreigners who may not even speak our language. Unlike most other industrial countries, the vast majority of our population speaks only English. Worse, few hotels, restaurants, or travel companies are well equipped for multilingual operations. It is also very difficult for foreign travelers to exchange money anywhere outside a major city (in Europe and much of the Far East, it is very easy to change dollars into the local currency). The environment in which we work is rapidly changing, and unless we keep up with the change, we are likely to miss out on a tremendous opportunity.

A second trend started in the late 1960s, gained steam in the 1970s, and seems to be going as strong as ever. This is the emphasis our society places on **consumerism** and lawsuits as the best way to work out differences. Consumerism refers to all of the activities and organized efforts related to protecting buyers from exploitation or mistreatment from sellers.

Consumerism is a fairly new concept in the business landscape. In fact, as recently as 1970, *Webster's 7th New Collegiate Dictionary* does not even contain the word. The old idea of **caveat emptor**—which translates from Latin as roughly "Let the buyer beware"—no longer governs the American social and business environment.

Despite the relative newness of consumerism, it is a powerful political and legal force in our environment. It has done much to make the exchanges between business and consumers more "fair," but at the same time it has resulted in legislation and regulation that can be quite cumbersome to a company and its employees. In some jurisdictions, it has also gone so far as to give the majority of rights to the consumer and the burden of much of the responsibility to the business. In some cases there are complaints that consumerism goes so far as to protect people from their own mistakes or stupidity. On the other hand, the consumerism movement has made it more difficult for dishonest businesspeople to make a profit at the expense of an honest citizenry.

Although to date, the benefits of consumerism have outweighed the burdens placed on doing business, the purpose of this discussion is not to debate its merits and weaknesses or to suggest public policy changes. Rather, it is imperative that customer-contact employees be aware of this powerful force in the environment. Similarly, they need to be sensitive to the litigious nature of our society. The United States has more lawyers than all other countries combined, and where there are lawyers, there are definitely lawsuits. Again, we do not have the time or space to debate the good and evil of this system. Rather, we will simply discuss a few important observations about the environment that result from this characteristic of our society.

Whenever there is a dispute in American society, the thoughts of the participants often move quickly toward the judicial system as the best place to get appropriate redress. The increasing tendency to sue has overburdened the courts, resulting in even longer waits for "justice" than ever before. The cost of defending oneself can be prohibitive, so that the threat of suit may be as powerful as actual court action. The unfortunate truth is that once a company is sued, it will lose substantial time and monetary resources as well as suffer adverse publicity, whether or not they are defended successfully. Since the outcomes of a civil court case can sometimes be arbitrary, a company may be willing to settle out of court regardless of the feeling in the company regarding the merits of the case.

The upshot of all of this is that companies are very concerned about avoiding the possibility of lawsuits—sometimes at any expense. Hospitality and tourism industries are particularly susceptible to lawsuits. The emphasis on information and the perishability of its products make it very easy for people to claim that the company did something wrong and caused them harm. This is made all the more difficult since most of our business is conducted verbally, and most consumer laws place the burden of proof on the company rather than the consumer. It is important that customer-contact employees understand that everything they say and do (and don't say and don't do) could be brought back by a customer later in a suit against their company.

SUMMARY

It is very important that we understand the environment in which hospitality and tourism companies deliver their service products. Like a physical environment, the service environment is the result of numerous forces that affect how businesses act.

Technological forces have had a profound impact on the service sector of American business. Automation, communications, and transportation technology play such a large role because the business of hospitality and tourism is the business of people. Anything that affects their ability to move people or information about them directly affects their ability to perform.

Competition, both direct and indirect, as well as other economic forces also affect their environment. Competition continually forces companies to find better, less expensive ways of providing the services they offer or new services the market may desire. These forces have driven many companies to develop different products to meet different market segments—budget, mass market, luxury—or to try to establish a niche within a single segment.

Social and cultural forces are the third category of forces affecting the environment. Companies must consider the demographics of their current and prospective customers when they develop and market their services. Their employees must behave in a manner consistent with the cultural norms of society and the company. And they must cope with that portion of consumer mentality that looks for deals and tends to distrust the business world.

Finally, the service environment is pressured by political and legal forces. Through regulations, the courts, legislatures, and local political initiatives, government and people in general affect the environment. In particular, the service environment is affected by consumerism and a legal structure that attempts to protect consumers and place the burden of proof on companies.

QUESTIONS FOR REVIEW

1. List the four categories of forces that affect the service environment.
2. List and describe three ways that technology has affected the service environment.
3. How does indirect competition affect hospitality and tourism companies?
4. Give three examples of hospitality and tourism businesses that have used demographics to their advantage.
5. What two basic objectives do political and legal forces try to meet?

QUESTIONS FOR DISCUSSION

1. Which of the four categories of forces has had the largest impact on hospitality and tourism over the past decade? The past 25 years?
2. What is America's consumer sociology today? How can a service company use this knowl-

edge to market its products? How can customer-contact employees use the knowledge to give better service in a single moment of truth?

3. Is consumerism good or bad? Has it gone too far or not far enough? Support your position.

REFERENCES

SCHEIN, EDGAR. *Organizational Culture and Leadership.* San Francisco: Jossey-Bass, 1987.

WEBSTER, MERRIAM. *Webster's 7th New Collegiate Dictionary.* Springfield, MA: G. & C. Merriam Co., 1970.

6

COMPANY RESPONSIBILITIES

OBJECTIVES

After reading this chapter, you should:

Understand the importance of the service setting.

Know the components of the service setting.

Understand the importance of selection and training in a service company.

Be able to distinguish between an effective service improvement campaign and mere theatrics or rhetoric.

Know how to implement and be a part of "customer-friendly" systems.

Be able to distinguish between service and services.

Understand how effective service systems are designed.

Understand the legal responsibilities that companies and employees have to customers.

Understand management's responsibilities to customer-contact employees.

KEY TERMS

service strategy

market research

business mission

driving value

smile training

customer-friendly system

experience factor

core services

peripheral service

visible service

invisible service	sales scale
system design	disclaimer
activity	waiver
decision point	safety
timeline	courtesy
fail point	show
corrective action	efficiency
service setting	

Much has been written about why companies exist and what their responsibilities are. Rather than discuss these general theories, this chapter focuses on responsibilities a company must meet for its employees to be able to deliver high-quality service. Unfortunately, many service organizations allow their operations to evolve in a haphazard and unmanaged fashion. Studies have shown, however, that the one thing that all companies known for their service excellence share is an approach that studies service excellence, plans for service excellence, and implements a service delivery system based on their plans (Figure 6-1). To do this, companies must:

1. Set a service strategy.
2. Select service-oriented employees and train them on the service strategy.
3. Design and implement customer-friendly service systems.

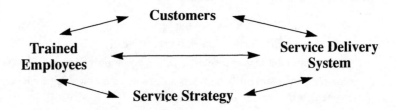

Figure 6-1 Successful service company.

SETTING A SERVICE STRATEGY

> One of the most important things an organization can do is determine exactly what business it is in.
>
> —Peter Drucker

In Part 1 we mentioned how today's corporations are experiencing a crisis of identity. The lines between traditional categories are breaking down, and the differences between "industrial" and "service" industries are less obvious. So before a company can do anything else, it has to decide what business it is in.

Who we are, what we do, what we believe in. Go sell. (© Derek Barnes. Reproduced by permission.)

Once there is a consensus in upper management about what the business is, the company can establish a **service strategy**. Albrecht and Zemke define a service strategy as "an organizing principle that allows people in a service enterprise to channel their efforts toward benefit-oriented services that make a significant difference in the eyes of the customer." This strategy can be used as a guiding principle throughout the hierarchy of the organization. There are many nonroutine customer service interactions and there is no time to review the problem with an entire company's management team to arrive at a decision. When employees must react to a situation in a timely manner, they can use the service strategy to answer the question: If the CEO of the company were here now to help, what would (s)he do? In this way, service strategies specifically let customer-contact employees know what is important and what is expected from them in dealing with customers.

Another view of service strategies is that they make the statement, "This is who we are, what we are, what we do, and what we believe in." They help establish a culture for employees, and identify to customers what they ought to expect. The former provides a unifying direction for the organization. It serves as a rallying point for understanding how each person fits into "the big picture"—meeting customer needs. The latter positions each company's service in the marketplace. It serves as a marketing tool for identifying to customers what is unique about this company and why customers should buy services here. It also helps control customer expectations—an important part of the satisfaction equation of the First Law of Service.

Elements of a Service Strategy

There are three important elements of a service strategy: (1) market research, (2) business mission, and (3) driving values of the organization. Companies have the responsibility to utilize all three effectively to arrive at an overall strategy.

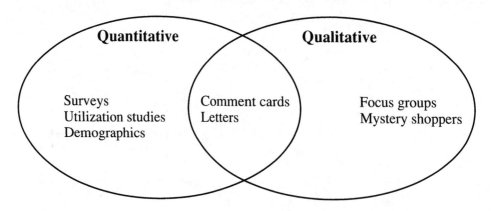

Figure 6-2 Market research techniques.

1. Market research. Good market research (Figure 6-2) is a cornerstone of any service strategy. It involves both an analysis of what the market wants and will pay for and an analysis of what the competition is doing. Since all good service strategies start from the customer perspective, market research must tell the company who the customers are and what they want. Market research should be a continuous process to understand customer needs.

Companies also need to understand where they are in relation to their competition. A service-oriented company does not suffer from "pride of authorship." Any idea that helps meet customer needs, even if the original concept comes from the competition, is more than welcome. Market research can help take the competition's ideas and do them one better.

2. Business mission. The business mission is a statement that clearly communicates the purpose of the company. Its length can vary, although the shorter the message, the easier it is to communicate without misinterpretation. The statement should identify the customer, the type of service to be offered, and the elements of the service approach that distinguish the company from other organizations. This statement should be specific. Simply stating that "XYZ company's mission is to be the best" without specifically identifying how it will be the best is not of much use.

3. Driving values. Driving values are a set of clearly stated, well-publicized corporate principles. These beliefs serve as a rallying point for all employees (and sometimes even the customers). The values underlie every basic decision. When corporate decisions are consistent with and complement driving values, employees are usually energized and focused to meet customers' needs. When decisions are inconsistent with these stated values, there is a conflict within the inner psyche of the company, which usually manifests itself in low morale and correspondingly inconsistent service delivery.

Ultimately, a service strategy helps establish an environment that empowers all employees to provide service excellence to the customer. It is the company's responsibility, then, to support the environment thus created with high-quality people and customer-friendly systems.

SELECTING AND TRAINING SERVICE-ORIENTED PEOPLE

Although many companies are quick to say how important customer-contact employees are, the truth is that many do not treat them as if they believe this to be true. Customer-contact employees often get the lowest pay, and the least education and training, and not surprisingly, have the most turnover. For companies to succeed at providing service excellence, they must first recruit and select appropriate personnel, then must train them to perform. While it takes employee participation to succeed, the company is responsible for making the opportunities available (and mandatory, if necessary).

Customer-contact jobs obviously require a high level of contact with other people. Good customer-contact employees must possess sufficient social skills to communicate with people, an ability to tolerate other people and other lifestyles, and an empathy for the needs of others. A strong desire to serve can be important as well. Most people who meet these criteria also have strong self-esteem.

Companies must select employees who have these requisite characteristics and skills. This is becoming increasingly difficult since most customer-contact jobs do not have the pay and prestige necessary to attract applicants from the best backgrounds. Although this is changing, companies must turn to a variety of sources to find the appropriate applicant pools: getting involved in programs to attract high school graduates, looking to colleges to provide part-time workers, increasing the pay and benefits packages to attract a wider variety of workers, and looking toward the retiree community for workers with a high degree of maturity who may desire only supplemental income.

As qualified applicants become more scarce, training becomes more important. Even when there is a sufficient talent pool, training is required for newly hired personnel to learn the specific processes and procedures indigenous to a company. Regular follow-on training is required as well, to remind and refresh existing workers. As customer-contact employees are continually bombarded by a variety of customer needs and requests over the course of time, it is natural for them to begin to insulate themselves. They can become "robotized" in their actions, overly defensive with customers, or worse, uncaring. Regular follow-up training helps remind them of their purpose, thus reenergizing their attitude. This follow-up training need not be as long and involved as initial training, but it must be done. Unfortunately, many managers turn to theatrics and slogans or other superficial techniques rather than implementing a cohesive development program to teach and reteach service basics to its personnel.

Dr. W. Edwards Deming, recognized as the major force behind Japanese quality developments after World War II, includes among his 14 points for implementing quality in a workplace: "Eliminate slogans [and] exhortations." Albrecht and Zemke state the same idea, somewhat less philosophically, when they say: "Brass bands and armbands don't work."

None of these experts are belittling the importance of excitement and vigorous championing of company goals by managers. What they are saying is that signs and messages that attempt to remind customer-contact employees of their job responsibilities are not a replacement for effective training. The money and creative energy spent on these efforts would be better placed where the company's real responsibility is—training the customer-contact employee to do it right the first time.

Often, theatrics are presented by managers in the form of a new "campaign" to provide better service. With almost religious zeal, employees are sent to new training classes, marketing messages are delivered to customers, and coffee mugs and buttons are handed out with the new "slogan of the month." However, since these "campaigns" have no real infrastructure and are rarely backed up with concrete changes in the way that management allocates resources and rewards, they usually peter out in 6 to 10 months.

The results over time are disastrous. Employees become trained to expect a new program every 12 to 18 months. They know that all they have to do is to tolerate the campaign for a few months and it will eventually go away. Morale is lowered with each passing fad. The only thing that allows the company to continue this process is that its turnover is so high. There is always a new bunch that haven't yet been jaded—but they soon will be.

Rather than copy this formula for disaster, today's service company has the responsibility to design and deliver a comprehensive training program that meets these criteria:

1. It delivers a specific message about the service strategy of the company that customer-contact personnel can act upon. This message is not merely a "motherhood and apple pie" statement, but rather, is an accurate reflection of how the company expects to treat its customers.

2. Managers and supervisors support this message in policy and action. By example and through coaching, they reinforce the training. Executive leadership champions the message and takes every opportunity to continue to communicate it throughout the organization.

3. There is a clear follow-up program to evaluate the performance of participants and the effectiveness of the training. Resources and rewards are allocated based on customer contact personnel's adherence to the strategy. Changes are made to the training program when deficiencies are noted or new systems are designed to meet new challenges (training is given *before* the new system is in place, not after).

Another common mistake that many companies make is to implement a training program that focuses on getting customer-contact employees to have "a better attitude." Dubbed **smile training** by Albrecht and Zemke, this method may get some small, immediate results; however, what few results are achieved are usually quite short-lived. The problem is that smile training consists mostly of teaching a few basic social skills of minor relevance and a few lessons on "how to get along with others" or "how to be nice to an angry customer." This ignores the much more basic motivation and personality characteristics that cause customer-contact employees to behave as they do. Worse, this kind of training is often forced on the staff by supervisors who don't follow the training themselves.

Smile training does not meet the criteria for effectiveness discussed above. A much better approach is for a company to engage its customer-contact employees in personal enrichment and self-awareness programs. Attitude is a very difficult thing to change. By using training that emphasizes personal satisfaction and an understanding of the dynamics of human interaction, a company will reap the benefit of employees with better attitudes. A company has the responsibility to further the growth of its employees, not merely teach them to "grin and bear it."

DESIGNING AND IMPLEMENTING CUSTOMER-FRIENDLY SYSTEMS

The creation and implementation of customer-friendly systems is the third major area of responsibility for companies. Systems include all the ways in which a company interacts with the customer. This is all the "stuff," physical and procedural, that is put into play in servicing customers. In Part 3 we examine in detail specific tools that are used in creating systems. In this chapter our discussion of systems is limited to a company's responsibilities in relation to customer-contact employees and customers.

Companies have the responsibility to design systems that implement the priorities they spelled out in their service strategy. As the title of this section suggests, good service companies design such systems so that they are "customer friendly." Systems that score low on the degree of customer friendliness tend to subordinate the needs and ease of access for customers in favor of the convenience of the people who work in the system. On the other hand, systems that score high for customer friendliness may create more work on the part of the company to increase the ease of access for, and value to, the customer.

A customer-friendly system addresses the needs and expectations of the customer. According to the First Law of Service, this is the only way to get a satisfied customer. Needs and expectations are dynamic, not static. They change as fads come and go, as the demographics of society change, and as the experience level and savvy of customers change.

Companies must address this **experience factor** on two levels. At the broader level, they must constantly monitor shifts and trends in society. Large-scale changes such as those identified in *Megatrends* and *The Third Wave* (discussed in Chapter 1) open up new opportunities for services and shut down old ones. Companies must continually reassess their service strategies, their selection and training activities, their systems, and their overall position within the marketplace.

On a smaller scale, companies must be prepared for each of their customers to change needs and expectations. As people get older, their perspective changes. More important, as F. Stewart DeBruicker and Gregory L. Summe point out in the *Harvard Business Review*, as customers become more experienced, they become more critical of the quality of the product and they become much more aware of other ways to satisfy similar needs.

The approach at Disney World is a good example of how a major tourism attraction tries to deal with this. Their continued growth is partially fueled by market research data that tells them that their average customer returns approximately once every three years. Therefore, for them to get the same high level of satisfaction, they need to top their previous performance level every three years—with customers who are now no longer as in awe of the product as they were the first time. Furthermore, the product must

It Takes All Types

Anyone who works in a customer-contact job for very long probably has many stories to tell about the variety of different requests they have received from customers—from the ridiculous to the sublime. This is particularly true for travel agents, who are uniquely situated in the hospitality and tourism industry. Because they help their clients make use of the many different segments of the industry, they are in many ways at the crossroads of a variety of requests.

In 1992, *Travellife* magazine ran a contest asking agents to identify "the wackiest client request ever received." The winning entries provide proof that no service system can cover every conceivable encounter.

Winning entry

- A brother and sister were sending their mother to her birthplace, Rome. She had told them how she enjoyed being pinched by male admirers there while she was growing up. The siblings asked their agent if they could arrange for such an incident. They set up for a hotel bellboy to go to one of the gardens on her itinerary and pinch her discreetly (the bellboy did it for a mere $5).

Among the runners-up

- A man wanted to book a vacation in Jamaica for his dog—just the dog. Apparently, the dog was "stressed out," and the man wanted to do his "best friend" a favor.
- A client being booked on a ski vacation wanted to know the colors of the condo's bedroom ahead of time so that she could color-coordinate with her lingerie.

Other strange requests

- After being told a flight was full, a client asked if she could "stand" on the airplane. Apparently, she was confused about the meaning of "standby" travel.
- A client once asked if she should take one or two birth control pills when she crossed the international date line.
- A client told she needed to get a "visa" to travel to a foreign country replied, "Oh, don't they take American Express?"
- A cruise ship client asked for a reservation to waterski behind the ship.
- A client called his Los Angeles travel agent from a New York hotel to ask them to ring room service to order him coffee and a croissant.

be varied enough to appeal to people as children as well as when they grow up. The company has taken the responsibility for keeping in touch with the changing face of its customers.

Services

There is a big difference between "services" and "service." We can easily create a laundry list of services. But merely providing services is not the same as providing service. Services are "things," whereas service is the result of a process. In fact, recalling the Third Law of Service, if we eliminate the need for some services, we are in fact providing good service. In designing service delivery systems, companies are responsible for deciding what to offer to whom and how to offer it.

A useful way to look at services is to categorize them as core versus peripheral. Another way of saying this is primary versus secondary services. **Core services** are the basic product(s) of value that a company offers its clients. Airlines offer air transportation, restaurants offer food preparation, hotels offer lodging, amusement parks offer entertainment, and travel agencies offer travel arrangements. These are the reason that each type of company is in business. Core services reflect the basic answers to the "what do we do?" question contained in service strategy statements.

Peripheral services are the other minor services and service "add-ons" that companies provide. Secondary services should complement, support, and add value to primary services. They should not be just a hodge-podge of extras. Through synergism with primary services, secondary services add leverage by increasing the value of the primary service in the eyes of customers.

Peripheral services may actually drive customer decisions. When two or more companies are competing in the same market for similar basic services, the only thing that distinguishes them is the peripheral services they offer. Customers may look for the company that offers the most peripherals for the same price, or they may be willing to pay a premium to get additional peripherals. Both a Motel 6 and a Hyatt Regency offer the basic service of a night's lodging. However, the peripherals differ drastically.

Less dramatically, there are a number of distinctions in the hotel industry, and many hotel companies have established new product lines to meet these different needs. Marriott developed a chain of Residence Inns with a package of peripheral services designed to give value to customers who need long-term stays. Radisson has five different categories of properties, each with a different set of peripheral services designed to meet the values of different types of customers.

Another useful way to categorize services is **visible** versus **invisible**. Visible services are those provided directly by customer-contact people (hotel check-in, ride supervision at a theme park, tour guiding, etc.). Invisible services are all the things that go on to support the visible system (accounting, billing, supply requisitions, etc.). The degree of visibility has a great impact on the perceptions of the customer. Customers tend to take invisible services for granted. They expect them to be there, and they have little patience or sympathy when something goes wrong. In fact, they get annoyed when these "invisible" services are suddenly visible.

System Design

Companies have a responsibility to design service systems to meet customer needs rather than allowing them to evolve haphazardly. To design their systems they must take the service delivery system and break it down from the customer point of view.

First, they should identify the **activities**. These are the "things" that happen during a service encounter. They need to be broken down to the lowest level possible and analyzed to determine which activities mean the most to customers (it is important to distinguish between what means the most to actual customers as opposed to what management or employees think customers should care the most about—the two are not always the same).

Within these activities, **decision points** should be identified. These are the points at which either customers or customer-contact employees must decide between one or more options. Decision points control the flow of an encounter since they guide the process from branch to branch of the flowchart.

After activities and decision points have been laid out, companies can identify **timelines**. Timelines take the general flow of the process and attach specific time intervals to each piece. This allows them to get a view of the dynamic nature of the entire encounter as well as analyze what types of resources will be necessary. Timelines are critical for ensuring proper staffing and supply.

By looking at this entire dynamic process, companies can then identify **fail points**, places where something could go wrong. For each fail point, companies have the responsibility for identifying **corrective actions** and for training customer-contact employees as to what they are. In this way, they proactively design and build in fixes for known potential problems rather than being forced to react to problems as they occur. In general, a designed-in response will be better than a "quick fix" determined in the stress of a moment. Although companies cannot possibly anticipate every single thing that could go wrong, they should be able to identify the vast majority of them. Furthermore, when a surprise occurs, the "lessons learned" from the experience can be used to add this new

Well, Joe, I'd call this a "fail point,"
wouldn't you? (© Derek Barnes.
Reproduced by permission.)

fail point and the appropriate corrective actions to the design of their systems. In this way, the company constantly improves its understanding and the quality of its service systems.

In designing service systems companies must also take into account their **service setting**. This is the setting in which they conduct business. It is the offices, lobbies, corridors, counters, and any place else that they may be sending their customers a message. Companies need to ask themselves, "What kind of first impression do we want to give?" and "What kinds of messages do we want to transmit to our repeat customers?" The first question is particularly important given the Second Law of Service. Service settings must be designed to be consistent with the answers to these questions.

Companies also need to think about their "behind-the-scenes" setting. This is the environment that their employees work in but that their customers never see. Although it does not have to meet the same exacting standards as the service setting, it should be consistent with the messages that companies expect employees to receive. Employees understand that customers are the most important people around and that they are paying for the additional care and quality that they receive. However, employees are also important to the company. If they work in relative squalor compared to the customer's environment, they are likely to come to resent it.

Finally, companies are responsible for balancing the **sales scale**: the balance between the cost of a service product and the revenue it generates. Companies must communicate this information to their customer-contact employees. Since their time is the company's money, customer-contact employees must be aware of how much service they can afford to give. An airline, for example, cannot afford to give the same level of service to an excursion coach passenger as it gives to a first-class passenger. A hotel is willing to have employees spend extra time providing service to guests on a VIP floor. A travel agency can spend much more time providing advice to the purchaser of a cruise vacation than it can to someone buying a round-trip discount air ticket from Baltimore to New York.

LEGAL RESPONSIBILITIES TO CUSTOMERS

Some of the responsibilities that a company has to its customers are the result of local, state, and federal law. Since the details of the requirements can vary significantly from one jurisdiction to another, company personnel need to be aware of the peculiarities of their particular environment.

At the most basic level, companies have a legal responsibility to represent their products accurately. There is a whole body of law that covers this area, often called "truth in advertising." Unfortunately, the travel and tourism industry has been an excellent target for unscrupulous people who manipulate advertising and promotions with disregard and contempt for this requirement. It is often a difficult thing for authorities to police. Fortunately, however, the overwhelming majority of tourism and hospitality companies work to comply with these requirements, but the industry is so complex that it is difficult to know and understand all aspects. All we need to do is to look at a travel brochure or try to read the health regulations for a restaurant to understand how difficult this is. Nevertheless, the requirements are there, and companies must deal with them. When in doubt, a company is better off underselling to a customer than overselling.

Otherwise, they risk taking on the responsibility for meeting a promise that could not be fulfilled.

Most of the remainder of the legal requirements that companies have fall in the area of basic contract law. A contract is an agreement between two parties (or people) in which something of value is exchanged. In the hospitality and tourism industry this usually takes the form of a service being exchanged for money. Obviously, as discussed above, companies take on the legal responsibility to deliver what was promised.

However, in today's litigious society, companies indirectly take on much more. In manufacturing, there is continued growth in product liability lawsuits. This is the case where someone sues a company because the company's product was somehow involved in the injury of themselves or a loved one. In some cases, particularly with chemical products and the like, the person suing doesn't even have to prove that the product caused the harm—only that it is capable of having done so.

This trend is finding its way into the service industry as well. In these cases, people are filing suits claiming that information was incorrect or misleading or that the negligence of an employee was part of the reason that something went wrong or somebody got hurt. To counter this, companies often use two different tools: disclaimers and waivers. **Disclaimers** are written notifications that a company is not responsible, or only partially responsible, for any damages caused by something. Although it is often unclear if many of the disclaimers are truly enforceable in court (particularly when they are very general, such as "swim at your own risk" signs), they are often effective in discouraging nuisance suits. These are suits where the merits of the case are seriously in doubt and the plaintiff is just hoping for a settlement.

Waivers are statements signed by a customer that acknowledge a particular piece of information and/or absolve the company and its employees of responsibility. These serve the dual purpose of protecting a company from undue risk and providing an excellent communication feedback tool. Many customers pay much more attention to the details of information provided when they have to sign for something than when they don't. It also makes it virtually impossible for them to claim later that they were not informed. Because waivers are signed acknowledgments that the customer has read and understood the information included, they are often much more enforceable than disclaimers. They are, however, more intrusive into the service process, and they take more time (and thus money) to obtain.

RESPONSIBILITIES TO CUSTOMER-CONTACT EMPLOYEES

In the traditional hierarchy, the focus was placed on what workers owed to the company. Although there are many examples of efforts to understand what employees need to be satisfied, the basic premise still is that the primary item that the company provides to workers is salary. In addition, a "good" company will look to provide for the higher-order needs of its workers: social needs, ego needs, and self-actualization needs.

In a modern, customer-oriented service company, management is responsible for providing one more critical thing—an environment in which the customer-contact employee can effectively and efficiently deliver positive moments of truth to customers.

The first thing that companies must do is communicate a clear, concise statement of objectives and priorities so that customer-contact employees can make decisions in the absence of supervision. The basic directions are contained in the service strategy, but companies need to elaborate. Disney World, for example, communicates four things that it expects employees to provide to their customers safety, courtesy, show, and efficiency. These categories are very useful for all businesses in the hospitality and tourism industry.

Safety is self-explanatory. Customers could not possibly be satisfied if they get hurt or even perceive that there is a substantial risk of injury (with the exception of "high adventure" activities, where the risk is an inherent part of the excitement of the experience). Remember, physical security is one of the customer's most basic needs on the Maslow hierarchy. It must be satisfied before any other needs can be fulfilled.

Courtesy is one of the seven basic expectations discussed in Part 1. In Disney's simplification for training purposes, courtesy includes the elements of empathy and personal attention as well. In essence, courtesy in this list includes everything that the customer-contact person does to make each individual customer feel comfortable and appreciated.

All the things that make customers' experience unique with a particular service company is called **show**. At Disney, it's everything they do to make customers feel as if they are in Fantasyland or Tomorrowland or whatever international pavilion they are visiting at Epcot. At a restaurant, it's the ambience and the way the waiters, busboys, or anybody else contributes to the experience. With an airline, it's the way the customer is meant to experience the pleasure of flying—from front counter check-in through in-flight

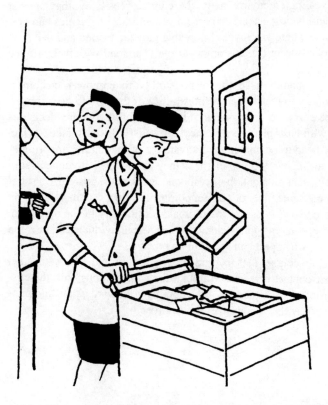

We're trained to ensure the comfort and safety of our passengers and you want me to serve them this? (© Derek Barnes. Reproduced by permission.)

service to baggage pickup and beyond. Show encompasses the customer's expectations for teamwork, consistency, and job knowledge.

Efficiency is also rather self-explanatory. It is similar to accessibility in the list of the seven basic expectations. It deals with all aspects of the service system and customer-contact personnel behavior that affect how much time it takes for the encounter to occur.

Furthermore, by explaining these in order of priority, the company now empowers employees to make decisions in the absence of management supervision. At Disney, a customer-contact worker knows that safety takes precedence over all else, even if it means that courtesy, show, or efficiency has to be sacrificed. On the other hand, even though efficiency is very important, it should never cause the customer-contact person to sacrifice safety, courtesy, or show. The Disney prioritization is appropriate for virtually all service companies, but management should still review it. For example, a fast food restaurant might choose to put efficiency ahead of show.

The next thing that companies are responsible for is the installation of support systems that allow customer-contact employees to get their jobs done. As discussed above and in Part 3, this includes a number of things. There must be the technical support systems—office equipment, computers, software, procedures, and so on—that serve as the foundation for effective and efficient service delivery. And there must be the feedback systems—an active aggressive program to query both employees and customers continually to determine what is good, what is bad, and what can be changed. More important, management has the responsibility to act upon the lessons it learns from feedback.

Companies have the responsibility to give and make available sufficient education and training opportunities to teach customer-contact employees how to do the job right the first time. Rather than creating an environment where employees know they are not trusted and that their work will be inspected 100 percent of the time, companies can create a more positive atmosphere where employees know that they are trusted and that they are ultimately responsible for assuring that customers are left satisfied with their service encounters.

To accomplish this, companies have the responsibility to empower customer-contact employees with authority to match their responsibility. If they are to be responsible for the success of service encounters, they need to have the ability to make decisions when they are face to face with customers so that they can satisfy the customers. When something goes wrong, they need to be able to take advantage of the unique opportunity the customer's expectation for recovery gives them. If they are saddled by unnecessary rules and regulations at that critical moment, their company loses as the customer's satisfaction quickly declines. At the same time, of course, companies must establish limits on what customers can be allowed so as to assure the ultimate profitability of the operation. If training teaches these concepts to customer-contact personnel, individuals can become "mini-executives" of their own when problems need to be resolved.

To do this effectively, of course, the pay and reward system must be consistent with the notion that customer-contact personnel, through their interactions with the customer, are ultimately responsible for the success of the company. Rewards, pay, and punishment must be dealt out in a way that emphasizes this approach.

SUMMARY

Leaders of service companies have the responsibility to (1) set the service strategy, (2) select and train service-oriented employees, and (3) design and implement customer-friendly systems. The first step in setting the service strategy is deciding exactly what business the company is in. Then the company can state the service strategy, which essentially says: "This is who we are, what we are, what we do, and what we believe in." This strategy should be based on sound market research about what their customers expect, it should incorporate the business mission, and it should express the driving values of the organization. This strategy then serves as a guiding principle for all activities and helps empower employees to make good customer-oriented judgments in the absence of clear direction.

Companies must select employees with sufficient social skills to communicate, tolerate others' differences, and empathise with customer needs. They must also provide the technical and service training required to orient new employees to their jobs and to refresh current employees. They must, however, resist the temptation to rely on mere slogans and "smile training." Theatrics are not an acceptable substitute for meaningful training. Successful training must deliver a specific message about the service strategy of the company; it must be supported through action by managers and supervisors; and there must be a clear follow-up program to evaluate the performance of participants and the effectiveness of the training.

Companies have the responsibility to design customer-friendly systems that consider the customers' perspective and experience level. These systems must deliver both the core services that customers need and the peripheral services they want. They should be designed with an eye toward understanding the activities needed to make a good service encounter, the decision points for customers and employees, the timeline for these activities and decisions, the points where things can go wrong ("fail points"), and the corrective actions that can be planned into the system. These systems must also take into account the setting in which service will be delivered. In today's increasingly litigious society, companies have a legal responsibility to customers to keep them fully informed. The use of disclaimers and waivers may help document when customers have been informed, thus protecting the company.

Finally, companies have a responsibility to their customer-contact employees to let them know what is most important. A good list for most service organizations, in order of priority, is safety, courtesy, show, and efficiency. However, there's nothing wrong with some companies wanting different things emphasized or a different order of priority, as long as they let employees know what is considered correct for that business.

QUESTIONS FOR REVIEW

1. List the three things that a company must do to implement a service delivery system based on a coherent plan for excellence.

2. What is the thing called that lets employees and customers know who we are, what we are, what we do, and what we believe in?

3. List the three elements that should form the basis for all service strategies.

4. List the three criteria that virtually all successful service training programs meet.

5. What is the difference between "core services" and "peripheral services"?

6. What is the difference between "visible" services and "invisible" services?

7. List the five elements that all service delivery system plans must contain.

8. What is the environment called in which service is delivered to the customer?

9. What is the "sales scale"?

10. Name two ways that companies limit their legal liability to customers.

11. Based on the Disney example, what are the four things that customer-contact employees must deliver? What is their order of priority?

QUESTIONS FOR DISCUSSION

1. How can a company develop a service strategy that will be accepted and acted upon by employees?

2. What is the best way for a company to run a new service training program?

3. How can a company encourage employees to accept training or seek relevant educational opportunities?

4. When is a company's responsibility to itself (to make a profit and continue to survive in a competitive environment) more important than its responsibilities to its employees? To an individual customer?

7

CUSTOMER-CONTACT EMPLOYEE RESPONSIBILITIES

OBJECTIVES

After reading this chapter, you should:

Know what customer-contact employee responsibilities are to customers.
Know what customer-contact employee responsibilities are to the company.
Know what customer-contact employee responsibilities are to themselves.

KEY TERMS

proficiency
failure
professionalism
pride
critical incident
introverted culture

Companies have their responsibilities, and so do customer-contact employees. In customers' view, customer-contact employees are the company. Whether it's 5 seconds or 5 minutes, the time they spend with customers determines what those customers think about the organization. When customer-contact employees exceed customers' expectations, they reinforce a positive image; when they fall short, they reinforce a negative one.

Customer-contact employee responsibilities fall into three general areas—the "three PRs": proficiency, professionalism, and pride. These are the ways that customer-contact employees can provide that little "something special" extra that turns a moment of truth with a customer into lifetime loyalty.

PROFICIENCY

As it sounds, **proficiency** is the ability to do the job. This is a combination of training and experience. But saying simply "training and experience" is doing neither of these important aspects justice. Since the lifeblood of service is the processing and flow of information and knowledge, postgraduate education is as important as, if not more important than, basic training. This is true whether the employee graduated from high school or from college. Proficiency, in the form of job knowledge and accessibility, is part of the seven basic customer expectations.

To excel, customer-contact employees must constantly update their knowledge. The opportunities for this are limitless. There are graduate schools, small and large undergraduate colleges, night classes, off-campus programs, seminars, and teach-your-self kits and books. Nor does the training need to be so formal. Reading a trade magazine or even the morning newspaper is often a help. This is particularly true in the hospitality and tourism industry because customer-contact employees need to have the knowledge and social skills to be able to interact with their customers. Knowing something about a current movie, for example, may be useful in casual conversation with customers. This helps meet their need for socialization and a high-touch interaction.

Experience itself is of some value, but it gains its greatest value when its lessons are applied. As the men and women that customers depend on for service excellence, customer-contact employees have the responsibility to approach everything they do in the proper frame of mind. There's an old cliché, "We learn more from our **failures** than from our successes," but most people don't really listen to this advice. As old as it may be, this cliché is still true.

Failure is not an end, it's a beginning. There's a story about how long it took Thomas Edison to invent the light bulb. Failure piled upon failure. Before he was finally successful, someone is reported to have asked him, "Mr. Edison, how can you keep going on trying to create this light bulb when you have failed hundreds of times?" Edison replied matter of factly, "Sir, I have not failed hundreds of times. I have found hundreds of ways not to make it work." Everyone can learn from this kind of attitude.

Customer-contact employees may enjoy successes and use them for career advancement or to prove they can do a particular job, but they also have the responsibility to heed the lessons of their failures and learn how to be better in the future. It's easy to say, "I'll approach my failures as a positive learning experience," yet few of us actually do that. People who are able to approach failures in a positive fashion (not just say it) have "something special" that will, in the long run, make them more proficient in their ability to meet and exceed customers' needs.

PROFESSIONALISM

Professionalism is the dedication necessary to put proficiency to work at its maximum potential. A hospital doctor does not expect the sick to operate on a 9-to-5 schedule. Similarly, customer-contact employees in hospitality and tourism may not be able to follow a strict 9-to-5 schedule to be able to meet customers' needs. They have a responsibility to be prepared to take some work home or to work on weekends, evenings, or "graveyard" shifts.

They also have a responsibility to seek out opportunities to put their education and training to work. Learning about the Laws of Service, the factors behind customer behavior, and the tools for delivering service excellence is wonderful for their own growth and understanding, but it does little unless they put it to use. There is no one "right way" to deliver good service (although there are many obviously wrong ways). Therefore, customer-contact employees have a responsibility to seek out situations where they can test their knowledge and experience in order to learn how to adapt them to suit their personality and clientele. Neither their company nor they can afford to sit around and wait for learning to come their way. Rudyard Kipling once wrote: "If you can fill the unforgiving

You keep me waiting for 3 hours, the blade is filthy, and your tunic is wrinkled. Don't you have any professional pride? (© Derek Barnes. Reproduced by permission.)

minute with sixty seconds worth of distance run, Yours is the earth and all that is in it. . . ." This dedication is another "something special" that will help meet and exceed customers' needs and expectations.

Also, as a part of professionalism, customer-contact employees have a responsibility to meet customers' expectation for teamwork and consistency. Arguing with a co-worker in front of a customer, intentionally trying to do an "end run" to avoid some internal or external requirement, or offering up a wild guess as fact are all examples of plainly unprofessional behavior. No matter how proficient customer-contact employees may be as individuals, they do not know everything and depend on others in the organization to help accomplish the overall goal of delivering service excellence. Similarly, others in the organization depend on them. A professional approach means that customer-contact employees have the responsibility to work with others and with customers as part of a big team.

Professionalism means having the responsibility to control your own ego. Effective teamwork requires that customer-contact employees and their co-workers work together toward the common goal of providing customer service—there is no room for personal egos or personal agendas. This is also true when dealing with customers directly. A customer-contact employee gains nothing from proving a customer wrong or showing them how dumb they are. It may satisfy the person's ego, but it undermines his or her purpose. Smart, professional customer-contact employees find a way to show customers a better way without getting involved in a conflict of egos.

PRIDE

Pride is the hardest of the three to define, but it is correspondingly the easiest to recognize. It is a contentment and self-confidence, only more. It is to a large degree intangible. It results from and causes inner motivation to be the best. When employees share pride with their fellow workers, the team atmosphere is unbeatable; and when they share a lack of pride, the morale could be no lower. In short, it is being happy and comfortable about what they are doing.

Pride manifests itself in two ways. First and foremost, it benefits relationships with customers. When customers see and feel pride, they are much more likely to have confidence in the company and want to return in the future. No one can expect their customers to be satisfied with their work if they are not. When customer-contact employees show pride in their job, those they serve feel good about being part of them.

Pride also manifests itself as an infectious spirit that promotes teamwork and group identity within an organization. When employees are in good spirits and think positively, it usually rubs off on those with whom they work. This helps build an efficient team rather than a collective group of individuals. Not only does the customer expect teamwork, but in many companies, teamwork is essential to deliver even adequate service. Conversely, a poor attitude and lack of pride often breeds a tense and uncomfortable atmosphere that will create the opposite effect. At the same time, workers should be careful not to mistake arrogance or conceit for pride. The ability and desire to serve all customers well, no matter what their abilities or needs, should be a source of pride—not the ability to show everyone how good we are or how bad they are. Pride in the job and the ability to serve is the third "something special" that helps meet and exceed customers' expectations.

The "three PRs" are an excellent guide to the general responsibilities that all customer-contact employees have. In a more specific sense, there are responsibilities of four other basic categories: responsibilities to external customers, responsibilities to the company as a whole, responsibilities to fellow workers, and responsibility to themselves.

RESPONSIBILITIES TO CUSTOMERS

As Jan Carlzon of SAS has written, customers' perceptions of a company are based entirely on their individual experiences with customer-contact personnel. These service encounters, or "moments of truth," are what make or break a company's ability to get repeat business. The customer-contact employee is the company in the eyes of customers. A company may meet all its obligations to design and implement customer-friendly systems, but each customer-contact employee can alter or influence the customer's perception with each encounter. As a result, the ultimate satisfaction of customers' needs is the responsibility of customer-contact employees.

The fact is that the vast majority of service encounters go by without much fanfare. Customers will be neither dissatisfied nor overly impressed. They will probably have a fairly neutral opinion about the organization based on this interchange and may even take what they get for granted. Any strong feelings—the kind that will cause them to give a rousing endorsement or a ringing condemnation to a friend—will usually be based on just a few individual service encounters.

These few encounters are the **critical incidents** that make or break a customer's perception of a company. Critical incidents can occur at almost any moment, although they usually occur whenever a customer is in a higher-than-normal state of stress. In such situations, customers are more judgmental and critical. This is obviously the case when customers are upset or angry, but it can also be simply because they didn't sleep well, are sick, or are being pressured from an outside source (job, family, friends, etc.). In general, when customers are in a more relaxed or normal state of mind, they are more willing to look at the bright side of things and let the little things slide by without being bothered.

An increased stress state also often exists when customers are dealing with a company, a particular customer-contact employee, or a particular service for the first time. The Second Law of Service tells us there is never a second chance to make a first impression. The stress experienced by a customer during the first encounter helps make this a particularly critical moment. This is one reason why learning how to answer phones is an important part of any employee's service training.

A customer-contact employee's responsibility, therefore, is to do whatever is necessary to avoid or minimize the impact of negative impressions and maximize the number and effect of positive impressions. The best way to do this, of course, is to meet the seven basic customer expectations while remembering the discussion in Part 1 about the psychological nature of both expectations and perceptions.

Since perceptions and expectations are psychological phenomena, customer-contact employees are not necessarily dealing with objective (or even rational) judgments from their customers. We discussed this in detail in Part 1. In Chapter 4 we examined the motivation theory behind some of this behavior. Now it's important to understand how customers form an overall opinion based on all of the experiences they have had with a service organization.

Customers do not generally form an opinion by "tallying up" the sum of their encounters. We've already discussed the importance of first impressions. In many cases, last impressions are just as important, or more important. Like most sports fans, many customers' favorite question seems to be, "What have you done for me lately?" The unfortunate fact is that one perceived mistake often counteracts many positive encounters. This is perhaps why recovery is so important. By apologizing for a problem, fixing things, and/or giving some sort of compensating "freebie," a customer-contact employee leaves the offended customer with a positive experience as a last impression.

In between first and last impressions, any encounter may become a critical moment in the memory of customers. These critical moments can be positive or negative. The moment itself may not even seem important to the customer-contact employee, but in the context of the situation it may be critical to the customer. Imagine the customer-contact employee who answers a question about where the rest room is with a quick, "Over there." This service encounter is accurate and efficient. But if the customer is tired and has just had a negative encounter with someone else, he or she may perceive such a response as being discourteous and indifferent. This may be "the straw that breaks the camel's back."

Looking directly at the customer and responding "Yes sir/ma'am, it's down the hall and to the right—just across from the bar" has little chance of being misinterpreted. It will probably not get a grand response of appreciation from the customer, but it might be exactly what is needed for a tired customer to start to feel good again. Or, combined with dozens of other equally courteous, efficient, and caring responses, it may ultimately leave the customer feeling, "Wow, XYZ company really knows how to take care of me." Customer-contact employees rarely know the state of mind of their customers, but they do know they deserve specialized, individual treatment to meet their seven basic needs.

When a company or its individual employees begin to focus more on their own needs than on their customers', the company is said to have an **introverted culture**. Such companies and individuals are not necessarily uncaring about their customers. Rather, they have committed the cardinal sin of placing themselves ahead of their customers. They make assumptions about what customers want without asking them. They make customers take the extra step to get results, rather than going the extra step to find out how to deliver their services to their customers with a minimum of customer effort. They expect that customers will tell them when something is wrong rather than going out themselves, aggressively seeking constructive feedback.

Customer-contact employees have the responsibility to avoid becoming introverted. Even if their organization tends toward introversion, they can still do a lot to compensate for that in their direct dealings with customers with whom they come into contact. The best way to avoid introversion is to remember: "Our logic is not necessarily the same as the customer's logic." Anything that customer-contact employees do to better understand and serve the customer's logic helps them with their responsibility to maximize positive impressions and minimize negative ones.

RESPONSIBILITIES TO THE COMPANY

Customer-contact employees also have responsibilities to their company as a whole. First and foremost, they should work within the service strategy set up by the company. It is impossible for a company to function as a team if each person is working to his or her own agenda. Furthermore, the company hopefully has empowered all employees with authority commensurate with their responsibility. A very serious trust has been placed in them, and they have the responsibility to exercise it wisely.

Customer-contact employees have the responsibility to seek out opportunities to improve their education and training and to accept these opportunities when they are made available. If their company is willing to spend the money, they should be willing to take advantage of the opportunity.

Finally, they have the responsibility to use their company's systems and tools as they are intended. Working against the system or misapplying the procedures may occasionally get some short-term gain, but in the long run it will undermine the ability of customer-contact employees and their co-workers to do the job. When systems or procedures seem ineffective, antiquated, introverted, or otherwise inappropriate, it is their responsibility to suggest improvements. This is the most effective way to help enact positive change.

RESPONSIBILITIES TO CO-WORKERS

Teamwork and consistency are two of the customer's seven basic expectations. Customer-contact employees depend on their co-workers to help do their job, and they depend on customer-contact employees to help them do theirs. In Part 5 we examine this issue in detail.

RESPONSIBILITIES TO THEMSELVES

It may not be immediately obvious, but customer-contact employees have some responsibilities to themselves as well. If they meet all their responsibilities to their company, their customers, and their co-workers but neglect themselves, they will not be able to maintain a very high level of service—not to mention keep their sanity. Service is a difficult job, made all the more so when one is in a customer-contact position. Employees must be in good condition physically, mentally, and emotionally to maintain peak capability. In Chapter 10 we look at these issues in detail.

SUMMARY

If a company meets its responsibilities for satisfying customers, customer-contact employees must meet theirs. They have the responsibility to be proficient, professional, and proud in their work with customers, fellow workers, and management. They should continually seek ways to improve their job knowledge and to learn from their failures as much as they build on their successes. They should be dedicated to service as a lifelong profession, seek out opportunities for challenge and growth, and act as part of the team. And they should project a spirited, proud attitude. This infectious attitude will make their customers more confident of their abilities and will help co-workers feel at ease.

Customer-contact employees have the responsibility to their customers to treat each transaction as the "moment of truth" that it is, thus striving to exceed expectations rather than merely meeting them. They should think of how they can make their customers' lives more easy, not complain about how they wish customers would make theirs more simple. They have a responsibility to their company to work within the established service strategy. Employees should always suggest ways for improvement but should never undermine the company's credibility. (If ultimately they cannot support their company's view, they should seek alternative employment.) They have a responsibility to their co-workers to work with them as a team. And they have a responsibility to themselves to be in good physical, mental, and emotional condition.

QUESTIONS FOR REVIEW

1. List five ways to improve job proficiency.
2. Teamwork, personal responsibility, and consistency are all examples of what personal development skill?
3. In what two ways does pride manifest itself on the job?
4. What is the term for a service encounter that makes the customer feel particularly good (or bad) about a company?
5. A company that focuses its systems on making things easier for employees rather than easier for customers is said to have what kind of culture?
6. List the three basic responsibilities that employees have to themselves.

QUESTIONS FOR DISCUSSION

1. In general, can employees learn more from their successes or more from their failures? Why?
2. What does "professionalism" mean? Give examples of both professional and unprofessional service that you have experienced.
3. What can a customer-contact employee do to make seemingly routine service encounters do more than merely meet customer expectations?

PART 3

SERVICE TOOLS

In Part 1 we began to understand the service product: its importance, its strengths and weaknesses, and some basic, universal theory. In Part 2 we came to know and understand the players involved and the environment in which they operate. Now we turn our attention to service tools. Tools are the "things" that make up the service experience—good or bad. They are the specific procedures to apply when delivering service.

The use of the term "tools" is a good analogy. Just like hardware tools, these devices do not create good or bad service on their own. They depend on human beings applying them in the manner for which they were designed. The old saying, "To a hammer, the whole world looks like a nail," applies. Just as we would never choose to use a hammer when we need a chisel, we must not apply the wrong service tool at the wrong time. And just like a saw that is never used eventually becomes rusty and useless, service tools that are not exercised become ineffective.

This section is broken into three major areas. In Chapter 8 we investigate all the basic service tools used by an organization to establish a system that allows its employees to provide service. These often relate to the environment in which customers deal with customer-contact employees or the environment in which customer-contact employees work. For a customer-contact employee to be able to provide good service, these tools must be designed and applied in a customer-friendly way.

Chapter 9 deals with all aspects of the interaction between employees and customers. We discuss exactly how to handle "the moment of truth," from initial contact through service completion, including handling difficult customers.

Chapter 10 covers some skills that are helpful in maintaining personal satisfaction and continuing personal development in a service career. One of the important variables in a moment of truth is the attitude of the customer-contact employee. A well-adjusted worker will, on average, provide a better level of service. Furthermore, one of the most common problems with customer-contact work is the tendency to let the repetitive nature of some aspects of the job lead to uninspired, almost robotlike delivery. We discuss some tools for avoiding this trap.

8

SYSTEM TOOLS

OBJECTIVES

After reading this chapter, you should:

> Understand the concept of service "hardware" and "software."
>
> Be able to identify major hardware components common to all hospitality and tourism companies.
>
> Be able to identify major policies and procedures common to most service delivery systems in hospitality and tourism companies.
>
> Understand how to help minimize the negative effects of customer waiting.
>
> Understand some of the unique challenges needed to offer equal access to disabled customers.
>
> Understand the importance of recovery systems when something goes wrong.

KEY TERMS

service hardware	toll-free number
service software	automated call routing system
Americans with Disabilities Act	fax machine
back office computer system	customer flow
front office computer system	telephone transaction
self-help system	enunciation
automated teller machine	coherence
peripheral	grammar

projection	work flow
personality	specialization
walk-in traffic	generalization
last in, first out	ombudsman
first in, first out	

In many ways, system tools are the technology of the service industry. They are the devices that are used as building blocks to create service delivery systems. To steal terms from the computer industry, there are "hardware" tools and "software" tools (Figure 8-1). **Service hardware** is the physical "stuff" of service businesses. This includes all the computers, telephones, fax machines, copiers, and so on, that make possible timely and efficient delivery of information. **Service software** comprises the methodologies and procedures, such as the telephone answering process, the handling of waiting lines, and so on. Just as a computer is useless without good programming, all the service hardware in the world is worthless without the practices and procedures—the service software—to make the physical things useful to customers.

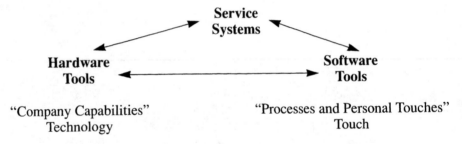

Figure 8-1   Service system tools.

HARDWARE

An outline of the service hardware tools is shown in Figure 8-2.

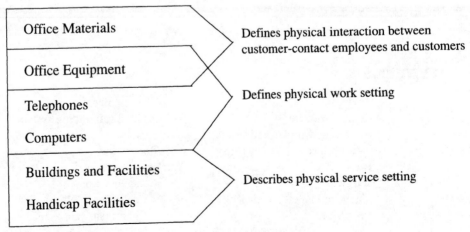

Figure 8-2   Service hardware tools.

Buildings and Facilities

These may not appear immediately to be hardware, but there is often nothing more important to a service organization than its building. This includes the exterior look, the interior decor, and the facilities. To a restaurant, for example, this may be the single most important item of hardware. Sophisticated restaurants spend large amounts of money to decorate their interior to suit their customers' tastes. But the importance of appearance is not limited to upscale clientele. McDonald's and other fast food restaurants work just as hard and often spend more money to create the look and feel they want.

The facilities are also very important. Such things as flow control of people, placement of bathrooms and water fountains, and the supply of trash cans all contribute to the image and feel of a company. Trash cans may seem trivial, but companies like Disney have found that outdoors, the average person will hold onto a piece of garbage for about five steps before dropping it. Once a few pieces of garbage are visible, it is like a sign to everyone that it is all right to drop their trash anywhere. With cleanliness being both one of the customer's basic expectations and one of the more important hygiene factors, the simple placement of numerous garbage cans substantially reduces the load on the remainder of the service delivery systems. Disney even designs the trash can to blend in with the atmosphere of the area in which it is located.

In the hospitality and tourism industry, "buildings and facilities" also includes such things as airplanes, hotel buildings and premises, and cruise ships. For the food and beverage sector of the industry, it includes the kitchen, dining room, and table and lounge setup. In Chapter 6 we discussed the responsibility that a company has to establish the service setting. The buildings and facilities are the most influential element of a service setting.

Many facilities are used for peripheral services as well. Luggage handlers and storage space, shuttle cars or buses to and from the airport, and information booths and concierge desks are all examples of facilities that get used to add value to the service delivered to customers. Hotels may have a VIP floor, restaurants may have a lounge to make the wait more enjoyable, and airlines have club lounges to meet the additional needs of some of their customers.

Handicap Facilities

Passage in 1990 of the **Americans with Disabilities Act** marked a dramatic change in the way that all businesses in the United States must design and use their physical environment. Now, handicap access is not just good business and social sense, it is the law. Although the act is not specifically a hospitality and travel law, travel agencies, restaurants, airlines, hotels, and tour, cruise, and entertainment operators all qualify in the broad category of "public accommodations" that are now required to make their facilities and services available to disabled persons.

Access for the disabled covers a wide range of physical things. The needs of the disabled are incredibly varied. They encompass everything required by the blind to that of the deaf and of the physically or mentally impaired. We are all aware of such aids as the special parking spaces we see at shopping centers, but providing a means of access is much more than that. It includes stair ramps, elevators, and handicap-accessible bathrooms and hotel rooms. On cruise ships, something as trivial to the "able-bodied" as the lip at the bathroom that prevents water from spilling into the room becomes a major barrier to those who require a wheelchair. Full access must include special phones for the deaf (a telecommunications for the deaf device, or TDD), smoke alarms for the deaf, message notices for the blind, and means of providing for guide dogs.

Computers

Computers have made possible growth of the service sector. Since all services involve some manipulation and/or transfer of information, computers have had an immeasurable impact on the industry. By speeding up the processing of information, they allow tremendous increases in individual productivity, thus making many more services profitable. With their ability to hold and manipulate large volumes of data, they allow targeted marketing and "instant memory" for repeat customers.

Well I don't know what the problem is. Didn't Joe say something about fixing the computer? (© Derek Barnes. Reproduced by permission.)

In general, computers are used in three ways (Figure 8-3). **Back office computer systems** support service operations by performing such functions as accounting and billing, payroll, and customer mailing list operations. Customers do not have direct contact with these systems, but they do see their effects—particularly as "dissatisfiers," as discussed in Chapter 4. It is exceedingly rare for customers to have their expectations surpassed by the billing system, but should anything go wrong, customers will become dissatisfied quickly.

Front office computer systems are those used directly by customer-contact employees in the course of working with customers. Examples of front office systems include car rental, airline, hotel, and travel agency computer reservation systems (CRSs). The CRS has become a critical link in the delivery of service in the travel industry. Customers often see these systems used, and they have the ability to provide input to customer-contact employees using these front office systems.

The third and least frequent use of computers is in **self-help systems**. These are systems used directly by customers without the aid of a company employee. The most popular use of these is the bank **automated teller machine** (ATM). In hospitality and tourism, there is some use of this type of computer application. A couple of car rental companies have experimented with customers handling their own check-in, and flight

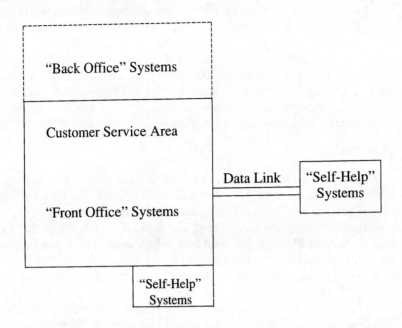

Figure 8-3   Computer systems.

insurance companies have had automated machines in airports for years. Some hotels and casinos have systems to access credit card advances directly. Self-help systems are usually put in place to reduce labor costs that limit the profitability of the service. The difficulty with self-help systems is that they must be designed so that untrained customers can operate them. No matter how hard a company may try, there is no such thing as a "foolproof" system. Someone will always find a way to do something wrong. In addition, the public has rarely embraced these machines in the way that their owners and developers had hoped they would. ATMs, for example, have been used mostly for low-level transactions: customers still prefer personal attention for larger transactions. Often, bank customers will use ATMs to get withdrawals, yet refuse anything other than personal contact for deposits—despite the ATM's capability and the bank's desire to reduce the number of teller deposit transactions.

Another important part of computer hardware are the **peripherals**. These are the printers, CRTs, disk drives, mouses, and a variety of other pieces that get attached to the basic computer system to provide input or get output. Information that is stored in the computer is useless unless it can be used by customer-contact employees and/or customers. Therefore, peripherals are often at least as important as the computer system itself. Company A may have a mainframe computer that is more modern and faster than that of company B. But if company A has only a single, centrally located printer that forces each worker to leave the customer to walk to and from the printer, and company B has a printer at every customer-contact employee's workstation, company B is probably able to deliver more efficient service.

There are many other types of peripheral automation devices that find use in a variety of special ways in different companies, such as bar code and magnetic readers used to speed up paper processing, people processing, and inventory. A large amount of information can be coded on either the universal product code (UPC) black lines and spaces or in a magnetic strip. Some amusement parks use the former for tracking tickets on entry, and many restaurants use the latter for processing credit cards. Airlines have already been using tickets that have the magnetic strip in place, but they have yet to implement the full capabilities of the system.

Telephone

Telephone systems are at least as important to most service organizations as any other hardware. In fact, in some facets of the industry, customers never come into direct face-to-face contact with service employees—they have contact only on the phone. This places a lot of emphasis on proper phone technique. Some studies have indicated that over 85 percent of communication in a conversation comes from nonverbal signals. Since the telephone robs customer-contact employees of their ability to communicate with body language, they need to be particularly effective with verbal communication over the phone.

Telephones have come a long way over the years in terms of the services available. **Toll-free (800) numbers** are now a norm in the industry. These allow for anyone in an area defined by the company to be able to call in, with the phone charges billed to the receiver.

Telephone systems also offer a wider variety of capabilities internal to companies. A company can set up one phone to ring immediately and others to ring only after a number of rings have passed. There are also call forwarding, call waiting, and conference calling. With digital phone technology, many companies have replaced phone receptionists with **automatic call-routing systems**. With these systems callers make selections from a menu as to where they would like their call to go. Once the call gets there, they can leave a message on a voice mail system if the person they want is unavailable.

Office Equipment

Another important set of hardware tools consists of office equipment. Although most people do not think of office equipment as being directly related to service, much of this equipment has a direct impact on the ability of customer-contact employees to do their jobs.

Copiers are probably the most expensive piece of general office equipment. This is particularly true when the cost of operating and maintaining a copier is considered along with the cost of acquiring it. The technology is proceeding to the point where color copiers are becoming more and more affordable. Color copiers may well have a substantial share of the market by the end of the decade.

Most companies are very careful about their purchase or lease of a copier. When considering copiers, they must look at the quantity of copies that will be needed, the capabilities and quality required, the maintenance and repair record of candidate machines, and the money available. There are copiers that can do more than one page per second, can collate and staple, and copy on one or both sides of the paper. Some companies save money by using lower-quality, less costly copiers for internal use, using high-quality machines only for copies that will be given to customers. Obviously, each function costs money and increases the size of the machine.

Telefacsimile machines are newer in the office environment, but their effect is already widespread. A telefacsimile, or **fax machine**, allows someone to send a written copy of a document over phone lines. The cost of sending a document is simply the cost of the phone call. Faxes are quicker and cheaper than express mail services. Most companies now consider a fax machine an essential piece of equipment. Many consider it as necessary as a phone.

Fax machines have many optional capabilities: automatic page cutters, transmission reports, and multiple dial and memory storage for sending a single document to many different locations. Although the cheaper machines require the use of special paper, there is a growing market for "plain paper faxes." These use laser printer technology to print on standard bond paper. As technology improvements and manufacturing reduce the cost, plain paper faxes will probably become the norm just as they have become with copiers.

Office Supplies

Just as with office equipment, most people do not think of such mundane items as scissors, staplers, and pens as part of the "hardware" of service, but they are. For example, something as simple as having a pair of scissors and a stapler at every desk or workstation might contribute to better service. If there are only one or two pairs of scissors or two staplers, customer-contact employees might have to leave customers and reduce the efficiency of their services in order to finish processing something for them. The same concept applies to filing cabinets, organizers, desk materials, and wastebaskets. They should be easily available, and where customer-contact employees have their own space, they should have some degree of flexibility to set things up to be comfortable for themselves and their customers.

Office Materials

Another important set of hardware tools consists of office materials. These include reference materials (books, pamphlets, brochures, etc.), forms (including those for internal use and those used by customers), and other consumable materials. It also can include such things as instructional material for customers (guidebooks, menus, telephone instructions, etc.). All of these materials support the basic service delivery system by providing information important to customers, facilitating transactions, or leaving a record of them.

SOFTWARE

Service software tools are the policies and procedures that are used in service delivery systems. They are the way in which companies string together individual hardware tools to create a complete delivery system. Whereas the hardware obviously places limitations on some ways of doing things and opens up opportunities for others, there is always a wide range of latitude in developing service software.

Service software tools are critical because they usually involve the personal touch. They are how companies design in high-touch elements to meet the social and personal attention needs generated by the high-tech elements. While service hardware tools generally meet the need to eliminate dissatisfiers for the customer, service software tools generally deal with those elements that are satisfiers. Service software tools usually govern the structure of interpersonal contact between the customer-contact employee and the customer. In a few cases, service software may actually design out much or all of this human contact. As long as there is no customer need for such contact, this follows the corollary to the Third Law of Service: If we can design out the need for service, we will probably be perceived as delivering good service.

Customer Flow

One of the most important procedures used by all service organizations is the method for handling **customer flow**. From first contact through the delivery of service, a customer may have contact with many different customer-contact employees. They may make contact and get the service in a single session, or they may continue to make contact over a period of days, weeks, or even months. The procedures used for handling them have a large impact on the quality of service they perceive they have received.

Basically, the flow can be divided into four distinct phases, all or some of which may be applicable to a specific situation: (1) initial encounter, (2) middle encounter(s), (3) final encounter, and (4) follow-on encounter(s). At times, the period between encounters is equal to or greater in importance than the encounter itself. The way the hand-off is handled and the amount of time between encounters are two of the most frequent sources of frustration and dissatisfaction. Conversely, when someone is anxious or upset, smooth hand-offs and little or no waiting can often go a long way toward recovering the satisfaction of the customer. The act of waiting is so crucial in many service exchanges that it is covered in detail later in the chapter.

The initial encounter sets the stage for all future exchanges. The Second Law of Service reflects its importance. The initial encounter can come by phone, by mail, or in person. Customer flow procedures must be set up to handle all of these in an effective manner. They must meet the customer's expectations for efficiency but at the same time identify enough about the customer's needs to determine how to proceed. In simple service encounters, this may be the only contact necessary. Any customer-contact employee ought to be able to give directions to the rest room or answer a simple question about the company's product.

In more complicated instances, the initial customer-contact person may not be able to do everything necessary to meet the customer's needs. This could be by design, as in the airport, where one customer-contact employee checks in a passenger and baggage, another does the security check, another takes the ticket on boarding, and still another provides in-flight services. Or it could be because the customer's request requires additional authority or expertise. Customer-contact employees may have to bring a co-worker into the conversation, or they may have to have the customer wait while they get their supervisor to listen to the request and make a determination.

Either way, the critical moments usually come early or late in the exchange. The most common causes of customer dissatisfaction with these procedures are a perception that they are "getting the runaround" or "nobody seems to know what they are doing." Stephen Koepp titled an article in *Time* magazine's February 2, 1987 issue, "Why Is Service So Bad? Pul-eeze! Will Somebody Help Me?" as an indication of how poor many service encounters are.

All service exchanges have a final encounter. Sometimes this is also the first encounter. But with most complex transactions it is not. Final encounters are important for two reasons. First, the importance of the Second Law of Service aside, people tend subconsciously to give more weight to their most recent impressions. This is what makes recovery such an important part of any encounter with a dissatisfied customer. If customer-contact employees show some care and concern and back that up with a tangible form of compensation, they make the final encounter a pleasant one.

Second, the final encounter is the last chance to communicate with customers. It is the last chance to tell them an important piece of information, and it is the last chance for customer-contact employees to receive information about what their needs are. If customer-contact employees make the erroneous assumption that the last encounter is merely a formality, they miss out on the chance to proactively assure good service. Even if the communication is redundant with previous exchanges, the repetition can only help.

Follow-up encounters are, unfortunately, often overlooked. For many services, it is critical to the company's ability to continue to perform in the future. Without follow-up, no organization could possibly analyze what their customers liked and didn't like. With follow-up, they can use this information to improve their systems and procedures. Also, they might uncover a dissatisfied customer who had not bothered to complain. Follow-up encounters give the opportunity to identify these people and attempt some form of recovery.

Telephone Answering System

Telephone answering procedures are an important element of customer flow. Since many service encounters occur over the telephone, the way this process is implemented within the overall service system will have a lot to do with how customers perceive service quality. In fact, almost all customers will deal with any specific company by telephone at one time or another.

Although telephone conversation may seem simple on the surface, many customer-contact employees are not very good at handling it. This is usually the result of poor (or no) training, not an inability of the worker. As a matter of general practice, there are a number of techniques to use to enhance the capability to handle **telephone transactions** effectively.

The first thing that customer-contact employees can do is practice good **enunciation**. All phone lines suffer some degree of distortion, making it difficult at times to understand what is being said. Customer-contact employees can reduce the impact of this by being certain that they are pronouncing words correctly, minimize the effects of any accent they have, and avoid the use of abbreviations and slang. They must not chew gum or eat while on the phone, and must avoid anything else that hinders the ability to speak clearly. They must also make sure that their speech is **coherent**. Often, people speak in sentence fragments. They interrupt themselves with "ums," "uhs," and "you knows" and sometimes change thoughts in midsentence. This can make it difficult to be understood in person, and is doubly difficult over the phone. Customer-contact employees need to be careful to avoid these tendencies.

Another important practice is the use of correct **grammar**. The use of nonstandard contractions such as "ain't" and other poor grammar can make customers feel uneasy about a person's capabilities. Subconsciously, they are concerned that if customer-contact employees do not even know correct English, they certainly cannot know their jobs. Even the use of such words as "yeah" instead of "yes, sir/ma'am" inadvertently convey a lackadaisical and uncaring attitude.

Finally, when customer-contact employees speak over the phone, they should concern themselves with **projection** and **personality**. A good telephone voice communicates a strong but warm and supportive attitude. Many people do not project a strong voice over the phone. They allow their mouth to do most of the work. However, if they concentrate on starting the sound in their abdomen and letting the larynx (the "voice box") mold the sound, they can get a strong, powerful voice without shouting. At the same time, they need to work consciously on conveying a helpful and caring personality. Generally speaking, the voice is 50 percent of peoples' personality as judged in initial face-to-face contact situations. On the telephone, it is 100 percent of their personality. Customer-contact employees need to speak with enthusiasm, alter their tone of voice to avoid a boring monotone, and speak slowly enough to be understood. Their voice should usually sound like a smile to customers on the other end of the telephone.

Now that we have covered general telephone handling skills, it is important to focus on specific procedures that all customer-contact personnel use at one time or another:

1. Answering the phone.   As the Second Law of Service states, first impressions matter. The best way to make a good first impression on the phone is to answer it promptly (within three rings) and professionally. A professional answer identifies the company, the person answering the phone, and their willingness to serve: "Good evening, Tivoli Restaurant, this is Jack speaking. How may I help you?" As we discussed, the last impression is often the most important. Therefore, customer-contact employees also need to end the conversation as professionally as they begin it. "Thank you for calling Tivoli, Mrs. Jones. I look forward to seeing you later tonight."

2. Putting customers on hold.   Unfortunately, there are always situations where customer-contact people must put somebody on hold. It may be because they are busy handling another customer, or it may be because they need to go get additional information to handle a specific question. Being put on hold can be stressful. When the person called, he or she knew that someone would hear the phone ring and would answer, but once put on hold, they have no idea when (or if) someone will come back. This lack of knowledge and control can quickly cause anxiety. Even short holds seem longer—just try looking at a watch for 60 seconds and doing nothing else. It's amazing how long a minute can be.

To alleviate this anxiety, customer-contact employees need to follow a couple of simple rules. First, they can ask customers if they would not mind being put on hold, being sure to wait for a response. It is very annoying to customers to be asked the question and then put on hold before they can answer. Second, they can keep the length of the hold to a minimum and continue to give customers an option. If customer-contact employees know they have to put customers on hold for awhile they can ask them if they would prefer a callback. When customers are on hold, customer-contact employees get back on the line every 2 or 3 minutes to let them know they have not forgotten them. At that time, again, they can offer the option for a callback.

3. Calling customers back. The procedure here is simple—all customers should be called back. Failure to do so is one of the seven deadly sins covered in Part 1. Even if the only information is that there is no new information, a callback shows customers that they are not forgotten and that the caller is actively working to meet their needs.

4. Screening. Screening phone calls is a common procedure for customer-contact employees who answer the phone and control the flow of customers to their supervisor or co-workers. Screening is the practice of filtering out calls from those callers that the supervisor or co-worker will want to talk to immediately and those callers that should be told automatically that they will be called back.

There is a right way and a wrong way to screen. The former tactfully deflects callers' requests with a credible excuse and a polite promise for call back. The latter leaves callers certain that they have been screened and potentially insulted. The best example of badly handled screens is when a customer-contact person asks for the caller's name and implies that the person he or she wants is in, then puts the person on hold for a little while only to come back and say, "I'm sorry, Ms. Arnold is in a meeting. Can I have her call you back?"

A better way to handle this screen is to ask the caller for his name and then say something like, "O.K. Mr. Greenbaum. Let me check if Ms. Arnold is in her office." In this manner, customer-contact employees let Mr. Greenbaum know that they are not sure if Ms. Arnold is around. When they come back to tell him that she is in a meeting, the excuse is more credible.

Another approach is to tell Mr. Greenbaum that Ms. Arnold is in a meeting as soon as he asks for her. Then the customer-contact employee asks for his name. If Ms. Arnold has let the customer-contact person know who she will talk to, either a message can be taken or Mr. Greenbaum can be told to hold a minute while the customer-contact person goes and gets her. If Mr. Greenbaum is not on the "list," he does not know it and cannot possibly be insulted. If he is on the list, it is clear that the customer-contact employee was screening, but since he is on the list, he may even feel privileged that Ms. Arnold considers him that important.

5. Interruptions from the phone. All customer-contact employees who handle both phone calls and face-to-face customers (often called **walk-in traffic**, or "walk-ins") will encounter situations where the telephone interrupts their work with someone who is physically with them. The procedure most commonly used is to interrupt the face-to-face discussion to answer the phone. The problem with this is that it sends a signal to customers who show up in person that they are not as important as customers on the phone. In cases where face-to-face customers have gone out of their way to come in, this may quickly be resented.

The best systems ensure that someone not with a customer be available to answer the phones. There may even be a receptionist whose job it is to screen phone calls and take messages for people who are busy with customers (they should be told that someone will call them back, not that they should call back later). Inevitably, however, there are times when the system is overloaded. When this occurs, companies cannot afford to miss phone calls—they may never hear from the caller again. In these cases it is perfectly proper to interrupt a face-to-face encounter, provided that they are offered the appropriate apologies. "Excuse me for a moment, we seem to be very busy today," gives customers the courtesy they expect and lets them know it is understood that they are being interrupted. Customer-contact employees should, of course, keep the interruption as brief as possible. When not abused, this usually avoids the resentment that customers feel if they perceive they have been "rudely interrupted."

Waiting Lines

Waiting is another integral part of controlling the flow of customers. Federal Express, one of the most famous and successful service companies (they were the first service company to win the Malcolm Baldridge award, the top award in the United States for high quality in business), once advertised: "Waiting is frustrating, demoralizing, agonizing, aggravating, annoying, time-consuming, and incredibly expensive." No one can doubt the veracity of the claim because at one time or another everyone has experienced the horrors and frustrations of waiting. In service industries, where customers depend on human interaction most of the time, waiting is unfortunately inevitable. The systems that companies put in place to handle waiting speak volumes about how important they think customers are. Interestingly, there is a large volume of previous study on the time and space dynamics of waiting—the objective reality—but very little on the psychology of it.

The former is called *queuing theory*. The goal of these studies is to determine the best way to handle people or things that are waiting for something. When dealing with people, the objective is to use a system that minimizes the waiting time while still being fair to each person. Queuing theory studies were particularly popular in studying how computers can deal with large volumes of information, but the studies are equally applicable to processing individual people as they are to studying individual pieces of data.

Last in, first out (LIFO).

In a LIFO system, the last person into the waiting area (or queue) is the first one out. A good example of this is the coach section of an airplane. Many airlines load up the plane from the back first to process the passengers in a more orderly fashion, thus reducing the wait before the plane leaves.

People sitting in the front spend less time waiting on the airplane. This results in some inequity since it is generally less comfortable to be waiting onboard. However, since passengers know that they will be waiting for luggage anyway, most are not bothered by this. In general, however, LIFO systems are not particularly good for handling people unless there is an overriding advantage, such as the efficiency of loading the airplane discussed above, to mitigate the unfairness.

First in, first out (FIFO).   This is the most popular queuing system used. It is really just a fancy technical way of saying, "First come, first served." Restaurants use it for people without reservations, and most check-in desks for airlines, hotels, and so on, use FIFO systems.

In general, it is both efficient and fair. However, the degree of fairness is highly dependent on the implementation. For example, there are many places that have a number of individual lines similar to a supermarket. In reality, each line is its own FIFO system. This leaves the customer to "guess" at which line will be fastest. Many people in this situation get frustrated by one of the corollaries to Murphy's Law: "The other line always moves faster."

The best way to avoid this inequity is to have a single line that feeds each customer-contact position. Most airlines and cruise lines use this at check-in. Hotels are increasing the use of this form of queuing as well. Restaurants and travel agencies have been using it almost exclusively.

There are some variations and exceptions to FIFO that are often used. The most popular is to have separate lines for separate processes. For example, airlines have separate check-ins for domestic versus international or ticketed versus unticketed passengers. This allows customer-contact employees to "get into a groove" dealing with a single set of needs, thus increasing efficiency. Similar to the express lane in a supermarket, it means that people who have quick transactions will not have to wait for those with longer ones. There is a risk that workers will get too bored with the mechanical nature of handling the same transaction, so care must be taken to avoid "robotization" of the moments of truth.

Another similar variation is the separate line for first- or business-class passengers or frequent customers. These special, separate FIFO lines that bypass the normal flow of people are set up to provide an additional level of service to those willing to pay for it or to reward repeat clientele. These same people may be allowed to bypass other normal processing orders as well. People in the normal flow generally do not complain about an inequity since they know they are more than welcome to purchase the higher-priced service level or use the company often enough to qualify for the benefit.

An example of an exception to the FIFO line is something technically termed a *priority interrupt*. This occurs when somebody with priority is allowed to interrupt the normal flow of a line. The best example of this is a ski school participant or a handicapped person in a lift line at a ski resort. The former is being given a benefit in consideration of the additional services she is paying for, while the latter is being given a benefit in consideration of his condition. As with handicapped parking at the supermarket, most of the people in the line do not view this as an unfair inequity.

Unfortunately, understanding the scientific study of queuing theory is far from sufficient for delivering service to customers. Although the objective realities of waiting may be easy to study and control, the psychology of waiting is not. This means that from the customer's viewpoint, "equal" waits according to queuing theory may seem very different. This is because in each person's experience the effect of the wait is highly contextual. What may be an acceptable wait for one person may not be for another; and worse, what may be acceptable for one person at one point in time may not be acceptable at a different point in time.

Remembering the First Law of Service:

Satisfaction = Perception – Expectation

both variables on the left side of the equation are psychological phenomena, not scientifically predictable "realities." Therefore, to maximize the probability of a satisfying experience, service delivery systems must consider elements far beyond the technical aspects of queuing theory.

There are a number of ways that the psychological aspects of waiting can be used to help customers feel like they are getting better service, even if the wait is no different in a scientifically objective sense.

1. Keep the customer occupied while waiting.   When people are doing something while waiting, the wait seems shorter than when they are left idle. As the philosopher William James once noted, "Boredom results from being attentive to the passage of time itself."

There are a number of different ways in which people can be occupied while waiting and thus avoid boredom. The simplest is to have some interesting reading material available. Magazines, today's newspaper or a book of short stories are all good ways to present something to do. A more useful way to occupy people is to have them fill out any forms, questionnaires, and so on, while they are waiting. Not only does this make the wait seem shorter, but it also will shorten the amount of time it takes to serve the person.

Another method is to make the waiting period a part of the activity. Disney has perfected this method for theme parks by building a number of "preshows" around the waiting area so that customers participate in the wait with a level of interest and activity approaching the show itself. In the food and beverage sector, a cocktail reception prior to seating for the main dinner is somewhat analogous. Instead of having people wait at their seats for the rest of the participants to arrive, they are able to enjoy a leisurely wait while they drink, eat hors d'oevres, and chat.

2. Avoid preprocess waits as much as possible.   People waiting to get their first encounter with a person at a hospitality or tourism company are more impatient than those who have already begun the service interaction. An excellent example is the wait at a restaurant. The wait before being seated is much more anxiety-ridden than the wait once seated and given a menu. The fear of many people is that somehow they have been forgotten. They are usually much more likely to go back and check with the maître d' than they are to call over a waiter to tell him or her that they are ready to order or to ask how much longer the dinner will take.

3. Minimize the sources of anxiety.   Anxiety always makes waits seem longer than they are. There are many sources of anxiety, particularly if there is a critical time factor involved in the service. The time just before a plane leaves is just such a situation. One of the most universally poor examples of dealing with this is almost every airline's handling of standby passengers. They take the tickets and then wait until the last moment to let passengers know whether they are going to get on or not. Not only are passengers anxious about the flight, they are now also anxious about whether they will get their tickets back.

In this case, passengers are not only worried about the time-critical nature of the flight, but they have also been asked to give up control of the situation. Although this loss of control is minor and the anxiety may be irrational, it is still very real. Customer-contact employees must understand what sources of anxiety (rational or irrational) their customers might experience. Then they can determine a way to minimize the effects.

4. Keep the customer informed of the length of the wait.   Uncertain waits are perceived as being longer than known, finite waits. Appointments are an excellent example of this. Customers will come early to an appointment and have no problem waiting 15 or even 30 minutes. However, once the appointment time passes, even a wait of 5 minutes can be excruciatingly painful psychologically. Up until the appointment time, the wait was known and expected, but once that time passed, it became uncertain when the appointment would finally take place. All a customer-contact person needs to do is tell the client that it will only be 5 more minutes. Customers may be bothered that they have to wait longer than they expected, but at least the 5 additional minutes will only feel like 5 minutes to them. This avoids the perception of a much longer wait driven by the anxiety of not knowing when the meeting will occur. This approach tends to work only once or twice. If customer-contact persons keep adding "5 minutes" on top of "5 minutes," they quickly lose credibility. This "rolling delay" may infuriate customers more than if the customer-contact person had just admitted it would be 25 more minutes to begin with.

5. Inform customers why they are waiting.   Unexplained waits always seem longer than explained waits. Unfortunately, even the best-designed queuing systems occasionally result in longer-than-desired waits. This may be due to a breakdown in the system or some external cause that was completely unavoidable.

Psychologically, when someone knows why they are waiting, the wait does not seem as bad as when they do not. The reason may be the sense of powerlessness that customers have, resulting in acute anxiety. By simply informing them why the wait is necessary, they now possess the same information as the company. They are able to make a judgment that the wait is understandable or at least beyond the customer-contact employee's control.

If customers are not informed of the reason for the wait, they will continue to feel uncomfortable. In the best scenario, this is not the impression that a service organization wants to leave at a moment of truth; in the worst case, customers have been known to get highly irritable, rude, and even physically violent.

6. Make waits equitable.   Nothing can irritate someone waiting more than the perception that he or she is waiting unfairly longer than someone else. In situations where there is little order to the waiting, anxiety is visibly present. When waiting for a crowded subway, for example, most people tend to be tense. Rather than relaxing, they wonder about where in the line they will end up and whether they will get a seat or have to stand.

To avoid this, an organized queue should be established. At the same time, customer-contact employees are responsible for ensuring that it is run fairly. Nothing is more aggravating to even the most passive person than the perception that someone has gotten away with "cutting into the line."

This idea can be extended to add that nothing can irritate someone waiting more than the perception that they are waiting unfairly longer than they have to wait. This is why many restaurants, theme parks, tourist attractions, and other service companies insist that employees take their breaks out of sight of customers. It appears very unfair for people to see employees standing around when they are waiting for service. This is also why in companies that provide good service, the supervisors of customer-contact employees are more than willing to jump in and help handle customers when lines get too long.

7. Keep the length of the wait from exceeding the value of the service. The more valuable the service, the longer customers are likely to tolerate the wait. This is the reason that airlines establish separate lines for ticket purchase and baggage check-in. The ticket purchase is more complex and valuable. People realize that they will have to wait longer, but those who just want to check in do not feel that the service is worth the extra wait.

This value versus wait concept applies to all facets of the tourism and hospitality industry. People think nothing of a 20- to 30-minute wait at a fine restaurant with a comfortable lounge, while a 5-minute wait at a fast food restaurant is often unacceptable. At the same time, it is important to realize that there are circumstances where although the service may be valuable, customers have also paid a premium. They therefore expect special consideration in the form of a shorter wait. This is true of the first-class traveler, the presidential suite guest at a hotel, or the purchaser of limo service instead of a cab. At all times, the customer-contact employee is the person responsible for the moment of truth when the customer either gets handled or does not get handled in what the customer perceives is an appropriate amount of time for the value of the service.

8. Wherever possible, have people wait in or as a group.   Solo waits always feel longer than waits as a group. There is something about waiting in a group that makes the wait more bearable. Perhaps it is just the knowledge that the person is not suffering alone. In fact, it is not rare that a group sits or stands silently waiting for something. No one communicates with anybody else. Then all of a sudden, a delay is announced, and people turn to each other with exasperated looks, wonder aloud about what is happening, and begin to console each other.

Although the wait is still uncomfortable, it is much less so than if each person were completely alone. However, caution must be given that a group of delayed people can also use each other as a source of strength to react actively rather than passively to what is annoying them. If customer-contact employees follow the first seven points of this list, however, they can be assured that the group wait will be a positive help, not the source of disaster.

Working with the Disabled

In the first part of this chapter we covered the "hardware" necessary to work with disabled persons—the facilities and building features. However, true access for the disabled involves the elimination of emotional and social barriers as well as physical ones. Real access combines physical features for access and communication with the same kind of personal care and service that all people expect from hospitality and tourism companies.

Unfortunately, many customer-contact employees have made disabled customers the victim of poor treatment. Sometimes this is because of their own insensitivity, and ironically, sometimes it is because of their oversensitivity. Worse, it is often the result of systems and procedures that result in uninformed and untrained customer-contact employees who are incapable of giving good service.

Bill Marsano, a contributing editor to Condé Nast's magazine *The Traveler* once went undercover as a wheelchair traveler to do a story on disabled travel from the user's perspective. He recounts: "I rented a standard-width, nonmotorized chair and started to plan. . . . I knew plenty of phone numbers to call for help, and I spent two days trying to get it—my ears were so sore I looked like a prizefighter with a losing record. I called a disabled friend and told him of the interminable minutes on hold or being switched from one extension to another. I spoke of conflicting, incomplete, and inaccurate information from clerks who were ill-trained and uninformed. I said I'd been treated as an inconvenience instead of a customer, and I was getting pretty angry." He laughed hollowly and said, "Tell me about it!"

At a hotel, Marsano recalls: "I addressed the clerk; the clerk replied to my daughter. . . . This is a peculiar phenomenon of wheelchair life. In a chair I was visible and invisible at the same time, and presumed mentally incompetent at all times. . . . One maître d´ asked my wife, 'Where would you like to sit him?' as if I were an unusual sort of furniture; waiters asked my children what I'd like to eat. . . . I had the feeling that able-bodied people preferred not seeing me at all, with some exceptions. . . ." Marsano is obviously not alone in his experience. Although he was in a wheelchair only temporarily, many others are not.

Providing service excellence to the disabled is perhaps the ultimate act of looking at customer-contact work from the customer's perspective. In most cases customer-contact employees do not have any direct experience in what it means to have a major disability. The important thing to remember is that people with disabilities are still people. Their physical disabilities do not change their value as people or their needs. As customers, they have the same seven basic expectations. Customer-contact employees can still commit the same basic seven sins. Disabled customers are motivated to act by the principles discussed in Chapter 4, and customer-contact employees can put to use many of the same tools. The difference is that service companies have the responsibility to provide a physical environment that is barrier-free for disabled customers, and customer-contact employees have the responsibility to treat them the way they would treat any other customer.

Document Processing

One of the most important, yet ironically also most taken for granted, procedures in all service organizations is document processing. Since all service organizations rely on the communication and processing of information, handling document processing is probably the next most critical thing to handling people. Documents are the only way they have to communicate the full range of details about the product they are marketing, the final choice(s) that customers make, and everything in between. Money gets transferred and services provided all on the basis of what is written on documents.

Documents can be broken down into three basic categories: mail, valuables, and others. Mail includes incoming and outgoing. The processing of both is critical to the success of any company. Incoming mail must be looked at, distributed, and dealt with. Checks need to be put into the bank as soon as possible— ideally the day they are received. Information requests need to get fulfilled. Bills must be paid within a reasonable time (almost never the day they are received). Complaints and compliments should get a response. The vast majority of customers never bother to send mail to complain or to compliment. When customers do write, they deserve the courtesy of a response—even if it is just to thank them for their letter. Refusing to send a response, whether by intention or oversight, is almost as bad as not returning a phone call.

Outgoing mail needs just as much care and control. When customer-contact employees are in a job that receives and generates a substantial amount of mail, it is very easy to fall into the trap of letting things pile up. Whether they are communicating with their customers or their suppliers, the intended recipients of their mail depend on them for prompt, accurate processing. Unlike phone or in-person conversations, they cannot easily remind a customer-contact employee to send the information needed. When customer-contact employees are sending payments or documents, it is also very important to check whether recipients need the mail in their hands by a certain date or just postmarked by a certain date. When rushed, there is the option of overnight and two-day mail services from a variety of companies. Unfortunately, most companies waste a lot of money on these services each year. They are so simple to use that people lose sight of the fact that they cost $5 to 10 for each piece under 2 pounds. At that cost, they should be used only when necessary—not because of poor mail management.

Today's technology has seen fax transmittals become as predominant a transmittal means as overnight mail. In some cases it is even being used in lieu of standard mail because of its advantages. It is faster than mail, and it is still novel enough for most recipients to view it as more important. Even when the novelty wears off, fax transmittals have to be picked up by somebody (and thus are noticed). This has caused an outburst of "junk fax" since much junk mail often does not get opened and read. If companies are not careful, however, the volume of faxes could get out of control. Therefore, they must set up procedures to handle the receipt, review, and generation of faxes just as they do the mail.

Customer-contact employees also send a lot of "valuables" in the mail. These include checks, airline tickets, vouchers for hotels or rental cars, tour documents, and a variety of other things. Sometimes these papers have an actual cash value; other times, they merely represent access to a service or proof of reservation and payment. While the latter case may make intentional theft of the documents unlikely, their loss could still cause great inconvenience for customers. To date, faxes have not been used for transmitting important or valuable documents, due to concerns over the security of the process. However, there may come a day when airline tickets, tour and cruise vouchers, and other ticketing documents will be transmittable by fax or similar electronic technology.

"Other documentation" covers a wide range of printed material. The most common and important include such things as brochures and other promotional materials. Their creation and use are important since they are the primary means for both marketing service products to prospective customers and communicating what is included and what is excluded from various purchases. Good service delivery systems use these as tools, not as an end in themselves. Rather than merely dumping these documents on customers, well-trained, professional customer-contact employees use the documentation as a guide to explain products. The documents can be left with customers for future reference.

Office Procedures

"Hardware tools" include office equipment, furniture, and supplies. These are all useless if there is not an analogous set of "software tools"—a well-thought-out, planned set of office procedures. Office procedures include things like work flow and team planning. Just as there is a plan for the flow of customers from one step to another, there also needs to be a structured flow of work.

One of the most important things about **work flow** is whether the office is structured based on individual **specialization** or **generalization**. In an environment based on specialization, customer-contact employees are trained to be experts at their specific job, with very little training in other tasks. The advantages include the facts that workers become experts at their jobs, training is less expensive, and the workers are usually more proficient. The disadvantages include their inability to cover for a co-worker who is overloaded, their inability to answer customer questions about other facets of the company's services, and the chance that they will actually suffer a loss of productivity if they get bored with the singularness of the job.

Over the past few years there has been an increasing move to allow workers to be as generalized as possible. With the exception of situations where the customer flow can be controlled so that no one with generalized knowledge is needed, this is usually the best way to ensure that customers will not "get the runaround." However, there are still cases where specialization is either required due to the complicated nature of the job or is desirable to the company for economic reasons.

When Things Go Wrong

As Murphy's Law so famously states, "Anything that can go wrong, will." Although perhaps a bit pessimistic, the truth is that some things will go wrong no matter how well customer-contact employees do their job. In Chapter 9 we discuss some ways that customer-contact employees can deal personally with customers who are victims of problems or mistakes. This will be more effective if there are procedures for dealing with problems in place that can be used as tools.

The best tools and procedures for dealing with problems start with a good understanding of what customers are looking for and what went wrong. Based on the First Law of Service, we know that problems occur when one or more of the seven basic expectations have not been met. Ideally, through the company's own efforts to ensure high-quality service, customer-contact employees have identified the problem themselves. They can control the situation much better than if they have to deal with an angry customer who comes to inform them of a shortcoming in their product or service. Companies that encourage open communication and engage in active, aggressive searches to discover what customers think about their product are generally better at ensuring proactive identification of problems than are those companies that sit back and assume that everything is O.K. unless told otherwise by customers.

Most customers understand that problems will occur from time to time. However, all customers expect them to be handled. As reported in *Service America*, British Airways did an extensive study of customer expectations in the early 1980s to answer the question: What factors did people really consider most important in their flying experiences? Donald Porter, director of customer service quality assurance for the airline at the time, said the study resulted in the identification of four key factors:

1. *Care and concern:* "We knew about this one."
2. *Spontaneity (and creativity):* "We hadn't thought much about this one."
3. *Problem solving:* "We were conscious of this one."
4. *Recovery:* "We hadn't thought of this one at all."

All four of these come into play when there is a problem. There is no surprise that customers expect care and concern as well as problem-solving skills from customer-contact employees. However, this study showed that they also expect creativity in solving those problems. They do not just want to be read chapter and verse on why nothing can be done. They want customer-contact employees to have the presence of mind and the authority to come up with ideas to make the system work for them. They also want "recovery"—an expectation that someone will take the initiative to do something to make up for the problem or mistake. Even if it's a simple apology, they expect companies to acknowledge their mistake and to make some amends for the inconvenience. Angry customers are usually just people who are fed up with their perception that one or more of their expectations are not being met.

Customer-oriented companies must make use of service delivery tools that help them identify problems before or just as customers realize them, enable them to solve these problems quickly, and allow them to make some form of recovery. The most common way they do this is to set up customer service offices, help desks, or similar areas where customers can go when they have a problem. When staffed with workers who know their way around the company, this can be a very effective and simple way to avoid giving customers "the runaround." One of the most frustrating things that can hap-

I'm sorry you're dissatisfied, Mr. Binkman. Would you like a refund? A credit voucher? The manager's head on a flaming skewer? We're very flexible here. (© Derek Barnes. Reproduced by permission.)

pen to customers is for them to be shuttled from one department to another, each worker saying, "I'm sorry I can't help you with that. Try Mary at extension. . . ." By the time they get to the fourth person, they are so angry they are beyond recovery.

Another very effective way that is not used as often as it probably should be is to have an **ombudsman**. Like a customer service representative, this is a person who is responsible for fielding customer complaints. Customer service reps, however, still act as employees—the company comes first. An ombudsman is supposed to act as the customers' agent—their needs come first. When the proper procedures are in place, ombudsmen can get access to any office and any level of management necessary to satisfy a customer. This gives customers a single point of contact to work with. The ombudsman does the runaround for them.

The upshot of trying to fix things when they go wrong is that there is real truth in the old saying, "There are no problems, only opportunities." As the British Airways study showed, experiencing problems and even getting angry about them are part of the expectations that customers have. When a customer-contact employee encounters an upset customer, there is a unique opportunity to either make or break a critical moment of truth. If they treat customers with care and concern, attempt to problem-solve with as much creativity as can be mustered, and if they make sure that someone attempts to make amends, all of the previous negative perceptions can be erased and replaced with positive perceptions in a single encounter. When things go smoothly, all companies seem roughly the same. Customers can really judge a company by how well its customer-contact employees solve problems.

SUMMARY

There are many different things that can be used to deliver service. On the one hand, there are the physical "things": buildings and facilities, computers and other electric equipment, telephones, and office equipment and supplies. With the ever-increasing pace of change in technology, customer-contact employees must constantly adapt to new equipment and new capabilities. Government is also increasingly dictating rules about the environment that businesses must give customers and employees (through smoking regulations, handicapped access laws, etc.), so customer-contact employees must continue to adapt to those changes as well.

On the other hand, there are many policies and procedures that are crucial to the ability to satisfy customers, no matter how modern and up-to-date equipment and facilities are. Controlling customer flow is particularly important in following the basic laws of service. So too is answering the telephone, where particular attention must be paid to the difficulties in communicating without the benefit of a face-to-face meeting. Customer-contact employees need to be able to answer the phone professionally, deal with the possible problems inherent in putting people on hold, call customers back, screen phone calls for supervisors and co-workers, and deal with interruptions from the phone.

They also need to handle customers who are waiting in person. In technical terms, there are choices about how to control their movement by looking at the various options for queuing them. More important, though, the negative impact of affecting customers' perceptions of a wait must be limited. Systems can keep them occupied while they wait, avoid preprocess waits, minimize sources of anxiety, keep customers informed about the length of the wait, inform customers why they are waiting, keep customers from waiting an unfair amount of time or an amount that exceeds the value of the service, and have people wait in a group when possible.

With the passage of the Americans with Disabilities Act, there is now a legal requirement for businesses to meet the needs of disabled customers. However, a lot more can be done than merely meet their needs for physical access.

Finally, there are myriad of routine daily occurrences, including document processing and other office procedures. Unfortunately, there are also those times where employees have to deal with a situation where something went wrong. In general, they will keep their customers goodwill if they demonstrate sincere care and concern, show some creativity, attempt to solve the problem, and offer some compensation for whatever wrong was done.

QUESTIONS FOR REVIEW

1. What law requires equal access for handicapped customers to all buildings and facilities?
2. What are the computer systems that support service operations? The ones that are used by customer-contact employees to serve customers directly? Ones that are used by customers to serve themselves?
3. Give four examples of computer peripherals.
4. What is the advantage of having a toll-free number?
5. What is the quickest way to send a written letter to a customer?
6. What is the single biggest disadvantage of using a telephone to serve customers instead of face-to-face transactions?
7. What are three things that a professional telephone answer does? Give an example.
8. What is the first thing that should be done before a customer is put on hold?
9. What is the most popularly used waiting-line (queuing) system in service organizations?
10. List eight ways we can make waiting as painless as possible for customers.
11. What is the best way to treat a disabled customer?
12. List four basic steps in dealing with a situation where something has gone wrong.

QUESTIONS FOR DISCUSSION

1. Which is more important, service hardware or service software? (You're not allowed to say 50–50.)
2. How have computers affected the service segment you most want to work in?
3. Give an example of a service encounter that you have had with a company with good customer flow. Give another example of where the customer flow was bad. How could it be made better?

4. Who is more important, the customer who is on hold or the customer who just walked up? Whose needs should be met first?

5. Why should disabled customers be served when they take longer to handle than able-bodied customers? If they don't pay any more for the services, should they be entitled to expect more time or attention?

6. Which is better, specialization or generalization?

7. Is every customer who has had something go wrong entitled to compensation? If not, where should the line be drawn? If so, how can companies afford it?

9

INTERPERSONAL COMMUNICATION

OBJECTIVES

After reading this chapter, you should:

Understand the importance of communication in service transactions.

Know the different purposes for communications.

Understand how communications work.

Understand the different kinds of communication and the different ways that communications flow.

Be able to recognize barriers to effective communication and be able to correct for these.

Understand the nature and importance of nonverbal communication.

Know how to improve communications with customers.

Know how to deal with difficult and angry customers.

KEY TERMS

communication model	communications process
sender	creating
message	encoding
channel	transmitting
receiver	decoding
feedback	using

communication flow	routing
upward	bias
downward	nonverbal communication
lateral or diagonal	body language
formal communication	emblems
informal communication	illustrators
grapevine	affect displays
structural barriers	regulators
authority/status barriers	adapters
imprecise/ambiguous language	tone of voice
difference in perception	proxemics
semantics	object language
jargon	climate
slang	KISS
stereotyping	active listening
filtering	open-ended questions
overloading	reflective statements
timing	probing questions

Communication is absolutely critical to the success of any service encounter. Service, after all, is mostly just the movement and processing of information. Even in a restaurant, which unlike hotels or airplanes, delivers a "consumable product," much of the service act is the transfer of information between the restaurant and the person dining about what is offered, and vice versa about what is desired. As with other service products in hospitality and tourism, the only thing left after the service is provided is a receipt for payment and, hopefully, a pleasantly memorable experience.

Without communication, excellent service cannot be delivered. Without communication, it is difficult to deliver even poor service. In fact, most problems between a service company and its customers can be traced back to some form of miscommunication or lack of communication.

Communication comes in many forms—both oral and written. Anytime that someone is listening, speaking, reading, or writing, he or she is engaged in an act of communication. The person may even be communicating just by looking (mimes, for example, communicate without speaking or writing or being required to listen or read).

REASONS FOR COMMUNICATION

Communication serves many different purposes (Figure 9-1).

1. Information. This is probably the most common use for communication. Informational communication is the lifeblood of service. It is used by customer-contact employees to serve customers, and it is used by customers to communicate their needs. In the written form, it includes everything from restaurant menus to itineraries. In a spoken form, it can cover just about anything that customers need or want to know.

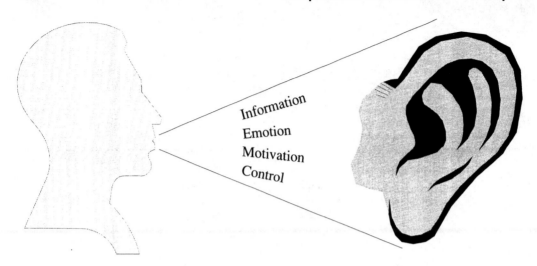

Figure 9-1 Why we communicate.

Vast resources have been spent to develop resource materials and information technologies which can get more information to customers more effectively and efficiently.

2. Emotion.   Communication occurs between two or more people, and much of what people communicate contains emotional messages. When customers are frustrated or happy, they are likely to let someone know. We've already discussed what motivates customers. Often, the act of communicating helps fill a social need for them. Customers want to be treated as individuals, and they want their unique needs understood. Therefore, they will often communicate their emotions. Customer-contact employees need to be prepared to deal with a full range of expressions in a professional manner.

At the same time, they need to be very conscious of the emotional messages they are sending to their customers. Often, they want to communicate a sense of joy or excitement, or even empathize with customers' frustration. However, they cannot afford to send negative emotional signals. The emotional content of a message is often the most powerful since it strikes a chord deep in the psyche of the recipient. Proper emotional signals can substantially increase the effectiveness of a message; improper ones can quickly make effective communication impossible.

Sometimes, the message that customer-contact employees send may connect with an image or a memory of the receiver's. In these cases, the receiver may get an emotional message that is very different (or maybe did not even exist) in the eyes of the sender. This is often a source of miscommunication, particularly between people of vastly different backgrounds or cultures.

3. Motivation.   Another purpose for communication is to motivate the recipient to take some action. Many customer-contact employees are also working at the point of sale. Aside from servicing customers, they are also expected to be salespeople. Much of the communication they engage in is laced with messages intending to motivate potential customers to make a particular purchase.

At the same time, customers are engaging in communication for which they are trying to motivate the customer-contact person to do something. They may be looking for routine service actions, special requests, or to have a problem solved. Whatever the reason or request, customers want the customer-contact person to be motivated to meet their needs as quickly and inexpensively as possible. As we discussed in Chapter 7, it becomes their job to balance meeting all the needs and wants of customers with what is allowable and profitable under their company's guidelines.

4. Control.   Finally, many forms of communication are designed to control the activities of the recipient. Communication can control the flow of people, their actions, or how they respond to a given situation. When a restaurant puts a sign up that says, "Please wait to be seated," it is controlling the recipients of the message. The same is true when an airline gate agent announces that the flight will be boarded from the rear of the plane first. A tour operator will print the terms and conditions of the tour as well as reminders that a passport will or will not be required. Hotels will print the checkout time in the room. A travel agent may verbally remind the customer of what is needed and may even print it on an invoice. All of these communications work to control the behaviors of the recipients.

It is also important to realize that customers may use communication in an effort to control customer-contact employees. When customers ask to be called only before a certain hour, they are communicating in an effort to control the customer-contact employee's behavior. In many cases, customer-contact employees will want to comply with the effort. On the other hand, there are cases where a customer might be trying to control behavior in an effort to secure an advantage that may be unfair (for example, through using veiled threats or other means of intimidation). In these cases it is probably wise for customer-contact employees to ignore tactfully the attempt to control or otherwise make it clear that they cannot be influenced that way.

A MODEL FOR COMMUNICATION

The simplest model for communication has only three elements: sender, receiver, and feedback. A more complete model (Figure 9-2) includes both the message being sent and the channel being utilized.

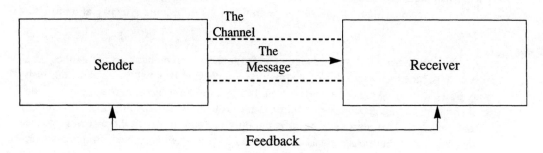

Figure 9-2 Communications model.

1. Sender. The person who originates a piece of communication is the sender. Customers become senders for any of the four reasons discussed earlier in this chapter and to meet any of the needs discussed in Chapter 4. For example, when customers ask a waiter to bring more water, they are conveying information and controlling the waiter's behavior in reaction to a physical need. When customers ask a travel agent what the age group on a cruise line is, they are probably reacting to a need for appropriate socialization, and the message is likely to be laced with emotional content.

2. Message. The message consists of words and nonverbal actions that convey meaning. The message can be oral or written. It can even be totally nonverbal, such as a shake of the head or a raise of the eyebrows. There is much written about the nonverbal messages that can be sent along with or instead of the spoken word. However, written communications can often send nonverbal messages as well. For example, grammar or spelling mistakes can convey an image of ignorance. An office memo may convey a sense of officialness. The entire art of typesetting and layout has grown around knowledge of how to build an image appropriate for intended messages. The message may seem to be the easiest part of the model to analyze and understand, but it is easily misinterpreted.

3. Channel. The method used to transmit the message is referred to as the channel. Channels for oral communication can be face to face, over a telephone, in a group meeting, or a teleconference. Written words can be via a letter, a memo, a rule or regulation, brochures, menus, newsletters, and so on. The choice of the channel is important and can affect the interpretation of the message. Using overnight mail conveys a sense of urgency greater than that of sending a letter.

Ideally, the channel should be free of **noise**. Noise is anything that can distort or distract the receiver, thus detracting from the message. Background noise during a conversation, interruptions, and unreadable handwriting are all excellent examples of noise in the channel.

4. Receiver. The ultimate destination of the message is the receiver. The people who receive the message may or may not be the people that the sender intended to get the message. Furthermore, they may or may not interpret the message as the sender intended. Since it is the receiver who interprets the message and ultimately gives it meaning, the sender must take care to assure effective communication. Throughout a service encounter, customer-contact employees constantly switch back and forth from sender to receiver. Therefore, they must learn the skills to become effective at both functions.

5. Feedback. Any message sent from the receiver back to the sender as a response is called *feedback*. Feedback may be a repetition of what the sender said, or it may be a question asking for a clarification. It may even be something as simple as a nod or a shrug indicating acceptance or confusion. Feedback is perhaps the most critical part of the model, for two reasons. First, it is the only method by which the receiver lets the sender know that the message was received and how it was interpreted. In this manner, feedback goes a long way toward encouraging effective communications. Second, it is often the most ignored part of the model. When either the sender or the receiver over-looks the importance of feedback, there is a substantially higher probability that some form of miscommunication will occur.

THE COMMUNICATIONS PROCESS

While the communications model is static (i.e., it's much like a "snapshot" of communication at a particular point in time), the communications process is really very dynamic. It is a process that occurs through time and is constantly changing back and forth between senders and receivers. For each piece of communication, the process runs through six basic steps (Figure 9-3).

1. Creating.   The first step in the communications process is the creation of an idea. The sender must think before speaking or writing since there is little point in sending a message that is not worthwhile for the receiver to receive or that is inappropriate for the situation.

2. Encoding.   Next, the sender encodes the message into a series of symbols. These symbols can be words (written or spoken) or nonverbals (body language, graphical layouts, color choices, etc.). The nonverbals may or may not be consciously and intentionally transmitted.

3. Transmitting.   Now that the idea for the message has been created and encoded, the sender transmits the message. This step in the process includes choosing the channel and the actual act of transmission. The effectiveness of the communication will be dependent on the quality of the transmission. This places a premium on the choice of the transmission channel, the minimization of noise during this part of the process, and the smoothness of the transmission act itself.

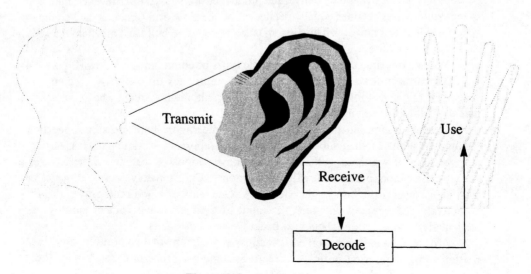

Figure 9-3 Communications process.

4. Receiving. The receiver is at the other end of the transmission. At this point, the message is received. This may seem like the simplest part of the process and the least likely to result in miscommunications. Unfortunately, many things can go wrong at this stage. Many people do not listen or read for comprehension very well. Worse, they may be listening or reading to receive the message they want or expect to hear or see—not what the sender actually intended to send. In all of these cases, the message is never received or is only partially received. The importance of effective listening to the communication process cannot be overstated, although it is often overlooked. We cover this later in the chapter.

5. Decoding. After getting the message, the receiver decodes it. In other words, the receiver takes the symbols that encode the real meaning of the message and translates it back into a meaning for the receiver. This process almost never results in a meaning identical to the original one the sender sent. Later in the chapter, under the subject of how communications can fail, we will see a number of examples where the receiver and the sender do not share the same view regarding the meaning of various symbols (words, gestures, etc.). These are all examples where the decoding is so different from the encoding that the message is not conveyed successfully.

6. Using. The acid test of the process is the last step—use of the message. Its success or failure may be shown by the receiver taking a specific action. It may cause the receiver to generate an idea for feedback or a completely new message. In these cases the receiver now becomes the sender, and the entire process starts over.

FLOWS OF COMMUNICATION

Customer-contact employees are concerned with many different types of communication flow. Obviously, the communication between them and their customers is very important because it is the way that they deliver the product customers desire. However, their ability to do their job is at times equally dependent on the flow of information and communication within their company. This flow must be effective to build and maintain the necessary support structure.

Within companies, there are three basic types of communication flow (Figure 9-4). **Upward communication** is that initiated by employees up the chain of command. Usually, it first goes to their immediate supervisor, although there may be circumstances that allow direct communication beyond that level.

Upward communication usually transmits messages about ideas or suggestions, feelings and attitudes, difficulties or problems, and reports on work in progress. They can take the form of written documents or oral conversations (sometimes in the form of a formal presentation, but more usually, one on one). Unfortunately, most companies and most direct supervisors rarely solicit feedback. One mark of a good company is that they do actively and aggressively seek the input of their customer-contact employees—particularly for suggestions about how better to serve customers.

Anyone who has ever worked is familiar with **downward communication**. In the written form, it is often policies, directives, memos, procedures, and other things

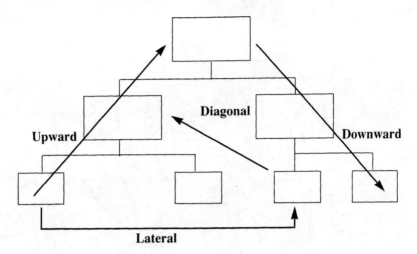

Figure 9-4   Flows of communications.

designed to organize, direct, and control the work of subordinates. In an oral manner, it also deals with organization, direction, and control but includes communication designed to motivate employees. Sometimes it may even be just general information that keeps everybody up to date on what is going on. Even this serves to motivate since it helps meet the need for socialization and a feeling of belonging.

The third flow of communication is called **lateral** or **diagonal communication**. This is the communication between people of equal position on the organization chart or between people in different departments of a company. Lateral communication can include anything from important coordination messages to simple conversations about customers. Lateral communication is often the most important flow to ensure that one organization is working together to meet its customers' needs (recall that teamwork is one of a customer's seven basic expectations). Paradoxically, it is the most difficult for management to control.

FORMAL VERSUS INFORMAL COMMUNICATION

Upward, downward, and lateral/diagonal communication are all examples of **formal communication**. Communication that exists outside the framework of formal communication is called **informal communication**. Informal communication ranges from the simple conversation at the coffeepot to the more notorious **grapevine**. The grapevine is perhaps the best known form of informal communication. Some people also refer to it as the "rumor mill." Like a vine, the grapevine strings itself along its way, sometimes vertical, sometimes horizontal, and sometimes diagonal. Also like a vine, once it starts growing it goes everywhere. No matter how hard someone tries, it is nearly impossible to stamp it out.

The main problem with the grapevine is that as messages get sent along it, they

I don't care what you heard on the "grapevine." I'm "dining with Charles"
not "dying with child"! (© Derek Barnes. Reproduced by permission.)

become garbled and mangled. Like the childhood game of telephone, the more times the message is sent from one person to another, the less the end rumor resembles the initial truth. The rumors that flourish may have no relation whatsoever to the message sent by the original sender. Yet the speed with which news can travel on the grapevine can be astounding. So, too, can the reach of the grapevine. Almost nothing is secret or sacred when it comes to a rumor mill. As we learned when we discussed the human motivation for socialization and status, people want to be "in the know." Studies have shown that many employees get most of their information from the grapevine.

Informal communication serves a number of purposes. It provides information not available through normal channels. Despite the propensity for the grapevine to distort messages, it is still surprisingly accurate. One study by Keith Davis, an authority on human relations, suggests that the grapevine is at least 75 percent accurate in a normal work environment. Particularly in organizations where management inhibits the flow of communication, employees may come to believe the grapevine more than official company communications.

Informal communication reduces the effects of monotony since much of what is discussed is somewhat sensationalized. As mentioned earlier, it satisfies a personal need for status and relationship. Many people take great pride in what they know about what is going on in their company.

One more problem with informal communication and the grapevine is that none of it is written. Therefore, there is no "audit trail." Without a record of who said what to whom and when, there is no way to verify the accuracy of the message. Even if informal communication is 75 percent or more accurate, this is not sufficient for customers.

Communications Gone Awry

Accuracy in receiving and transmitting messages is critical to any customer-contact work in the hospitality and tourism industry. Most of the business revolves around the receipt, processing, and retransmission of data. The "data" can be as simple as the food ordered at a restaurant to the complicated tour itinerary of multiweek exotic vacations.

It may seem that this should be a relatively easy thing for customer-contact workers to do. After all, how difficult is it to remember a few simple details and transmit them to someone else? Unfortunately, reality is not so kind.

Most people remember playing a childhood game called telephone. The game has a simple premise. A few kids line up in a line and the teacher gives the first one a message that the others cannot hear. This child's responsibility is to repeat verbatim the message to the second child, who then repeats it to the third, and so on. At the end, the last child repeats the message, and everyone gets to laugh at how ridiculously garbled the message ends up being.

Although just a child's game, telephone teaches us a lot of adult lessons. It emphasizes the frailties of human memory as well as the fact that the more people involved in between the first transmission and the last reception, the larger the distortion. Communication in the service business is never just a simple game.

Imagine how long an airline would stay in business if its front desk agents were not correct about flight departure information or if a hotel concierge gave correct information to VIP guests only three times out of four.

Ultimately, however, informal communication and the grapevine are here to stay. In fact, it can be a very useful source of initial information. When used correctly, it can allow access to information faster than any other method. The important thing is to verify through a more reliable and formal source anything learned from informal means before relying on it to meet a customer's needs.

BARRIERS TO EFFECTIVE COMMUNICATION: HOW WE FAIL TO COMMUNICATE

There are many different reasons that communications fail. In some ways, when one looks at the sheer number of ways that communications can go wrong, it seems a wonder that they ever go right. By studying the ways in which they can go wrong, though, customer-contact employees can work to minimize the problems. Since the transfer and processing of information is their major product, the increase in effective communications will substantially improve the services they provide.

We discuss next (in no particular order) the ten most frequent reasons that communications fail.

1. Structure. The structure of companies can encourage inefficient and ineffective communication—particularly with larger companies. The larger the company, the more the number of people and offices within the organization that are involved or may have an interest in a particular message. As more people get involved, the chances for people to misread the message or get left out increase exponentially.

The problems related to this manifest themselves in a number of ways. The most obvious is miscommunication from one office to another within a company. If a message has to go through multiple departments within a company, or if many departments have to work together to achieve a common objective, there are likely to be misunderstandings. There is often a case where "the left hand doesn't talk to the right hand." This happens when two or more departments generate conflicting information about similar situations.

Customers are affected by structural inhibitions to communication in two basic ways. The first is when they get two different answers about a question or a problem from two different people in the same company. This directly violates their expectation for consistency and is sure to generate dissatisfaction if not corrected immediately. The second and more subtle effect is that the company is unable to provide as high a standard of service as they could. If the organization is not communicating effectively internally, there is no way that its people can be developing optimal service practices. Although the first way is easy to see and attack, the second way is more critical for the overall long-term functioning and success of the company.

2. Authority/status.   When the receiver and the sender are not of the same authority or status, either one or both may listen or speak in a less than full and open manner. Customer-contact employees are all too familiar with this situation within a company. They are not often expected to act as equals when communicating with their bosses. Unfortunately, this often leads to poor communication—they may withhold or change information because of a desire to impress or a fear of reprimand.

The authority/status problem may also exist between them and their customers. On one hand, customers may view them as experts and yield to their judgment when they would be better off expressing their uncertainty with the customer-contact employee's recommendation. If the customers express their concerns, the customer-contact employee may learn something about their needs that otherwise would not have been discovered. It is important, therefore, for customer-contact employees to work hard to make customers immediately feel comfortable about discussing any concerns.

On the other hand, customers may consider themselves to be of a higher status than that of any customer-contact employee. This can be a problem particularly when dealing with experienced or upscale clientele. They may view customer-contact employees as being less experienced and beneath their social level—particularly if the customer-contact employee is young. It will take a great deal of tact and diplomacy to get them to open up enough to give the information needed to serve them well. In some circumstances a customer-contact employee may have to turn to an older, more experienced co-worker or even a supervisor to deal with a particular customer.

A related source of miscommunication is the degree to which the sender and the receiver know each other. This can be an advantage or a disadvantage. When senders know the receiver well, they tend to "click." That is, they understand each other well and can often communicate complex ideas more quickly through abbreviations and mannerisms or reactions that are quickly understood. Unfortunately, the saying "familiarity breeds contempt" can also hold true. Either party may take too much of a shortcut and assume that the other party understands something. The feedback part of the communications model is often ignored. Many people in business have learned the hard way that when it comes to money, they should not assume anything about how a friend or family member will either understand something or provide support in the event of miscommunication. The best rule is to take just as much care to go over every detail of the service encounter, no matter what the level of familiarity.

3. Language problems.   While the content and importance of nonverbal communication cannot be overstressed, the majority of messages are encoded using words as symbols for the intended meaning. Customer-contact employees are therefore highly dependent on language for their ability to convey messages. Although they may think that this is not likely to cause a problem (after all, a word is just a word, isn't it?), language problems are one of the most common causes of miscommunication.

One of the most common problems is that language can be **imprecise** or **ambiguous**. Although a statement such as "The airplane will depart at 6:45 P.M.," may be very precise, the statement "XYZ tour company offers an excellent range of options for the budget-minded traveler" is not. What might be a wide range to one person may not be to another, and what may be low-priced to one traveler may not be to another. Furthermore, people have a tendency to throw around superlatives without regard to their real meaning. Many times, restaurant-goers have been told about a new restaurant that offers "the best food in town at the most reasonable prices," only to be disappointed.

Ambiguities can be a particular problem with the written word. Senders may know what they want to say, but receivers cannot read their minds. Without the benefit of nonverbal cues such as tone and body language, it is much easier for the receiver to misinterpret something in writing. It is always a good idea to have a second person read any writing before someone sends it, particularly if it addresses potentially sensitive matters.

On the other hand, oral communication has its own problems with ambiguities. Because there is no record of exactly what was said, verbal communications can lead to a "He said. No, she said," exchange in which no one will ever really know what the original message was. Therefore, it is always a good idea to have a written record of meetings or conversations that occur. Many a miscommunication has been avoided by sending a written follow-up to the receiver regarding a recent conversation. This gives the receiver a chance to correct any misperceptions regarding what was said or agreed upon.

Many of these misperceptions are the result of a **difference in perception**. This usually manifests itself as differences in the subtle interpretations of the connotations of the words. Sometimes this is referred to as **semantics**. While there is general agreement between the sender and the receiver about the basic message, there are differences in the implications of the message. An individual message may not be garbled badly by this, but a series of messages each interpreted by the receiver slightly differently than intended by the sender can result in major miscommunication.

Differences in perception come from a number of sources. The sender and receiver may come from different regions of the country or world and interpret the words differently. This is very important today as we enter an era of unprecedented transglobal business and communication. There may be a cultural or religious difference that causes semantic misunderstandings. Or a difference in gender may result in a word or sentence being interpreted in a dissimilar fashion.

The sender's choice of words can be a source of problems as well. The use of technical language or **jargon** is a common problem. If a travel agent tells a customer that there is a risk of being "bumped" off an airplane flight or "walked" at a hotel, there is no reason to expect the customer to know what is meant. Many customers may get a picture in their mind of falling out of the airplane from rough turbulence or being taken for a stroll by a nice employee at the hotel when in reality these are the industry's technical terms for the airline and hotel being overbooked and responsible for providing alternative arrangements. A related problem is the use of unnecessarily complex words. Just as with jargon, there is no reason for a sender to assume that the receiver will be familiar with complex words. Sometimes, however, people either feel comfortable using that kind of language or want to demonstrate their level of vocabulary in order to meet a need for recognition and status. If customers are using words that customer-contact employees cannot understand, they must ask for clarification. And vice versa, when sending messages to customers, employees must use words that are as easily understood as possible.

Another problem is the use of **slang**, nonstandard or substandard English. The sender's meaning of the words may or may not be known by the receiver. Many slang words exist in standard English with completely different meanings, and many slang words are unintelligible to anyone who isn't aware of their use. Slang is not appropriate for a business or professional environment.

A final and growing source of miscommunication in society is the use of foreign words. Over the past years, both the number of foreign nationals in the United States and the number of people of foreign background who are in the middle class have increased. This, coupled with an emphasis on bi- or multilingual education, has affected communications in many areas. In Miami, for example, it is easier to get a job if you speak only Spanish than if you speak only English. In most service jobs in that area, there is a premium on bilingual customer-contact employees.

Even workers in a work environment where English is the only language are coming into more contact with people who do not speak English well. There are a growing number of foreign visitors to the United States (from Europe, South America, and Japan in particular), as well as resident aliens and new citizens. Also, within the United States there are a growing number of subcultures in which people either do not speak English well or mix in foreign words with otherwise English sentences. Dealing with these people in a service environment can be made very difficult since customer-contact employees depend so heavily on language to get their message across.

4. Stereotyping.   **Stereotyping** occurs when a group of people are attributed with a similar set of characteristics. Although this may make it easier psychologically to deal with them, the problem is that a stereotype is often negative and untrue. Customer-contact employees who think of all upscale customers as "snobby" or all budget-minded persons as "uncultured" or "dumb" do a disservice both to themselves and to the people stereotyped.

More important, customer-contact employees who believe in a stereotype undermine their ability to provide customer service. At the least, they are very likely to send out negative nonverbal messages which are sure to be picked up by the receiver. A customer-contact employee may act upon the stereotype and assume certain things about the needs and capabilities of a customer that are untrue. Worse, the worker may accidentally or intentionally voice the stereotype, thus insulting the customer.

Personal attention, courtesy, and empathy are three of the seven basic customer expectations. With one misguided thought, stereotyping violates all three.

5. Filtering.   When a sender intentionally sifts through information and presents only a portion of it to the receiver, it is called **filtering**. In the hospitality and tourism industry, all customer-contact employees must engage in some form of filtering. They cannot give the entire flight schedule for an airline, list every activity on a cruise or tour, or go over every hotel in a major city. Instead, they make assumptions about how much information a customer needs, or they ask questions to determine what to give specific customers and what not to give them.

However, filtering becomes a barrier to communication when information is intentionally sifted in an effort to present only one side of the story—usually to ensure that the receiver gets only positive information. Information may be filtered to convince a customer to choose a particular option, or it may be filtered so that a boss is impressed with how a particular situation was handled. This is a very dangerous practice. If the receiver ever finds out that the information was filtered, they will come to doubt the sender's integrity and consistency.

6. Overloading.   If too much information is sent across a channel at one time, the channel and/or the receiver is **overloaded**. When customer-contact employees provide more information than the channel or the receiver can handle, messages may get lost

I've removed all danger of information overload! I unplugged my modem, my phone, my fax, my television, my radio, and I swiped the paperboy's bike! (© Derek Barnes. Reproduced by permission.)

or garbled. The rules and regulations regarding the purchase or use of specific hospitality or travel services may be numerous and complex. Customer-contact employees need to be careful that they don't just "dump" these on customers and expect them to understand it. If they do, the chances are that they will become the victims of their own mistake— overloading the receiver with too many messages. If people are overloaded with information, they may back away and avoid the situation altogether or they may draw incorrect conclusions based on understanding and remembering only a part of the information.

7. Timing.   The **timing** of a message can be a problem, particularly with service systems as complex as hospitality and tourism. Sometimes, when a receiver gets a message is just as important as what the message is. The sender also needs to decide which messages can be sent in parallel (the receiver gets them at once) and which to send in series (the receiver gets them one at a time). The important thing is they avoid "catching someone at the wrong time," or confusing a receiver with issues that are not important at that time.

8. Routing.   Another common problem with communication is **routing**. Routing problems occur when the right message is sent to the wrong person/people (receiver) or through the wrong medium (channel).

9. Bias.   Any preference or disdain for particular persons or things solely on the basis of who or what they are is called **bias**. Bias on the part of senders will cause them to choose the wrong message to send or encode it in an incorrect way. Bias on the part of the receiver causes the decoding process to be faulty, resulting in a misinterpreted message. Similar to stereotyping, customer-contact employees need to avoid acting on biases.

10. Unwillingness of receiver to admit ignorance.   A final cause for miscommunication is the receiver's unwillingness to question what the sender has said. This is usually the result of a fear that the sender will think the receiver is ignorant, uncultured, or stupid. Unfortunately, although this fear is very powerful, it also directly undermines the entire communication process. When receivers do not provide feedback to senders, or worse, provide feedback that the message is understood when in fact it isn't, they have virtually guaranteed that the communication will be ineffective or incorrect.

NONVERBAL COMMUNICATION

Nonverbal communication between sender and receiver occurs without the use of speech or word language. Such messages play an important role in communication—particularly in conveying the emotional state of the sender. In fact, *Psychology Today* once reported that about 93 percent of emotional meaning was conveyed through nonverbal communication—only 7 percent through speech or written words.

Nonverbal communication continues to be a major area of interest and contention in psychological and communication studies. Although a complete review of the theory and modern understanding of the subject is beyond both the scope of this book and the needs of customer-contact employees, a brief review is helpful to understand how nonverbal communication can positively or negatively affect the effectiveness of communication and the quality of service.

No discussion of nonverbal communication would be complete without covering the concept of **body language**. Body language consists primarily of facial expressions, gestures, and posture. Body language can convey a message very quickly and effectively. The problem is that body language can be very ambiguous. Crossed arms do not necessarily mean that senders want receivers to maintain a distance from their private space. It could just mean that they are cold. Similarly, a smile can just as easily convey sarcasm as it can amusement. There are often only subtle differences in expression that convey large differences in meaning. This makes misinterpretation easy.

Furthermore, body language is intensely cultural. What may mean one thing to an American could mean something very different to an Arab or a Chinese person. A wave, a smile, or a simple touch can be interpreted drastically differently depending on the culture.

There are five basic ways in which people use body language. They can use it as an **emblem**, in place of words, as when they point to something. They can use it as an **illustrator**, to reinforce the message that is being spoken. **Affect displays**, such as movements or expressions of the eyes and face, convey emotional meaning. **Regulators** are used to control communication of and with others. For example, someone who suddenly stiffens and takes a breath may indicate that they want to cut in, or they may nod their head slowly to say, "I understand. Please continue." Finally, **adapters** change from person to person and situation to situation. They are used to satisfy personal needs that arise as people relate to others. As people communicate with others, they may change their expression, posture, or gestures in an effort to feel more comfortable with the communication process.

Much of the emotional content of a spoken message is conveyed by the **tone of voice**. This includes the pitch, speed, volume, and the way in which senders change from one tone to another. Happiness, excitement, anger, sorrow, and dismay are only a few of the wide range of emotions that are easily conveyed by tone of voice. Even on the telephone, where there is no use of body language, the tone of voice can effectively transmit a message. When used consciously, it can effectively complement the intended verbal message. However, if allowed to operate subconsciously, the tone of voice may contradict the spoken words and compromise the speaker's ability to get the desired reaction from the receiver.

Proxemics, the study of territoriality and personal space, can also send nonverbal messages. In the American culture, the space from touch to about 2 feet is an "intimate zone." This is usually reserved for close, personal encounters. The space from 2 to 4 feet, called "personal space," is reserved for a variety of formal and informal conversations. "Social distance" extends up to roughly 12 feet (Figure 9-5). This is recognized as the appropriate distance for people to conduct regular business activities. "Public distance," which extends beyond 12 feet, is only used for public-speaking situations. It is important to remember that proxemics change greatly from one culture to another. Many other cultures (Greeks, Arabs, and others, for example) allow or even require much more direct contact or presence within what Americans would consider to be their intimate zone.

Object language refers to the messages sent by the things with which people surround themselves. Desks, tables, filing cabinets, and other office furniture say something about the owner and the company. The use of uniforms sends very strong messages. Clothes, jewelry, makeup, and hairstyle also send strong signals, as does the presence of

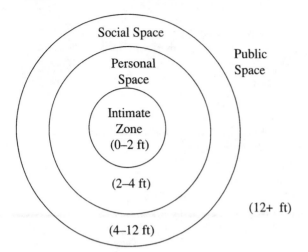

Figure 9-5 Proxemics (American culture).

any religious symbols. These are but a few examples of the types of "things" around customer-contact employees that can communicate a nonverbal message.

HOW TO IMPROVE COMMUNICATIONS WITH CUSTOMERS

Until now, we have merely reviewed the basic theory of communication as well as the sources of miscommunication. Although this is interesting in a descriptive manner, it is not useful unless we prescribe some ways to guarantee maximum communication effectiveness, particularly since it is the critical tool used to give customers excellent service. While this section focuses on the keys to establishing effective interpersonal communications between customer-contact employees and customers, the basic principles apply equally when dealing with communications within the company (supervisor to subordinate, and vice versa). As we learned earlier, the behind-the-scenes support structure provided by a company (which is highly dependent on intracompany communication) is necessary if a customer-contact employee is to be able to deliver excellent service consistently.

The result of all the potential barriers discussed above is miscommunication. Therefore, anything that can enhance the clarity of communication, thus preventing miscommunication, will improve the ability to deliver consistently excellent service. Customer-contact employees should use the following as guidelines for maximizing the effectiveness of their communications.

1. Set the climate. One of the first and most important things that customer-contact employees can do is to set the climate and conditions for effective communication. Setting up a climate of trust between themselves and customers goes a long way toward establishing the groundwork for effective communication. When customers trust someone, they are much more likely to be open about what they like and don't like about what is said. Customer-contact employees need their customers to be open with them so that they get all the information they can about how to meet customers' needs. When customers question the motives or integrity of customer-contact employees, they are not likely to share with them their innermost feelings—feelings that are probably critical to the ability to meet their needs.

The first step in setting a communications-friendly, service-oriented environment is to create a physical area that sends positive messages through object language. Physical objects should be spaced in such a way as to invite customers to communicate with customer-contact employees—not to make it difficult for them to come into contact. At the same time, there should be an appropriate distance and privacy between different customers' space. This gives customers a sense of security with regard to their ability to speak freely. In some cases the appropriate distance is only a couple of feet and there is no need for any barriers; in others, there may be a need for more distance and a completely isolated room with walls and a door. The important thing is to match the environment with the clientele and the services being offered.

The next step is to choose furnishings and attire that are appropriate as well. An amusement park in the summer may issue uniforms of T-shirts and shorts, whereas an office environment might require tie and jacket, and equivalent for women. The former is appropriate for setting the climate since the amusement park wants its guests to feel casual and outdoorsy, and it wants its employees to be noticeable but very approachable. The latter is just as appropriate for the service office because there it is desirable that the customer feel a sense of security in the professionalism and knowledge of the staff.

Designers of the service setting can also take advantage of our knowledge of proxemics to establish a physical environment that is nonthreatening to customers. If the service encounters will be limited to purely businesslike, professional discussions, they will want to set up an environment that allows customer-contact employees to be close enough to be in their customers' social zone, but not so close as to invade their personal zone. If the designers expect customer-contact employees to get into detailed, somewhat personal conversations, they may want the customer-contact employee to be able to move so that they are able to enter their customers' personal zone. At the same time, many service encounters happen between customer-contact employees and a group of two or more customers who know each other. If customer-contact employees will be dealing with multiple customers who are close friends, spouses, or significant others, designers will want a physical setting that allows multiple customers to be within each other's intimate zone.

Finally, the first few messages that customer-contact employees send should convey a sense of sincerity. By showing customers immediately through words, nonverbals, and deeds that they sincerely care about their customers' individual needs, customer-contact employees go a long way toward meeting the expectation for personal attention and courtesy. Furthermore, given the Second Law of Service ("It's always hard to play catch-up ball"), the first impression made will last a long time. An impression of sincerity will help get customers to open up immediately. An impression of insincerity will take a very long time to overcome.

2. Plan the communication.   Simply put, customer-contact employees should think before they speak or write. Before they ever begin a conversation or start to write something, customer-contact employees should have a plan for what information they want to get across and what actions they want the receiver to make. For written communication, it is even more important to plan. The customer-contact employee involved will not be able to be there when the receiver gets the message to make immediate corrections based on feedback. Receivers may not even be able to get hold of the customer-contact employee to ask for clarification, or they may not realize they have misinterpreted the message.

3. Use the appropriate media.   Another important element in ensuring effective communication is to make sure that customer-contact employees choose the proper channel. There are times when it is appropriate to speak and times when it is appropriate to write. Furthermore, there are times when customer-contact employees should address a customer face to face and times when it is better to use a telephone. There is also a time for taking a customer away from everybody else and a time for talking in front of the group or other customers. The choice of media should also include considerations of such things as the importance of speed and the need for acknowledgment or other specific feedback.

4. Consider the receiver's frame of reference.   When customer-contact employees plan their communication and try to choose the appropriate communication channel, they need to consider the receiver's frame of reference or perspective. The true mark of a good service organization is that it looks at everything about its business from the perspective of its customers and their needs. Customer-contact communication and interface is no exception.

Receivers will have biases, filters, stereotypes, and other barriers at work. Customer-contact employees cannot allow a customer's listening weaknesses to negate their ability to get a message across—in the end, they are responsible for delivering the service, despite any weaknesses in a customer. Customer-contact employees will need to take all of this into consideration as they decide what to say, how to say it, and what to emphasize.

Another consideration is the customer's state of mind. A waiter servicing a couple with 7:30 reservations who are there to celebrate their twenty-fifth wedding anniversary will encounter a very different customer from the hotel front desk clerk who deals with the same wife a week later at 11:30 P.M. after she has survived one flight cancellation and another 3-hour delay.

5. KISS.   With all the complexities and difficulties involving the use of language, the best bet is to apply the KISS principle. KISS is an easily remembered acronym which is short for "Keep it simple, stupid!" Written and spoken messages should use the lowest vocabulary possible to convey the message accurately without sounding condescending or insulting to the receiver.

When the KISS principle is applied, customer-contact employees avoid the use of insider jargon, slang, and words that could only be found in a vocabulary test. Napoleon is rumored to have developed his own form of the KISS principle—often referred to as the Napoleonic Principle of Communication. According to the legend, whenever he was about to go into battle, he would give his battle orders to the lowliest, most ignorant corporal he had and ask him what he had written. He figured that once the orders were written so that the corporal could understand them, they were ready to be sent to the generals. That way, he was sure that his generals would not be likely to misinterpret his orders.

6. Use repetition for key ideas.   Nothing is more disastrous for service than a miscommunication between customer-contact employees and customers on a critical point. The best way to avoid this is to repeat messages. Repetition accomplishes many objectives:

  a. When receivers are not really listening or are "tuned out" during the first message, they will have another chance to get the critical idea.

  b. When receivers are victims of overload, repetition provides further opportunities to receive and "ungarble" the key ideas.

  c. Human beings learn and remember better through repetition. If the key ideas are at all complex, repetition is necessary for receivers to get the full context of the intended meaning.

  d. When receivers hear the same message a number of times, they will infer that the message is important and worth remembering or thinking about.

  e. If customer-contact employees repeat the same basic idea but send it in slightly different ways (either through multiple channels—written and spoken—or by using slightly different words and descriptions), receivers will get the opportunity to decode it differently. People absorb information differently. Some do it best in audio form, and some do it best in the written form. This often uncovers misinterpretations that receivers would not otherwise realize occurred in a single transmission. It can also help to compensate for any stereotyping, bias, or similar barriers from receivers.

7. Encourage feedback.   As discussed in the communications model, feedback is a critical part of the communications process. As customer-contact employees serve customers, they need feedback to assure that what they are doing or advising meets their customers' needs. The ability to get feedback is related directly to two things: the extent to which customer-contact employees "allow" receivers to give feedback, and the extent to which they seek it.

The former is highly dependent on the first item discussed in this section—the service climate. But beyond the physical climate, there is a lot that can be done to create the kind of relaxed atmosphere that is conducive to getting valuable feedback. It's always a good idea for anyone to pause between sentences or thoughts. This cues receivers that it is acceptable to cut in and say or ask something. Also, no one should do all the talking. After all, how can customer-contact employees learn anything about customers' needs if they never let them speak?

Customer-contact employees need to be aware that new customers may not be comfortable with their lack of knowledge about the customer-contact employees or their products. The hierarchy/authority barrier is likely to come into play unless customer-contact employees take specific action to let these people know that there is no such thing as a dumb question or comment.

Another key element to establishing a relaxed, open environment is how questions and feedback are handled. If customer-contact employees disregard customer feedback, act gruff, or worse, respond in a condescending fashion, they shut down future feedback. On the other hand, if they respond in a way that shows sincere concern about customer questions or concerns, they encourage continued feedback. It's often amazing how a simple response such as "That's a very important question, and it's important for you to understand . . ." will both get the message across clearly and establish a bond between customer and customer-contact representative that will continue to pay dividends long into the future.

The latter, the extent to which customer-contact employees actively seek feedback, is equally important. To get much of the information they need, customer-contact employees must take the initiative. Sometimes, their company may formally seek out feedback through questionnaires and surveys. Usually, though, customer-contact employees seek feedback in a much more informal manner. They may prompt their customer in a general way:

"Do you have any other questions?"

"Is there anything else I can do for you?"

"Please feel free to call me?"

Or they may ask something more specific:

"Have you already been told that a passport is required?"

"Did you say you would be paying by cash or charge?"

An interesting side benefit to this type of interchange is that it also helps establish rapport between customer-contact employees and their customers. This helps demonstrate sincerity and contributes to creating an environment conducive to future positive encounters.

8. Practice active listening.   While talking to customers is an important part of any customer-contact job, listening to customers is even more important. Customer-contact employees are expected to exercise tactful control over the flow of communication in order to understand customers' real needs and provide for them. This customer-oriented approach places a premium on skilled listening. Although people have two ears and only one mouth, they unfortunately seem to be more willing and effective at using their mouth and not their ears. Listening is an art that requires just as much schooling and practice as good public speaking.

Active listening is a technique that encourages customer-contact employees to get as much information and feedback from customers and helps assure that the messages they intended to send are indeed the messages customers received. There are three specific ways the technique can be applied to optimize communication: (1) open-ended questions, (2) the reflective statement, and (3) probing questions.

In its most basic form, active listening takes the form of asking customers **open-ended questions**. "Closed" questions are those which suggest that a limited response is desired. For example, "Did you enjoy your stay?" implies that the only response that is really appropriate is "yes" or "no." A better way to ask is, "How did you enjoy your stay?" This implies that the sender would like to hear some of the details about what was liked or disliked.

Unless there is a specific reason to the contrary, customer-contact employees should avoid questions that require only a simple "yes" or "no" or questions that offer simply a choice between two things. It takes more time to ask and receive the answer, but much more useful information is provided.

An excellent technique for ensuring that the message the customer wanted to send is the one that was received is to repeat what the person said and ask for agreement. This is called a **reflective statement** because the original message is "reflected" back to the sender.

> "What you seem to be telling me is that you prefer a place with lots of sun and beach but not too much noise and activity at night."

> "Since you would like to try a nice, fruity wine, I would recommend a Johannesburg Riesling."

These are examples of how a travel agent or a wine steward or waiter might use the reflective statement. Note how it gives customers the opportunity to step in quickly to correct a miscommunication before any damage has been done. This is a way that customer-contact employees can turn the difficulty of customers being involved in the production of service into an advantage.

When customer-contact employees need to get more information out of a customer, the best way is to use **probing questions**. A probe elicits a more specific answer than does a reflective statement.

> "What was it that the flight attendant did that bothered you?"

> "How did our lobby particularly impress you?"

A reflective statement checks for accuracy in the interpretation of a customer's statement; a probe asks for additional information so that the customer-contact employee may better understand the statement.

Customer-contact employees can also take advantage of the difference in their ability to process language faster than they can speak. People can process 300 to 500 words per minute, yet the person speaking usually says only about 120 to 180 words per minute. The extra time can be used to think about what is being said, take notes, or otherwise make sure that there is a complete understanding of the intended message.

SPECIAL PROBLEMS IN COMMUNICATION

There are two special circumstances that customer-contact employees routinely encounter that take special handling to avoid potential disaster: dealing with difficult customers and dealing with angry customers. While the basic principles for avoiding communication problems provide a general background for working in these difficult environments, special skills and approaches must be put to use as well.

Every customer-contact employee comes into contact with difficult customers—those who are unusually demanding, always complaining, or just can never make up their minds. Sometimes it becomes obvious that a new customer fits into this category, but usually customer-contact employees know that a particular customer is difficult because they (or their co-workers) have dealt with them before. Because most companies in the hospitality and tourism industry work on low margins and depend heavily on repeat clientele, it is important that difficult customers be dealt with as effectively as anyone else.

There are a number of ways to attempt to work with difficult customers. However, there is rarely any chance to do anything that will turn a difficult customer into one who is easy to work with. Therefore, customer-contact employees must control their own expectations. They cannot take difficult customers' unwillingness to change their behavior too personally. Not only won't they be able to give better service, but they will drive themselves insane trying.

1. Pay special attention to expectations. Although customer-contact employees are always concerned with their customers' expectations, they need to pay special attention to difficult customers. The chances are they are difficult because they view as normal something that customer-contact employees see as being beyond an ordinary expectation, or they may not trust anyone and expect to be cheated. In such a case, customer-contact employees should adjust themselves to understand what is important to the customer—not to themselves. Even if requests seem irrational, they are still a very real need for the customer.

At the same time, customer-contact employees should understand that some people in the world will never be happy. They actually enjoy worrying and/or complaining. In these cases, customer-contact employees can identify their need to get a response to their worry.

2. Use repetition and active listening. Many difficult customers are either "looking for an angle" or just plain don't remember things too well. It is critical that customer-contact employees use these tools to ensure that there is a very clear and mutually understood exchange of information. In many cases, it may be necessary to get something down in writing (a follow-up letter, a waiver of insurance, or a signed understanding of the terms and conditions of a particular service) to protect the company's exposure to liability. More important, careful active listening will get the information needed and avoid misunderstanding.

3. Be specific on what is included and excluded. The most common cause for confusion, particularly in complex service delivery, is a lack of clear communication over exactly what the customer is buying and not buying. Whether it is something as simple as french fries coming with a burger or as potentially expensive as meals being included in a tour package, it is important to the customer. There is little in American society more universally annoying to customers than the feeling that they were "ripped off"—even if the dollar amount is small. Difficult customers sometimes look for the customer-contact employee to make a mistake on what is included. By doing so, they make themselves feel good by being "smarter than the employee," they look to get something more than what they deserve, or they simply confirm their belief that everyone is out to cheat them.

4. Be empathetic. In a customer-oriented company, customer-contact employees must focus on everything from the customer's perspective. This is particularly true when dealing with difficult customers. Although their needs may seem unreasonable and/or irrational, they are nonetheless real to them. Except when supervisors instruct customer-contact employees to encourage a specific customer to look for services elsewhere, customer-contact employees have a job to meet those needs. By trying to "put themselves in a difficult customer's shoes," customer-contact employees may be better able to understand where they are coming from. Hopefully, this translates into being better able and more willing to deal with them. In many cases, these customers are only temporarily difficult because of something that happened just before. A little sensitivity can quickly make friends of them.

5. Try to limit options.   Another common problem with difficult customers, particularly the ones who can never make up their mind or are always changing it, is that they have too many options. Often in these situations, customer-contact employees abdicate the responsibility to control the exchange by allowing customers constantly to make new demands or change their demands. Although it is important to keep customers satisfied, this does not mean that customer-contact employees can allow them either to take so much time that their business is not profitable or to take time away from the need to service other customers.

A good tool to use here is to tactfully limit the options available. If customers who cannot make up their mind have fewer choices, they will be able to come to a decision more quickly. The trick is to combine the information already known about the customer with a few well-planned probing questions to be able to narrow down the full range of choices. It is also a good idea not to offer any choices until the full extent of their needs and desires has been determined. With difficult customers it is important to wait until all the information is gathered before proceeding to a "decision" stage. This way, customer-contact employees can get customers to focus on the decision process without any distractions or the feeling that they have not identified everything they want. If the customer does not like the choices offered, customer-contact employees can use reflective statements to reestablish their needs. If the customer tries to offer up some possible solutions before getting to a decision stage, the best bet is to deflect the input tactfully with something like, "That sounds like a good option, but I'd like to fully understand what you're looking for before I can really give informed advice." In this way, customer-contact employees maintain control of the situation without ignoring the customer's needs and without insulting them.

Another common problem with difficult customers is that once they make a decision, they change their mind or cancel frequently. Management may choose to limit their options after their initial decision. This can be done by attaching a cost to any changes. Nonrefundable fees (all the way from a few dollars to 100 percent of the service price) will often force customers to make a firm decision. When customers are allowed to make constant changes that cost the company money, but not them, there is no reason to expect them not to make changes. In extreme cases where a customer is known for shopping but not buying, they may even be required to put up a nonrefundable deposit before the service will be allowed to begin. Obviously, this is not a tool that customer-contact employees can unilaterally decide to use, but there may be a time where management instructs a customer-contact employee to employ it tactfully.

6. "Know when to say when."   The last couple of tools discussed above run a risk of losing customers if they do not feel that these restrictions are appropriate. The fact of the matter is that there comes a point in time when a business may need to make a decision that a particular customer's (or prospective customer's) business is not worth the time and hassle. It is not profitable and/or it requires a degree of extra handling that is not fair to the customer-contact people. Although this is an extremely rare situation, it does occur.

Needless to say, this decision is up to management and should never be made by a customer-contact employee. Without clear direction to the contrary, it is any customer-contact employee's job to provide as good a service exchange as possible, no matter how difficult the customer.

COMMUNICATING WITH ANGRY CUSTOMERS

No service system is perfect, so every so often customers will get upset. It may be because they had unreasonable expectations, or it may be because something happened that gave them good cause to be upset. Just as often as not, customer-contact employees end up dealing with customers who are angry about something that they did not do themselves or that they have no real control over—but now it is their problem to handle.

As discussed earlier, angry customers present unique opportunities to rewin their allegiance. Somewhere one or more of their basic expectations were not met, and they are looking for solutions to the problem and some form of recovery. These basic facts are guiding principles for figuring out how to turn the negative into a positive.

Handling Angry Customers

The first step in handling angry customers is to understand why they are upset. They have probably perceived that one or more of the seven basic expectations listed below have not been met.

- Accessibility
- Courtesy
- Personal attention
- Empathy
- Job knowledge
- Consistency
- Teamwork

To understand enough about the nature of the problem, customer-contact employees will have to use many of the communication tools discussed in dealing with difficult customers (in many ways, angry customers are just one type of difficult customer). Active listening will be a particularly important tool.

Since handling the complaint is also a moment of truth, angry customers have some idea of what they want from this service encounter. The only difference between this encounter and a routine encounter is that these customers already have a low opinion of the company and may try to take that out on the customer-contact employees. This means that customer-contact employees will have to pay particular attention to meeting the seven basic expectations. They cannot allow themselves to miss meeting any expectations if they want a chance of keeping the customer's business.

In one way, customer-contact employees can take advantage of the customer's low opinion. In many cases, customers complain but expect they will not be able to change anything. The First Law of Service says that their satisfaction will equal their perception minus their expectation. If their expectations are close to zero, it does not take much to exceed them. This is why an empathetic ear and a simple apology are often all that is needed.

Once customer-contact employees enter into an encounter with a disgruntled customer, there are many tools and techniques at their disposal.

1. Let them blow off steam.   One of the reasons why customers complain is that they have a need to do something about a problem they perceive. The act of complaining alone may be all that they want. Other times, they may be so worked up that they are not rational enough to deal with in a professional manner.

They can't repair diddly-squat, I just came here for a little sympathy! (© Derek Barnes. Reproduced by permission.)

In either case, one of the simplest techniques to apply is just to let them blow off some steam. In the case of the former, a few kind, understanding words from a customer-contact employee and a promise to make sure that management is aware of the complaint may be all that are necessary. In the case of the latter, customer-contact employees need to let such customers get to a point where they are willing to work with them to solve the problem. Like a child who can't keep crying forever, angry customers will eventually rant and rave themselves to exhaustion (or at least a point where they become more rational). Obviously, if the customer's actions interfere with the ability of customer-contact employees involved or their co-workers to service others, they will first need to bring the customer into a more private area.

2. Smile.   When customers get angry, customer-contact employees may have a tendency to get angry or defensive themselves in response. This is unprofessional and cannot be allowed. An excellent technique that customer-contact employees can apply to counter this feeling is to force themselves to keep a smile on their face. The reason for this is not to placate the customer, but rather because it is absolutely impossible for customer-contact employees to look or sound angry when they are smiling (provided that their tone is not mocking). Even when burning up inside, customer-contact employees can maintain both their professionalism and their control of the situation. This is just as effective when on the phone as in person.

3. Focus on facts, not emotions.   In many situations, customers let their emotions get the better of them. Everything becomes "absolutely the worst thing that ever happened," or similarly exaggerated. The best thing that customer-contact employees can do is to try to get customers to focus on the specific facts at hand—what can and can't be done and what did or did not happen. Emotional outbursts and vague generalisms will not help customer-contact employees help them. Although customer-contact employees may need to let them use these to blow off some steam, eventually customer-contact employees need to have them get down to the specifics. Similarly, customer-contact employees should want to avoid getting emotional themselves. Instead, they should maintain a professional, though empathetic appearance. Reflective statements can help put things in perspective. When customers hear their own words repeated back without the emotional overtones, it frequently shows them how exaggerated their actions are.

4. Don't be afraid to admit a mistake. As studies have proven, customers do not expect companies or their employees to be perfect. Although they will not tolerate chronic errors, they usually expect customer-contact employees to do the best they can and to correct quickly for any mistakes. Therefore, there is no reason for customer-contact employees to pretend that they or their co-workers are perfect when they are not. An admission of error is not a sign of weakness or incompetence, and sometimes it can actually diffuse a difficult situation:

> A customer complains, "I can't believe what you guys did to me! You mixed up my bill with somebody else's!"
> To which a customer-contact employee responds, "You're absolutely right, ma'am. We had a new person in accounting, and we made a mistake. We will get a new,

corrected bill to you within the day reflecting your actual payments. Please accept my apologies."

There isn't much left for the customer to do except thank the customer-contact employee for quick attention to the matter.

There is one thing to be very careful about when it comes to admitting mistakes. When customer-contact employees admit a mistake, they are often accepting liability on behalf of their company for any damages to customers. Therefore, when any real sum of money is involved, customer-contact employees should *never* admit a mistake without first getting approval from management.

Customer-contact employees can still react to a situation with care and concern with something like, "I'm very troubled by what has happened to you. Please let me look into it and check with my supervisor. I'll call you before the day is out and we'll see how we can help you." In this way, customer-contact employees show care and concern as well as willingness to solve the problem and make any recovery efforts necessary. However, they have not admitted guilt or accepted any legal liabilities without first getting approval.

5. Get customers to focus on solutions, not problems.   There is a tendency for many people to harp on what has gone wrong. However, "there's no need to cry over spilled milk." Customer-contact employees cannot change the past, nor do their customers expect it (no matter how much they complain).

The real expectation is for problem solving and recovery. The sooner that customer-contact employees can focus on solutions and get customers to focus on solution alternatives, the sooner they can go about meeting customer needs in this critical moment of truth. Customer-contact employees are the ones who are in control of the situation, so it is their job to guide the conversation toward the topic of possible solutions. Should the communication stray away from this topic, it is their responsibility to bring it back.

6. Offer options.   If there is one thing that most people hate more than anything else when something goes wrong, it is when they are put into a position of having no choice as to how they are handled. When faced with a bad situation, they still like to have some say in how they will get treated.

The best technique to use is to offer them options. Even if customer-contact employees think there is only one acceptable alternative, they can show them what the other "less attractive" alternatives might be. This accomplishes two things: (1) it shows that the customer-contact employee is taking into consideration the customer's personal needs (thus meeting their expectation for personal attention), and (2) it gives customers a sense of "ownership" about their fate. When they have a say in what's happening to them, they share some of the responsibility. This significantly reduces how they perceive the blame later.

7. Put the ball in the customer's court.   Customer-contact employees will come across customers who insist on being mad no matter what. They let them blow off steam, smile, focus on the facts and on the problem, and offer options. Yet these people do not want to accept any recommendations. Nothing will satisfy them, and they want customer-contact employees to know that.

At this point, a nice little trick is to throw the problem back into the customer's hands. By simply asking, "What would you like me to do to satisfy you?", customer-contact employees often take the wind right out of their sails. They are likely to react with a negative statement about how there is nothing that can be done, or how it's not their job to solve the problem, but usually this is just a quick reaction to the unexpected question. More often than not, it leads these customers to think about solving the problem from the customer-contact employee's point of view, and they often come up with excellent ideas. Customer-contact employees may need to get authorization from their supervisors, but there's nothing like the old adage, "Two heads are better than one." Customer-contact employees might as well use the customer's own creativity to meet the person's needs.

8. Offer freebies. A great tool for leaving a positive feeling with customers after solving a problem is to give them a "freebie." This is the ultimate form of recovery—it gives customers something tangible to make up for the inconvenience of the problem. Sometimes the freebie is a gift, sometimes cash back. More often, it is in the form of a discount on the product that caused a problem. Restaurants have been known to give discounts on future meals, airlines give script for future travel, and cruise lines give a coupon for savings on a future cruise. Usually, the freebie includes a personally written note thanking customers for their patience and understanding. A particularly effective thing to do is to make a statement like the following:

> "We apologize for the inconvenience you experienced. Your patronage is particularly important to us. Enclosed is a certificate good for _____. We hope you will use it in the future to give us another chance to show you the service excellence we usually deliver. Once again, my apologies. . . ."

Obviously, customer-contact employees should never promise a freebie to angry customers unless they have the authority to deliver.

9. Refer the customer. When absolutely necessary, refer the customer to someone else. This usually occurs in two situations: (1) when a customer-contact employee doesn't have enough knowledge and must refer them to another department, and (2) when a customer-contact employee does not have enough authority and must refer them to a supervisor. In both cases, customer-contact employees must take extreme care to ensure that they are not making customers perceive that they are getting the runaround. The best way to do this is either to give customers detailed information about who they need to contact, why that person or department can help them, and then connect them directly (this works particularly well with the appropriate telephone system), or explain why they need to talk to someone else, take their name and number, and have their company's appropriate person call them back—soon. Under no circumstance should customer-contact employees merely "pass the buck."

SUMMARY

Communication is perhaps the most important tool for ensuring customer satisfaction in a service encounter. Communication can be used to convey information or emotion, to try to motivate the recipient to do something, or to control the person's actions or thoughts.

All communications can be broken down to a simple model that includes the sender, the message, the channel, the receiver, and feedback. The communications process occurs when an idea is created, encoded, and transmitted by the sender, and then received, decoded, and used by the receiver.

Communication exists in many different ways and forms, both oral and written. It can be formal or informal. Within an organization, it can flow upward, downward, diagonally, or laterally. Although most companies attempt to control formal communication, its success in delivering service often depends on informal communication. This is a "double-edged sword" since informal communication (or the "grapevine") can spread very destructive rumors as well.

There are many different reasons why communications fails in organizations. The structure of the organization and the authority or status of the sender can inhibit communication and feedback. The message itself may be the source through imprecise or ambiguous language, semantic misunderstandings, and the use of slang or jargon. People can let stereotypes interfere with communication, can filter information, or can overload the receiver. They may not choose the appropriate timing for sending their messages, they may route it incorrectly, or they operate from a biased viewpoint. Finally, the receiver may be unwilling to admit ignorance or lack of understanding and therefore refuse to give feedback.

Communication does not have to use words to occur. Body language and proxemics (the relationship between people, space, and territoriality) can speak volumes. Customer-contact employees have to be very careful, however, because it is easy to misinterpret nonverbal communication or inadvertently send the wrong message.

The best pieces of advice to implement on the job revolve around how communications with customers can be improved. A climate conducive to effective communications should be set, communications should be planned ahead, the appropriate method of communicating should be used, and senders should consider how their messages may be viewed by receivers. They should also keep their messages as simple as possible to convey their desired meaning, repeat key messages to emphasize their importance and make sure they are understood, and encourage feedback as much as possible. Customer-contact employees need to learn how to practice active listening—through the use of open-ended questions, reflective statements, and probing questions.

Finally, there are techniques for handling both difficult customers and angry ones. No matter how well a company delivers service, its employees will have to work with difficult and/or angry customers at times. By employing these techniques, they can still deliver excellence.

QUESTIONS FOR REVIEW

1. Name four purposes of communication.
2. Describe five elements of the communications model.
3. Describe six steps in the communications process.
4. Explain the differences between upward, downward, and diagonal communication.
5. How can the structure of a company cause problems with communications?
6. Why might customers tell customer-contact employees that they understand what they have been told when, in fact, they are unsure?
7. List three different ways that the use of language can cause miscommunication.
8. How do stereotyping and bias contradict the seven basic customer expectations?
9. How can filtering, overloading, timing, and routing hamper effective communication?
10. List three different ways that people send messages without using written or spoken words.
11. What are eight steps to improving communications?
12. Give an example of an open-ended question, a reflective statement, and a probing question.
13. What are six ways to handle especially difficult customers?
14. What nine techniques can be used to turn an angry customer into a satisfied customer?

QUESTIONS FOR DISCUSSION

1. How can a service organization use the communications model to communicate with customers more efficiently and effectively? How can it use the model to communicate internally more effectively?
2. Is the "grapevine" dangerous to management (i.e., does it make it more difficult to control employees and ensure that they are productive)? Why?
3. Can large companies communicate effectively? If not, why not? (Relate directly to the barriers covered in this chapter.) If so, how can they overcome these barriers?
4. Pick a service company and describe why the layout, decor, and furnishings of their office are conducive to good communications. What might they do to make this better?
5. Describe a service encounter that made you angry. How did the customer-contact employee handle you? How would you have handled it?

10

PERSONAL DEVELOPMENT

OBJECTIVES

After reading this chapter, you should:

Understand how attitudes and abilities combine in determining work performance in customer-contact jobs.

Understand the physical, mental, and emotional components of attitudes and abilities.

Understand the importance of self-esteem in customer-contact job performance.

Know the characteristics of successful, well-adjusted people.

Understand how people interact with each other based on their emotional state.

Know how to apply personal growth and development concepts to improve your own attitudes and abilities.

KEY TERMS

ability	transactional analysis
attitude	ego states
fear of success	complementary transaction
self-esteem	crossed transaction
sell-fulfilling prophecy	ulterior transaction
conscious	active watching
subconscious	mentor

time management   emotional maturity

money management

Many of today's jobs require a mix of technical and human relations skills. The human relations part of the mix is particularly important in the hospitality and tourism industry since all customer-contact employees deal with customers, co-workers, and supervisors on a routine basis. Human relations refers to all aspects of people-to-people interaction. Skills at human relations in a work environment generally include (1) job-specific skills and knowledge, (2) communication skills, and (3) personal attitudes and abilities. We covered the basics of the first two in the preceding two chapters. In this chapter we cover personal abilities and attitudes.

UNDERSTANDING PERSONAL ATTITUDES AND ABILITIES

Jobs do a lot more than merely provide income. They provide the opportunity to learn and enhance skills, to have some control of one's fate and, perhaps most important, to gain a sense of self-worth, a sense of carrying one's own weight.

—William Rasberry

The ability to perform customer-contact service jobs is heavily dependent on personal attitude. If customer-contact employees view work as a nuisance that must be suffered through, they are likely to give short shrift to customers. If, on the other hand, they take the attitude that William Rasberry expressed, they will view work as an ongoing process that is a key part of their lives. It helps identify who they are to others; and it helps identify what they are to themselves. Children are always asked questions like "What do your parents do?" and "What do you want to be when you grow up?" By choosing a job in the hospitality and tourism industry, customer-contact employees make a statement about who they are and what they like and believe in.

Abilities refer to skills and capabilities, whether natural or learned. They can be seen, measured, and tested. **Attitudes** refer more to the individual person's frame of mind (Figure 10-1). They are relatively stable predispositions to evaluating objects (people, organizations, new processes, issues, etc.) in a particular manner. They are much more difficult to measure, because they are impossible to see. No one can observe a person's attitude—only the behavioral results of it. On the job, performance is dependent on

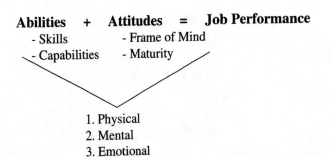

Abilities + **Attitudes** = **Job Performance**

- Skills   - Frame of Mind

- Capabilities   - Maturity

1. Physical

2. Mental

3. Emotional

Figure 10-1 Personal capabilities.

a combination of abilities and attitudes. When either one is lacking, performance suffers. Personal attitude and abilities have three components: physical, mental, and emotional.

Physical Component

The physical component of abilities and attitudes incorporates both internal and external parts. The internal part includes health, nutrition, and exercise. The effects of a healthy and fit body on the mental and emotional components cannot be underestimated. There is no doubt about the link between nutrition, physical fitness, and stress.

Unfortunately, the typical American lifestyle is wholly inappropriate for personal development. As a society, Americans tend to eat too much fat, sugar, caffeine, and other additives. Numerous government and health agencies have recommended reducing the amount of fried food eaten and increasing the consumption of fruits, vegetables, and fish. When necessary, vitamin and mineral supplements have also been recommended.

As a society, Americans also tend toward a lack of exercise. Most customer-contact jobs in hospitality and tourism do not involve a lot of strenuous physical work. Too often, this results in a sedentary lifestyle. Researchers have demonstrated that a good exercise program will not only increase life span and decrease susceptibility to sickness, but will significantly reduce stress levels. A combination of good nutrition and physical fitness can allow customer-contact employees to operate at peak efficiency—both physically and mentally. This gives them the ability to take maximum advantage of their mental and emotional skills in meeting customers' and company's needs.

The second part of the physical component is external physical appearance. Although this is not a book on "how to dress for success" or "how to win friends and influence people," there is truth to the fact that people often make judgments based on appearance—both customers and supervisors. This does not mean that any single appearance is "good" or "bad." Just as customers' expectations vary with a situation, the "correct" physical look varies depending on the job. In many cases (airplanes, chains of restaurants, etc.), customers expect to see a uniform dress of some sort. In a travel agency that caters to an upscale clientele, customers would expect to see very well-dressed staff. But T-shirts and jeans may be perfectly acceptable in an agency that is located in the student union building on a college campus.

It all depends on the image the company wishes to convey. Customer-contact employees' ability to impress both customers and supervisors may depend on how well they read what styles of dress fit in well with co-workers and customers. Although it may not be fair to "judge people by their covers," the plain and simple fact is that physical appearance is the first thing that anybody sees; and as the Second Law of Service says, first impressions *do* mean a lot.

Mental Component

The mental component of abilities and attitudes includes both knowledge and overall outlook. General service knowledge has been covered already, and job-specific knowledge comes from company training and on-the-job experience. The best thing that customer-contact employees can do for their own personal knowledge and growth is to seek out these training opportunities wherever they are. It is important, however, to realize one unique difference between the education and training environment and the real-life work environment. Too often in a school environment, students settle for a "passing" grade. If a "C" is good enough to pass, there is limited incentive to do better. Unfortunately, there is no such thing as a "C" in service delivery. Service delivery is either acceptable to customers or it is not (Figure 10-2). It is highly doubtful that customers will accept employees being right 70 percent of the time—yet that is usually acceptable in school. To grow as capable service employees, customer-contact employees must adapt a new attitude which says that anything short of an "A" is a failing grade.

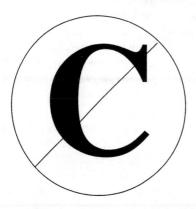

Figure 10-2 In a service environment, customer-contact employees either get an "A" or they fail!

Overall outlook is much more difficult to define and deal with. The entire field of psychology is devoted to better understanding the nature of human mental health and personal mental growth. Customer-contact employees cannot pretend to understand all the intricacies of this field, but they can learn a few things about those elements of their psyche that most affect their ability to do the current job and grow into the next step on the ladder.

We discussed earlier how the need for achievement can be a primary motivator. Ironically, in some people the **fear of success** can be equally effective as a motivation to avoid achievement. The first clinical evidence of this phenomenon was presented in a study by M. S. Horner in 1970. Horner asked female college students to write stories that start with the sentence, "At the end of first-term finals, Anne finds herself at the top of her medical school class." At the same time, Horner had male respondents write about "John" instead of Anne.

The study showed that 62.2 percent of the females wrote stories based on "fear of success" imagery versus only 9.1 percent of the males. These themes in the female responses included stories about social rejection that Anne experienced, negative self-images developed by Anne about her unhappiness, abnormality, and lack of femininity, and denial of Anne's success or outright hostility toward it.

Subsequent research has indicated that there is no correlation between a person's gender and the likelihood to exhibit "fear of success" behaviors in general job or social situations. All of these studies are in agreement that some people are motivated to avoid success. Related behavioral tendencies include fear of "being in the limelight" and a reluctance to "close the deal," "deliver the knockout punch," or otherwise "win" at someone else's expense. Whatever the underlying cause, the end result of a fear of success is a behavior pattern that is nothing short of self-sabotage. Therefore, if customer-contact employees are to grow, they must reject this fear and embrace the excitement of opportunity and success.

A number of more advanced studies looking for links between personal abilities and attitudes and job performance and success have discovered a more universal attribute. This attribute is **self-esteem**, a person's view of who he or she is. There is an ancient Chinese proverb that says, "A child's life is like a piece of paper on which every passerby leaves a mark." Self-esteem is often a result of all these marks. It is highly dependent on how parents brought the person up; it is molded through adolescence by friends, family, and the media; and it can be modified (with difficulty) in adulthood. There is also a growing body of research which suggests that genetics plays a significant role in self-esteem. Many studies have shown that the years between the ages of 12 and 18 are the most important in developing self-esteem as an adult because of the movement from close family relationships to an understanding of life as an independent person.

In general, the studies show that people who have high self-esteem feel confident and free to express themselves without worrying about others' reactions. On the other hand, people with low self-esteem behave suboptimally. They do not tend to lack ability—rather, they set lower expectations for themselves, feel self-conscious, and attribute their successes to external factors ("I was lucky") and their failures to internal factors

Hi, I'm Sara. I'll be your bitter, professionally unfulfilled waitress this evening. May I take your lousy order? (© Derek Barnes. Reproduced by permission.)

("I'm not good enough"). They tend to choose occupations for which they are not well suited, they perform below their capabilities, and they don't derive as much satisfaction from success. This reinforces their low self-image, thus fueling a circle of missed opportunities and other failings.

The notion of self-image and its effect on behavior is so important that in 1987, the California State Assembly formed a 25-member task force on self-image and personal and social responsibility. This demonstrates the government's understanding that for people in society to grow and mature into productive citizens, they must develop a positive self-image.

There are a number of ways that people with low self-esteem can eliminate their self-imposed performance barriers.

1. They increase their expectations. People with low self-esteem tend to expect less from themselves and therefore settle for less as well. When people expect things to go wrong, they often create a **self-fulfilling prophecy**. Raising basic expectations and looking for things to go right can break this form of subconscious self-sabotage.

2. They are instructed to attend diligently to the task. By focusing on the task, people with low self-esteem can shift attention away from themselves. This can allow them to use their abilities to accomplish the task without the interference of a negative attitude. Subsequent success will help begin to create a more positive self-image.

3. They are not placed under evaluative pressures. People with low self-esteem tend to perform best when not under the pressure of "big brother" watching them. Just like people who know a subject well but do not perform under the pressure of a written test, people with low self-esteem are much more self-inhibited when they know they are being judged. Removing this external pressure can allow them to focus more on the task and less on what people think about them.

4. They are helped to attribute success and failure realistically. People with low self-esteem need to be coached to better understand the true source of their successes and failures. By learning how to assess their own performance more realistically, they can better evaluate what they need to do to improve and grow for the future.

Customer-contact employees can also learn much about what they need to do to grow by examining the abilities and attitudes of people with high self-esteem. By better understanding what characteristics these successful, well-adjusted people have, they can identify potential weaknesses in themselves and learn to overcome them. People with high self-esteem exhibit most, if not all, of the following characteristics.

1. They are future-oriented. People with high self-esteem do not worry about past mistakes and failures. Rather, they look to the future. They believe in the old saying, "There's no use crying over spilled milk." Instead of brooding over past mistakes or complaining about the unfairness of their circumstances, they choose to apply the lessons from these experiences to future attempts.

2. They react to problems as challenges.   High self-esteem people are both able and willing to deal with the problems and disappointments that life is certain to deal them. They understand that success requires hard work and that annoying setbacks are part of the process. They believe that "There is no such thing as problems—only opportunities." They see these problems as challenges to overcome on their road to success. They do not focus on the doors that these problems close, choosing instead to concentrate on the doors that remain to be opened.

They do not accept failure as an end result. When they do fail at something, they look at the failure as a new beginning. They concentrate on the need for a different approach. They do not give up because of a failure. This attitude lets them try new ideas without fear. General H. Norman Schwarzkopf, Commander of Allied Forces in the Persian Gulf War, comments, "Good leaders cannot allow their people to expect failure, but they must give them the latitude to learn."

3. They control their emotions.   People with high self-esteem do not allow their emotions to interfere with their job performance. They feel the same emotions as anyone else—they just keep them under control. Some people with high self-esteem may even experience more intense emotions than others, but they will channel that energy and intensity into a positive behavior. They will use their anger or frustration to fuel a passion for future success.

4. They help others.   High self-esteem people derive satisfaction from sharing their skills and knowledge with others. They feel just as good about helping someone else do the job as they do about doing it themselves. Perhaps just as important, people with high self-esteem are willing to accept help from others. They do not pretend that only they are capable of doing something best. They know that they must rely on others to get complicated tasks accomplished, and they look forward to sharing the effort (and the credit) with other competent people.

5. They accept others as unique, talented individuals.   The best sign of the maturity that people with high self-esteem exhibit is the ability and willingness to accept other people for whom they are. They do not expect everyone else to act as they do, and they are not threatened by people who do things better than they do. In fact, they usually view meeting these people as a welcome opportunity to learn.

These abilities and attitudes possessed by people with high self-esteem lead to a variety of self-confident behaviors. People with high self-esteem are neither overly self-critical nor self-serving. They feel free to express themselves, even if they disagree with others; and they appreciate others' expressions, even if they differ.

Emotional Component

The emotional component of abilities and attitudes includes all those ways in which people react to outside stimuli. Emotional maturity refers to the ability to control "feelings" and reactions to these feelings in any given situation. It includes the ability to leave private problems at home. Too often, customer-contact employees bring along the "baggage" of problems at home and inadvertently take these out on customers or co-workers. It includes the ability to treat each situation as a distinctly unique encounter of its own. Although it is fine to bring the positive feelings from a good previous encounter, it is not acceptable to bring over a tense and argumentative attitude from a previous negative encounter. Each customer is unique, and so is each transaction.

Much study has been dedicated to better understanding the emotional content of human personality and behavior. Many people are aware of the fact that their responses to various stimuli are influenced by both **conscious** and **subconscious** elements of their mind. Conscious elements are those reactions and feelings that they control directly; subconscious elements are the memories, ideas, and desires that operate beyond direct knowledge and control. In a stressful situation, the subconscious elements often exert a more powerful influence on behavior than the conscious ones.

Sigmund Freud is largely credited with developing the early psychological theories about how these two parts of our mind influence daily behavior. Unfortunately, much of this theory did not easily translate into ideas that laypeople can understand and put to use. Starting in 1969, with Thomas Harris's famous book, *I'm O.K., You're O.K.*, the development of a theory now known as **transactional analysis** began to explain these approaches to understanding human psychology in ways that can be practically applied. Transactional analysis is explained in a variety of other books, including Eric Bernes's *Games People Play* and *What Do You Say After You Have Said Hello?*.

Transactional analysis is based on a three-part model of the human ego state (*ego state* is a psychological term for a consistent combination of feelings and related behavior): parent, child, and adult (Figure 10-3).

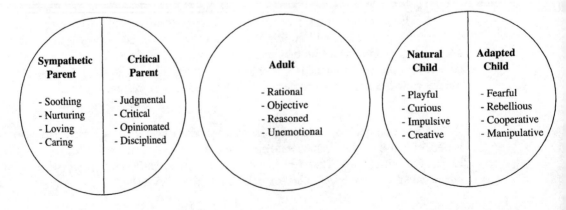

Figure 10-3   Ego states.

The **parent ego state** is operating whenever people feel, think, or act as they saw their parents (or other adults acting in a parental manner) operate. These include the "do's and don'ts" that all parents teach their children. The parent ego state consists of two basic sets of attitudes: the **sympathetic parent** is a soothing, nurturing attitude, and the **critical parent** is judgmental, opinionated, and disciplined.

The **child ego state** is the major source of emotional responses. It is a result of memories of joy and happiness as well as sorrow, fear, and despair. Figure 10-3 shows that the child ego is also broken into two very different sets of attitudes. The **natural child ego state** consists of those emotions and behaviors that one would expect to see from an uninhibited child—playful, impulsive, prone toward fantasies, and eager for fun. The **adapted child ego state** consists of behaviors that result from the child's attempt to change and adapt to the demands and requirements of others. These attitudes include anger, fear, jealousy, cooperation, and rebelliousness. All of these attitudes and behaviors are learned responses to the world around children—they are not natural behaviors.

The **adult ego state** describes the part of an emotional being that is at work when dealing with a situation in an objective fashion or otherwise thinking and acting in a rational manner. The adult ego state is not encumbered by personal feelings, opinion, or other irrational reactions to external stimuli. Dorothy Jongeward and Philip Seyer describe this state that allows people to think and reason through a situation: "Whenever you are gathering information, reasoning things out, estimating probabilities, and so on, you are in your adult ego state. While in this ego state you are cool and collected: you make decisions unemotionally. You just want the facts."

Transactional analysis is as much a theory of communication as anything else. The heart of the theory is not merely the description of each ego state described above. Rather, it is a model of the behavior among people as their different ego states interact with each other. In this theory, each communication between two individuals is referred to as a "transaction." Each transaction (there are many transactions in each conversation or other work encounter) can be analyzed on the basis of which ego state is talking to which ego state in each person.

Using these figures as a guide, there are three basic categories of transactions: complementary, crossed, and ulterior. **Complementary transactions** occur when the ego state of the sender gets a response from the desired or expected ego state of the receiver.

Conversely, **crossed transactions** are those exchanges in which the receiver gives a response to the sender that was not expected. This will obviously create stress between the two participants. It is very important that customer-contact employees avoid sending crossed transactions to customers. When they receive crossed transactions from customers, they need to be careful how they react. Because they are servicing customers, they do not have the luxury of reacting to a crossed transaction the same way as they would to friends or family.

The term **ulterior transaction** covers those situations where a message says one thing but really means another. This is usually done when one of the participants wants to disguise the hidden message in socially acceptable terms. Just like crossed transactions, ulterior transactions usually create tension and stress. They should be avoided in the work environment since they serve no useful purpose in meeting customer expectations. In fact, they usually lead directly to dissatisfaction.

Generally speaking, customer-contact employees are at their most professional when they deal with customers, co-workers, and supervisors communicating adult ego state to adult ego state. However, there are many cases where it is perfectly normal to engage in transactions from one of the parental states to one of the child states, and vice versa. The important thing is that the transactions be complementary.

Almost by definition, emotional maturity comes as customer-contact employees understand their five personality states and as they begin to be able to recognize them in others. The best way to recognize customers' ego states is to listen closely when they communicate. Putting to use all the communication tools learned in Chapter 9, customer-contact employees can interpret both verbal and nonverbal signals.

Once the ego state of the other person has been identified, customer-contact employees must choose the appropriate ego state with which to respond based on a reading of the customer's desired transaction response. Emotional control occurs when customer-contact employees are able to choose the correct response for each situation, even when emotionally they want a crossed or ulterior transaction. This can be particularly difficult in customer jobs in hospitality and tourism. Ccustomer-contact employees are involved in a large number of customer contacts each day. The tendency is to suffer from "emotional burnout." This is characterized by increased irritability, decreased tolerance for the differences between customers, and decreased willingness to accept the little annoyances that come with every job. But the job depends on getting along with people, and getting along with people depends on emotional maturity.

PERSONAL GROWTH AND DEVELOPMENT

Having discussed the three components of personal growth, the question left to ask is, "What specifically does it take to grow?" Life is a continuing process, and people are always presented with new opportunities to learn and grow. There are, however, a number of specific things that customer-contact employees can do to seek out these opportunities and take maximum advantage of them when they become available.

1. Set goals.   Goal setting is an important foundation for any successful career. Just as any business must first state what its purpose is, customer-contact employees must decide what it is that they want to do. Developing career goals and a career plan serves many purposes. It focuses attention on what is important and helps decide which opportunities are worth accepting. It gives something to measure progress against and reinforces actions that lead toward accomplishing those goals.

At the same time, customer-contact employees should be careful not to develop goals or plans that are too restrictive. Goals should be difficult to attain but realistic. If the goals are too easy, they do not really force them to stretch their abilities to their limit. If they are too hard, they may limit capabilities by being a source of discouragement. Also, customer-contact employees should not be tied too strongly to a specific plan of action. Life has a strange way of throwing up unexpected roadblocks and opening up new, completely different opportunities. If plans are too narrowly focused, the planner may become overly frustrated at a temporary setback while missing out on new, exciting opportunities.

2. Improve observation skills.   Observation skills can be very useful for both performing the current job and developing the abilities and attitudes needed for the next position. Although seemingly simple, observation is a very complex and difficult task that requires skill and concentration.

As discussed above, the ability to read customers' moods and to provide desired responses is critical to customer-contact employees' ability to meet customer needs and expectations. To do this, they need to practice **active watching**. Just as active listening is a communication tool that encourages customer-contact employees to get as much information and feedback from verbal transactions, active watching is a technique that gets them to focus on receiving as much information as possible from visual sources.

People by nature see things, but they don't observe them. This means that while they are looking at a situation, they have really tuned out most of what they are seeing. They focus on those things they want to see, perhaps to the exclusion of more important things. They also tend to view scenes subjectively, using their emotions to influence what they believe they see. There is much more data in a visual encounter than in a verbal one, so it is almost impossible to notice everything. This is why eyewitnesses to the same scene can often describe completely different circumstances.

To practice active watching, customer-contact employees must consciously work to observe all the aspects of what they see. They can try to apply principles of behavior and communication to interpret what they are watching and to learn from it. Rather than being a passive "looker-on" who notices only the exceptions to what they expect to see, customer-contact employees can become active observers who see all the elements of the environment and notice the subtleties of the observed behaviors.

Active watching can be a particularly effective tool in helping customer-contact employees develop as service providers. They can pick out certain people among their co-workers who they know are effective service providers. By watching what they do and imagining themselves doing the same, customer-contact employees can improve their own abilities. They can also watch co-workers who are not as good and try to analyze what it is they do that hurts their performance. This may identify some attitudes or habits to avoid. Customer-contact employees can use this information to examine themselves and determine where and how their own abilities and attitudes could be improved. This form of honest self-criticism can be instrumental in personal growth.

The same approach can be taken with supervisors or other people in the organization who hold jobs or positions that customer-contact employees hope to get someday. They can examine what it is that they do right and what they do wrong. They can watch how they handle customers, co-workers, and subordinates. From this, customer-contact employees can develop a set of "do's and don't's" for these jobs. Again, through honest and open self-criticism they can identify their own strengths and weaknesses relative to this list. They can try to take maximum advantage of strengths while learning to overcome and improve on weaknesses.

Many organizations put this form of active watching into a formal structure. They assign someone (or allow employees to choose someone) who has been where the employees want to go and who is willing to take people under a wing and show them how to get where they want to go. These **mentors** act as teachers, coaches, and sponsors. They develop a personal relationship that allows junior workers to get to know and understand what it took for this person to succeed. Junior people get the benefit of the experience of someone who has already learned how to navigate the complex and dangerous waters of corporate advancement and internal politics. There is no longer a sense of being "alone against the world."

Mentors can serve as a sounding board for ideas and can also generate questions and advice of their own. Mentors are equally important and effective in small companies as well as large. Although not mandatory for success, research has shown that mentors certainly do help.

For mentoring to work its best, there are a number of criteria that should be met:

a. Mentors should not be the boss or in the chain of command of the employees assigned to them. A boss/subordinate relationship interferes with the openness required of a mentor relationship. Participants in a mentor relationship cannot worry about their mentor being responsible for job evaluations.

b. Mentors must be authorities in their field. Mentors cannot effectively teach junior employees, nor can they have the credibility required if they are not authorities in their field. The whole point of acquiring a mentor is to provide access to expertise that otherwise could not be gotten.

c. Mentors must be higher up on the professional ladder. They cannot be co-workers. They need to have the knowledge and experience that comes with having progressed through the organization. This is the very knowledge and experience that junior employees seek in establishing a mentor relationship.

d. Mentors must be influential in the organization. Again, mentors cannot have the credibility or experience level required unless they have risen to an influential position.

e. Mentors must have a genuine interest in junior employees' personal growth. Without a genuine interest in their growth, mentors are just going through the motions. Only with true commitment can they recognize opportunities that will meet the potential of the junior employee they are helping.

f. Mentors must be willing to commit time and emotion to the mentoring relationship. People learn so much from their parents and other influential adults because of the time and care these people invested. They put a little bit of each of them into their children, and mentors must be able and willing to do the same.

g. The mentoring relationship should not be permanent, but it cannot be too short-lived either. As junior employees grow and advance, their needs for new knowledge and experience change. So, too, will their requirements of a mentor. Therefore, they must be willing and able to change mentors. At the same time, if they change too often or too soon, they will never develop the full personal involvement that makes mentor relationships work. A good rule is to consider changing mentors whenever their boss or job changes. Sometimes they can keep the same mentor if there is still a level of difference between them.

3. Develop high self-esteem. Some customer-contact employees are blessed with high self-esteem already. However, most suffer from some of the effects of low self-esteem. This does not mean that they hate themselves or their parents. It only means that almost everyone can improve their self-image and apply that improvement toward leading a happier, more rewarding life—both on and off the job.

The first key to increasing self-esteem is for customer-contact employees to accept the way they are and look toward the future. Bemoaning their current weaknesses or past failures does nothing to help development. They must understand that it took many years to get where they are today. It will take a long time to get where they want to go. There are no "quick fixes" or easy answers, but there are a number of basic principles that can help them achieve their goals.

a. *Identify and accept limitations.* No one is capable of doing everything. Everyone should realize what their limitations are and look toward others to help them do those things they cannot do themselves. Accepting limitations does not mean that aggressive goals cannot be set, but it does mean that customer-contact employees are comfortable with who they are and what they do.

b. *Visualize desired results.* Most great athletes share an ability to visualize their desired actions before they create them. Customer-contact employees can do the same. By visualizing the success they want, they set an image in their subconscious that supports their efforts. They can create positive self-fulfilling prophecies.

c. *Engage in positive self-talk.* Everyone engages in self-talk—the act of speaking to oneself either silently or verbally. People with negative self-images continually feed themselves negative messages. They reinforce their negative images with thoughts like, "I just don't have what it takes," "Why does this always happen to me?", and "I'll never be able to do that." Before anyone can gain self-esteem, he or she must develop a positive self-image. Positive self-talk can help accomplish this by internalizing goals and dreams in a positive light. Statements such as "I have the capability to overcome that obstacle," "I know there are other opportunities that I can take advantage of," and "I enjoy sharing success with my work team members" are all useful, forward-looking self-talk messages.

d. *Make decisions.* Many people miss opportunities by refusing to make a decision or to take a positive action. They then bemoan their lack of movement or improvement. This then reinforces their negative self-image. People with high self-esteem are not afraid to make decisions. They welcome the opportunity for change and look forward to taking the risks and overcoming the obstacles. Very often, they find that the fear of risk is larger than the actual risks themselves. "Fear of success" problems often manifest themselves as an unwillingness to make decisions. One of the best ways for anyone to begin to establish and reinforce good self-esteem is to make a decision and then go full steam into dealing with the new situation rather than second-guessing.

e. *Develop expertise.* Nothing increases self-esteem more quickly than becoming an expert in something—and nothing makes customer-contact employees more valuable to their company as well. They can easily pick something (a specific job skill, a general service skill, or a general skill such as a new language) to concentrate on first. Once mastered, they can take pride in their accomplishment and apply it to a second skill. They can choose to specialize in a particular part of the company's operation or cross-train into a multitude of skills. Developing this expertise requires them to take full advantage of education and training opportunities, and it may not come quickly. But when it comes, it will pay off handsomely.

Other areas worth concentrating on include **time management** and **money management**. Very often, problems related to time and money lead to general stress and specific feelings of inadequacy. There are many seminars and other adult education opportunities that provide detailed training in time and money management (in fact, more and more companies today are offering after-work seminars to their employees on these areas). It is very difficult for customer-contact employees to feel good about themselves if they do not have control of their finances or if they feel they never seem to have the time to catch up and do the things they like to do.

4. Develop emotional maturity.

Customer-contact employees are continually bombarded by outside stimuli. To grow as individuals and professionals, they must be able to develop an ability to respond appropriately to each stimulus. The ability to mature depends on their ability to pick the correct response to stimuli. This can be quite difficult when they are tired, ill, under stress, and so on. It requires self-discipline, especially in jobs that have many transactions per day.

The most important lesson for customer-contact employees to learn is to realize that they are the masters of their own behavior. Nobody can make them lose their cool in any situation—they choose to either keep it or lose it. Customers are allowed the luxury of being able to lack emotional control because they are the ones who pay the bill. Customer-contact employees cannot be allowed that luxury. Even when customers are completely out of line, customer-contact employees cannot afford to lose that potential future business because of their inability to control themselves.

Another important lesson is to treat each encounter as a separate and uniquely challenging opportunity to meet customers' needs. Customer-contact employees should not let the last encounter affect the current one. The fact that the last customer was discourteous is not sufficient cause to be curt with current customers. After all, it is not their fault. Just as important, customer-contact employees need to deal with customers' questions and requests as if they were the first to ask. They may know that they have already been asked 45 times today where the bathroom is, but the forty-sixth customer does not know it. That customer still deserves just as friendly an answer as the other 45.

Another important part of emotional control is the ability to handle criticism. Too often, people respond to criticism by getting defensive—whether that criticism comes from a supervisor, a customer, or even a friend. Customer-contact employees need to recognize criticism for what it is—communication from someone who wants them to do something differently (and in their mind better). That's all it is. Getting defensive does not help learn from the experience, nor does it change the opinion of the person who made the criticizing remark.

5. Develop a willingness and ability to cope with change.

Change is the one constant in the world today. If customer-contact employees want to continue their personal growth, they have no choice but to learn how to deal with change—both in their company and in themselves. There are many reasons for change in both organizations and people.

Although the reasons are numerous and complex, the dynamics of change are fairly similar. Resistance to these changes is a normal part of human psychology. Understanding the reasons behind resistance to change can help customer-contact employees better use the other lessons learned about personal growth to learn to cope better with change. The reasons that people resist change fall into five basic categories:

a. *Feelings of inadequacy.* Change makes obsolete much of what people used to know and be able to do. This can have a big impact on their feelings of self-worth. If their skills and knowledge are no longer useful, there is a fear that they will no longer have adequate value as a person.

b. *Threat to personal security.* At a minimum, change may lead to feelings of inadequacy. But if changes result in demotions or layoffs, it becomes a threat to their basic need for physical and psychological security—the most basic needs in Maslow's hierarchy. A newfound need to re-fulfill these needs will override all other social, status, and self-actualization needs.

c. *Fear of unknown.* Everyone fears the unknown. Change is uncertain, and it is very difficult to predict its results. The threat of layoffs, restructuring, social isolation, and so on, can be more scary than their reality. Even when they are unhappy, human beings often fight change. They seem to feel deep down that "the devil we know is better than the one we don't know."

d. *Lack of trust.* Change can break down relationships between people that have been built up over years. The anxiety over the change can be directed at those who make decisions about how to manage that change (like union–management struggles) or at those who are the messengers of the change. Trust is an important part of teambuilding, and change can decimate a company's ability to function as a team.

e. *Inability to see the big picture.* When change occurs without some people's input, those people often are not able to see the full extent of reasons for change and their impact. They only see their little part of the world and understand and fear the impact of the change on them.

Universally, the one thing that change does is cause stress. In fact, many studies show that people who have had a major change in their life recently (death of a close family member, change in job or home situation, marital status, etc.) are much more likely to suffer from a major sickness than are those who are leading relatively stable lives. The stress level experienced is independent of whether the change is a happy one or an unhappy one. As a result, basic stress management techniques can help customer-contact employees cope with these changes. In general, they should:

a. *Stick to positive values.* Change often causes people to question their values and beliefs. They must be open to considering new ideas and updating antiquated beliefs to match new realities. However, there are still some universal positive values that successful people believe in—values such as honesty, hard work, and fair play. By focusing on the positive foundation of these values, customer-contact employees can build a new structure within the changed environment. Sometimes this new structure ends up better than the old one they were so fond of.

b. *Gain control.* One of the most frightening things about change is the loss of control that people experience. They feel as though they have been thrown into a situation they no longer know how to handle. It can be very helpful to take any action that helps gain control.

c. *Maintain or improve physical health.* The stress of change is bad enough. But when people are in poor health or have poor nutritional intake, the mental and emotional stress of change can quickly cause them to become ill. Exercise and good nutrition can help them feel much better about themselves, thus making it easier to adapt to the change.

d. *Use mental relaxation techniques.* Simple meditative exercises can also help deal with the stress of change. Customer-contact employees can take just a few moments out of the day to close their eyes, consciously relax their muscles, and take slow, deep breaths. These simple actions can help keep their emotions under control in otherwise difficult circumstances.

e. *Seek outside help and counseling.* There are many ways to do this. Customer-contact employees can join a social club or support group. If they can afford it (or are covered by medical insurance), they can seek professional counseling. In many large companies, there are employee assistance programs (EAPs) which are available free or at substantially subsidized rates to help employees cope with problems—in and out of work.

SUMMARY

Most customer-contact jobs require a mix of technical and human relations skills. Because these jobs involve continual interaction with customers, co-workers, and supervisors, the human relations part of the mix is particularly important. This, in turn, is based heavily on the personal abilities and attitudes of each service provider.

"Abilities" refer to somebody's skills and capabilities; "attitudes" refer to their preferences, beliefs, and frame of mind. Abilities can be tested and measured relatively easily; attitudes cannot be seen—only their effects can be seen. Attitudes and abilities have three components: physical, mental, and emotional.

The physical component includes health, nutrition, and exercise as well as dress and outward appearance. In general, when people feel good and look good, their behavior reflects these positive feelings.

The mental component includes knowledge—both general and job specific—and overall outlook. The latter, often referred to as self-esteem, is particularly important. Studies have clearly linked high self-esteem with high job performance and low self-esteem with self-defeating behaviors. Low self-esteem, however, is not unchangeable. There are many different ways that people with low self-esteem can learn the attitudes and behaviors that high self-esteem people demonstrate.

The emotional component affects how people react to outside stimuli. Through transactional analysis, researchers have been able to develop a model that explains human interactive behavior. Emotional maturity is often the ability to choose to respond in transactions that are complementary rather than crossed or ulterior.

People continually grow and develop as they progress through life. To help grow quickly and effectively people should set goals, improve their observation skills, develop high self-esteem, emotional maturity, and a willingness and ability to cope with change.

QUESTIONS FOR REVIEW

1. What is the difference between attitudes and abilities?
2. Describe self-esteem.
3. List five major characteristics exhibited by people with high self-esteem.
4. What is an ego state?
5. According to the transactional analysis model, what are the three ego states?
6. Describe a complementary transaction; a crossed transaction; an ulterior transaction.
7. What is a mentor?
8. What are time management and stress management?
9. For what five basic reasons do people resist change? Name five ways to overcome that resistance.

QUESTIONS FOR DISCUSSION

1. What is meant by "It's not a 'C' world?" How accurate a portrayal of the real world is it, and why?
2. Why is self-esteem important for job performance and personal development?
3. Is transactional analysis a valid model for learning about human interaction?
4. How can a company set up a mentoring program? How can a person find a mentor if there is no formal program?
5. How important is personal growth and development? What can you do to grow and mature?

REFERENCES

BERNE, ERIC. *Games People Play.* New York: Ballantine Books, 1964.

BERNE, ERIC. *What Do You Say After You Have Said Hello?* New York: Bantam Books, 1984.

HARRIS, THOMAS. *I'm O.K., You're O.K.* New York: Harper & Row, 1969.

PART 4

INTERNAL SERVICE

The preceding three sections have covered the topic of service in great detail. In fact, anyone who masters the concepts and techniques of these sections is ready to deliver excellence in service from the customer-contact positions of any hospitality or tourism company. However, this alone is not enough for companies in hospitality and tourism to deliver excellent service consistently.

Many people have conducted studies over the past 30 years in an attempt to distinguish the characteristics that separate truly excellent companies from the mediocre. Over the past five or ten years, the understanding of these results in the United States has grown to include the quality of the service that employees give each other within a company. This concept of **internal service** may be included within the basic expectation of teamwork. However, it does not do it justice merely to include it as part of one of the seven basic expectations. Furthermore, customer-contact employees can exhibit characteristics of teamwork in front of customers while not really working well with each other or with support personnel behind the scenes.

The creation of an organizational culture that supports internal service is the responsibility of management, but execution depends on the attitudes and capabilities of all employees. Because internal service is such an important discriminator between those companies that are truly good and those that are not, it is important that all customer-contact employees understand its basic principles and practices. The next two chapters are dedicated to this.

INTERNAL CUSTOMERS AND SUPPLIERS

OBJECTIVES

After reading this chapter, you should:

Understand the differences and similarities between external and internal customers.

Understand and be able to apply the Internal Service Laws.

Know what it takes to practice internal service excellence.

KEY TERMS

internal service

external customer

internal customer

supplier

customer focus

system focus

continuous improvement

Up to this point, we have discussed the subject of customers: their needs, desires, motivations, and how hospitality and tourism companies in general, and customer-contact employees in particular, can go about satisfying them. Yet we have never really defined what a customer is.

This may not seem like much of an oversight. After all, everyone knows who customers are. They are the people that companies serve. They are the people who pay for the services that customer-contact employees provide. In essence, they are hospitality and tourism's reason for existence. And although each customer is unique, they all share seven basic expectations.

To meet expectations, organizations must work as a cohesive unit (in fact, teamwork is one of these expectations). In the traditional hierarchy approach to business, customers are those people external to the organization who get served by its employees. Management may pay attention to how well their customer-contact personnel deliver service, but they rarely look toward anyone else in the organization as being directly responsible for the company's performance in the eyes of customers. In fact, there is often friction between such support personnel and customer-contact personnel. It is very easy for each to blame the other for any problems, thus building walls that encourage animosity.

However, all successful service delivery systems require both customer-contact employees and support employees working together to meet customers' needs (Figure 11-1). It is true that customer-contact employees are visible to customers and support workers are not. However, just as with back office systems, the effect of the work that support personnel do is very visible. Wherever support people are employed within the organization, they are critical to the success of the ultimate goal of meeting customers' needs, although customers will tend to become aware of them only when something goes wrong. A mistake in billing can undermine the most pleasant interaction that a customer may have had with the company. If the human resources department is not effective in developing and maintaining employee development and morale, the effect will soon show in customer-contact interactions. Even the washer maintenance person at a hotel is critical to customer service. If housekeeping can't clean the sheets and towels, there is no way they can deliver efficient and effective cleaning services.

The role of support personnel is so important, Albrecht and Zemke have said: "If you're not serving the customer, you better be serving someone who is." This brings us to a very important (and relatively new) concept in the design and implementation of

Customer-Contact Employees	Support Employees
- Visible to external customers	- "Behind the scenes" (i.e., invisible to external customer)
- Involved at time of service delivery	- Rarely involved at time of delivery
- Easy to observe and measure effect of performance	- Much more difficult to observe and measure effect of performance

Neither can succeed without the other!

Figure 11-1 Customer contact and support employees.

service products. It broadens the definition of what a customer is: A **customer** is anyone who receives or benefits from the output of someone's work. Within this definition, there are two broad categories of customers. The first is **external customers**, the customers that most people think of in the traditional sense as discussed above. The satisfaction of external customers ultimately measures a company's success since they are the people who are willing to pay for its services.

The second category is **internal customers**. These are the people inside any company who receive or benefit from the output of work done by others in the company. Examples of this include the meeting manager of a hotel, who depends on food and beverage people to deliver their product, or amusement park ride operators, who depend on repair and maintenance employees to keep the machinery operating. Internal customers must be viewed by support personnel not merely as co-workers but as customers in their own right. Figure 11-2 shows this relationship for the examples discussed above. Internal customers share the same seven basic expectations, get turned off by the same deadly sins, and follow the same Laws of Service as do external customers. The only difference between internal and external customers is that they cannot just take their business elsewhere when they are dissatisfied. The internal **supplier** has essentially a monopoly on providing the necessary product or products. Often, the only recourse that internal customers have is to quit; and that, more often than not, is not a realistic option.

Unfortunately, because internal customers do not have many alternatives when provided with poor service, they are often not perceived as having the same level of importance as external customers. Although it is true that poor internal service is often not directly visible to external customers, its effects quickly become apparent.

In understanding internal service and its relationship to delivering service excellence to external customers, it is worthwhile to review some basic internal service laws.

FIRST LAW OF INTERNAL SERVICE

At each point in time, in each work situation, everyone is either a customer or a supplier.

There is no category of "disinterested bystander" or "other" (Figure 11-2).

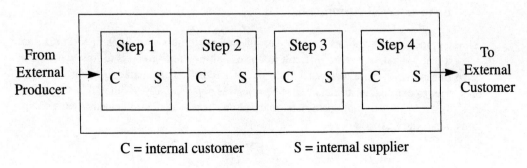

C = internal customer   S = internal supplier

Figure 11-2   Service delivery process.

As defined, "customers" are "people who receive or benefit from work." "Suppliers" are the people who do that work. It therefore stands to follow that everyone at work is either a customer or a supplier. In many jobs, suppliers may change from customer to supplier and back again quite frequently (Figure 11-3). In a single conversation, they may change roles many times.

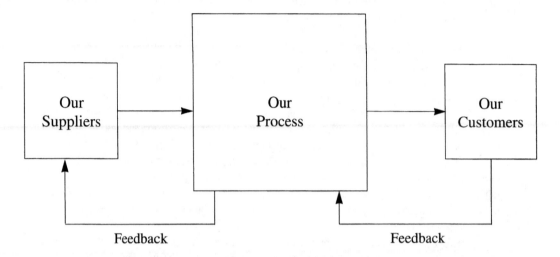

Figure 11-3   Everyone acts as both customer and supplier.

In a customer-driven situation, suppliers focus on providing quality output for their customers' use—independent of whether the customer is external or internal. At the same time, internal customers communicate with their suppliers to let them know what it is that they need. In this way, suppliers are able to understand the customer's perspective—internal customers participate in the production of service products for themselves just as external customers participate in the production of their products.

SECOND LAW OF INTERNAL SERVICE

The three Laws of Service apply to internal customers as they do to external customers.

Although most organizations do not treat internal customers as well as they do external ones, it really is not any more difficult to do so. All they need to do is to follow the same Laws of Service as those discussed in detail in Chapter 3. That chapter implicitly focused on service to external customers, but the principles apply equally to internal customers.

Just as with external customers, internal customer satisfaction equals their perceptions minus their expectations:

$$S = P - E$$

Both of these variables are still psychological phenomena and may or may not have any relationship to reality. Just as customer-contact employees must try to put themselves in the shoes of external customers to understand what they expect, internal suppliers must put themselves in their customers' shoes. This ability to empathize with the needs of internal customers is critical to smooth and efficient team coordination. It also means that internal suppliers must manage internal customer expectations so that they are aware of what to expect realistically.

Internal customers have the same seven basic expectations as external customers:

- Accessibility
- Courtesy
- Personal attention
- Empathy
- Job knowledge
- Consistency
- Teamwork

Internal suppliers can also quickly poison relationships with their internal customers by committing one or more of the seven deadly sins:

- Leaving someone expecting a reply
- Arguing with the customer
- Presenting a dirty or unprofessional look
- Giving conflicting or incorrect information
- Arguing with a co-worker in front of the customer
- Implying that the customer's needs are unimportant or trivial
- Passing the buck

In most service organizations, the success of the team depends on the relationships that exist between the various people and departments. With few exceptions, the full range of customer needs cannot be met by a single customer-contact person. Inevitably, every employee of a service company acts as both an internal customer and a supplier. The age-old golden rule, "Do unto others as you would like them to do unto you," is very applicable since each person will experience both sides of the relationship.

The Second Law of Service, "First impressions are the most important," and the Third Law, "A service-oriented attitude alone will not assure good service," are also applicable. Many an internal turf battle has started with a minor misunderstanding. Then, as each side builds walls, the differences become almost insurmountable. No matter which side wins, the external customer loses.

THIRD LAW OF INTERNAL SERVICE

For an organization to deliver consistent service excellence, internal customers must be "nearly equal" to external customers in importance.

The first two internal service laws may make it appear as if internal customers are just as important as external customers. In a good service company, this is almost true. There are only a couple of exceptions. The first is that internal customers understand that external customers come first. In other words, they do not expect any of their internal suppliers to meet their needs at the expense of servicing an external customer. This is not, however, a carte blanche for internal suppliers to plan poorly for the allocation of their time so that their internal customers rarely get proper attention.

The second is that internal customers do not expect the same level of comfort in the service environment. Companies "go the extra mile" to make sure that the service environment where customer-contact employees interact with external customers is flawless in space, decor, and cleanliness. Behind the scenes, however, the environment may be far more spartan or crowded. It does not make sense to waste money on unnecessary space or expensive decor. Workers understand that they do not need the same kind of environment that external customers may be willing to pay for. They do still deserve a clean, comfortable, and functional environment. The fact that they are only "nearly equal" to external customers does not give management the right to provide a dirty or unsafe environment or one that does not give enough work space to accomplish the job.

HOW DO PEOPLE PRACTICE INTERNAL SERVICE?

Thus far we have described what internal service is without prescribing the actions necessary for people to deliver excellent internal service. To do so, they must adopt and reinforce a service philosophy based on the following:

1. Customer focus. The obvious lesson from the discussion above is that the customer comes first in all successful service organizations. This is true whether the customer is an internal or an external one. This cannot be a passive activity that goes on independent of the day-to-day operations. While passive awareness of the customers' importance is useful, it is not enough. When things get busy or stressful, people tend to respond with their most basic motivations. In such situations, workers may quickly revert to ignoring their customers while they focus on "the real work."

Rather, focusing on the customer must be an active process. A company and *all* its employees must focus on understanding their customers' changing needs. The service product is as dynamic in nature for internal customers as it is for external customers. Internal service suppliers must constantly seek out their customers and solicit feedback on their needs, perceptions, and satisfaction level with internal service. Everyone from the president to the janitor is a customer-contact employee!

2. System/process focus. We have already covered the importance of designing systems for service. Just as companies had to focus on service delivery systems for external customers, they need to do it for internal customers.

All work is part of a process. All work takes some form of input, processes it, and produces some output. Whether large or small, every job assignment has customers who receive it, suppliers who provide input for it, and people who perform the tasks that add value to the output. As the First Law of Internal Service states, everyone is always either a customer or a supplier.

The first step for providing good internal service is to focus on the needs of customers. But having done that, all employees need to understand the systems and processes that make up their work. They need to understand how to go about changing or modifying systems to improve performance in meeting any customers' needs.

Information and communication are critical to any system or process, and in many ways they are the main components of a service business. Unfortunately, the tendency is to focus on the physical aspects of systems and processes. This results in a product-oriented culture. However, the real purpose for existence (and value to the customer) is the ability to process information.

In Chapter 9 we talked about the importance of interpersonal communication tools. Nowhere is this more important than in our internal supplier–customer interactions. Because employees are so familiar with their own company, and perhaps because they take for granted that their internal suppliers and customers have few options other than to continue to work with them, many people often pay less attention to how they communicate with co-workers than to how they communicate with external customers.

The reality is that external customers rely on all employees' ability to communicate with their internal customers and suppliers almost as much as they rely on customer-contact employee's ability to communicate with them. Employees must therefore make as much effort to communicate effectively with these people as they do to communicate effectively with external customers. The ultimate success of any company depends on it.

3. Measurement and feedback system. It is absolutely impossible to have a system and process focus without a good measurement and feedback system. As we saw in Chapter 5, the hospitality and tourism business environment is exceedingly complex. Companies can no longer afford to operate on "gut feel." They must be able to measure their ability to accomplish goals and act on those measurements.

First, they must identify the criteria they wish to measure. These criteria must be important to customers and measurable. They may range from something as specific as response time (e.g., number of rings until the phone is answered, average hold time, number of days to respond to a mail inquiry, etc.) to something as general as measures of overall customer satisfaction. Obviously, the more specific the criteria, the easier it is to enact specific corrective actions. However, they must be careful that they don't focus on a few specific criteria that are easy to understand and act upon, but which have little bearing on overall performance. They also do not want to end up focusing on quantity at the expense of quality. What companies choose to measure sends a very strong message to all employees about what is considered important.

Next, companies should identify the tools they will use to measure these criteria. They may involve technology such as a phone monitor or be very simple such as a return survey card. They can include labor-intensive face-to-face interviews. There are two important points to remember with respect to measurement tools. First, the tool itself should not change what it is supposed to measure. For example, a company should not want a customer-contact employee to conduct a face-to-face interview on the service they delivered since most customers would not be likely to give their real feelings to the person being evaluated. The second thing to consider is the cost of the measurement tool. This includes both the financial cost and the cost in time to customers. The value of the information gained by the tool must be worth the dollar cost to the company and worth the time to participating customers. If it is too intrusive, customers will not want to participate, or they will give whatever answers are necessary to get done quickly (rather than what they really feel).

4. Continuous improvement.   Though listed last, this is probably the most important thing that companies noted for excellence do that others do not.

Quality and quality improvement is not a single program with a starting point and an ending point. It is a never-ending process that requires everyone's participation. One of Deming's Fourteen Points says that organizations must "constantly and forever improve the system." Others talk about the "commitment" required for continuous improvement.

The struggle for continuous improvement requires an understanding of the dynamism of today's environment. What was good yesterday may no longer be sufficient today. Companies and their employees must plan for new services and processes to replace those of today. If they don't, someone else will. They also must remember from Chapter 10 that there is no such thing as "good enough." If it can be done better (and still be profitable), it should be improved. A "C" is not a passing grade in business. And what is an "A" today may only be a "C" in the future.

Companies that are committed to continuous improvement manifest this in everything they do. It shows in their corporate policies, their meetings, public relations, decisions, rewards, and recognition systems. They have a process by which new employees are taught the fundamentals of quality and continuous improvement as part of their orientation. They also have a culture in which the continuous improvement process is not stunted by changes in personnel, short-term crises, and other daily activities that relegate the improvement process to the position where it is given attention only "when we have the time."

SUMMARY

Customers are anyone who receives or benefits from the output of someone's work. This includes people internal to the company as well as external. The latter are the ones we think of traditionally as customers, but the former are equally important for the functioning of today's complex service delivery systems.

The First Law of Internal Service states that everyone is either a customer or a supplier at any point in time. There is no other category. The roles may change back and forth over time, but each person is acting as either a customer or a supplier in any single transaction.

The Second Law makes it clear that the Laws of Service discussed in Chapter 3 also apply to internal customers. Internal customers have similar expectations, similar "turn-offs," and their needs and motivations are developed by similar psychological phenomena. Finally, the Third Law says that internal customers should be treated as "nearly equal" to external customers in importance. Obviously, servicing external customers must take priority. However, internal customers deserve the same level of respect and dedication that we expect employees to give external customers.

Good internal service is practiced by focusing on customers' needs (both internal and external), the systems and processes used to meet those needs, and the measurement and feedback systems used to determine how effective the systems are at meeting those needs. Then the company must continually strive to improve these systems and processes. They realize that just because it is good enough for today, it may need to be better tomorrow.

QUESTIONS FOR REVIEW

1. What is the difference between internal and external customers?
2. Explain how the Laws of Service in Chapter 3 apply to internal customers.
3. List the four steps necessary for effective practice of internal service.

QUESTIONS FOR DISCUSSION

1. What is meant by the statement, "Internal customers should be treated as 'nearly equal' to external customers?" Do they deserve better treatment? Less treatment? Why?
2. How can hospitality and tourism companies strive for continuous improvement?

PRINCIPLES AND PRACTICES OF INTERNAL SERVICE: THE KEY TO QUALITY

OBJECTIVES

After reading this chapter, you should:

Understand what it takes to build a successful quality plan.

Understand the various ways that companies decide to make changes and how they implement them.

Know how to function as a productive member of a continuous improvement team.

KEY TERMS

quality plan	employee involvement
constancy of purpose	customer feedback
operational term	employee opinion survey
leadership	suggestion system
human resources development	synergy
trade press	process improvement team
refresher training	quality circle
business relationship	open-door policy
management-driven change	

Much has been written in the United States over the past decade on the subject of quality, particularly on what a company must do to achieve excellence. Virtually all of the origi-

nal writing dealt with the manufacturing sector. W. Edwards Deming, who is often credited with institutionalizing the quality culture in Japan, for example, did his work almost
exclusively with large volume manufacturers (automobiles, electronics, etc.).

Increasingly, however, attention has been turning to quality in the service sector as
well. Before examining the question of how to achieve quality in the hospitality and
tourism industry, however, it is necessary to understand the term. People usually think of
quality as some measure of how "good" a product is (i.e., the inherent value of the product). As we've discussed before, this is a product-oriented view.

A more applicable concept for hospitality and tourism companies defines quality
as "a measure of the ability to meet the customer's needs." This is a customer-oriented
attitude that listens to the "voice of the customer" and measures quality as it is perceived

---

"Gold Standard" Service

The year 1992 was notable for recognition of the importance of service in the hospitality and tourism industry. That year, the Ritz-Carlton Hotel Company was named a
recipient of the Malcolm Baldridge National Quality Award. It was the first time in
the history of the award that a hospitality or travel and tourism company received the
prestigious award. The award was established in 1987 by federal legislation and is
meant to recognize U.S. companies that have exemplary systems for managing their
operations and satisfying their customers.

The continual push for service quality starts right at the top at Ritz-Carlton.
Horst Shulze, president of the company, is directly responsible for quality planning
and involves himself personally in instructing employees at a new hotel on Ritz-
Carlton's "Gold Standards" for service. The "Gold Standards" set out the basics of
Ritz-Carlton's premium service standards. Employees receive over 100 hours of quality training a year designed to teach them how to prevent problems rather than just
react to them. Customer-contact employees are not just encouraged to solve problems
but are actually required to act at first notice—regardless of the type of problem or
customer complaint. Since service often requires team effort, other employees must
drop everything, no matter what their duties, to assist another employee who requests
help in solving a customer problem or complaint.

Backing all this up is a system designed to measure quality standards to provide
early warning of any shortcoming. Daily quality production reports derived from data
submitted by each of the 720 work areas in the hotel system help monitor service status. Monitoring systems are also used to enhance service to customers. Customer-
contact employees are trained to note guests' likes and dislikes and enter them into a
computerized preference profile system. The system contains profiles of over 240,000
repeat customers and guarantees that, as one Ritz-Carlton spokesperson puts it, "If
you ask for rocks in your pillow in Sydney, you won't have to ask for them again
when you stay in New York."

The aim of all this effort is to ensure that guests receive a "memorable visit."
According to independent research done for Ritz-Carlton, 92 to 97 percent of guests
leave with that impression—and that is a large reason why the hotel company is the
first in the industry to receive the Baldridge Award.

by each individual customer. In this definition, a quality service product is one that satisfies customers—nothing more, nothing less.

There is no single "right way" for companies to implement a program for quality. However, there are many examples of successful service companies that can be used to model what works and what does not. These have been used to create a set of guidelines for the minimum things that should be included for the success of any quality program. Although most of these things are the responsibility of management, it is important for customer-contact employees to understand what they are and why they are necessary. As the link to customers during moments of truth, customer-contact employees are ultimately responsible for the success of any quality program, and the better they understand what management is trying to do, the more easily and enthusiastically they can support their efforts. Also, most managers of service companies begin their careers as customer-contact employees. Today's customer-contact employees may someday have the responsibility tomorrow to support and train employees on delivering excellent service.

Although many different theorists have included many different aspects in their **quality plans**, there are seven basic characteristics that they all include:

- Create constancy of purpose.
- Cease reliance on inspection.
- Remove barriers.
- Practice leadership.
- Educate and train, reeducate and retrain.
- Build long-term business relationships.
- Take positive action.

Each of these elements is necessary for a successful quality program. No single element is more or less important than the others. Although it is possible for a company to give good service with one or more of the elements missing, it is highly unlikely. Not only is each element important in its own right, but it combines with other elements so that the whole is greater than the sum of the parts. Like a well-balanced sports team, taking away a single element hurts more than the importance of the value of that element alone. Interaction between that element and the other six is lost.

1. Create constancy of purpose.   We already know that management has the responsibility for setting a service strategy. We also know that employees are motivated to work for higher-order needs not for money alone. This service strategy needs to be the purpose toward which all customer-contact and support employees are working. This purpose becomes a rallying cry around which all co-workers band together.

Just like a building must be built on a solid foundation, service organizations must be based on strong, clear, and concise statements of their purpose. These statements must be developed with their customers' needs in mind. They can be used as a standard against which to measure which course or courses of action should be taken (Figure 12-1). Management can use them to decide what to do and what not to do. Those things that do not contribute effectively to meeting the purpose should be eliminated no matter how emotionally attached some managers may be to them, while those that do contribute to meeting the purpose probably merit additional attention and resources.

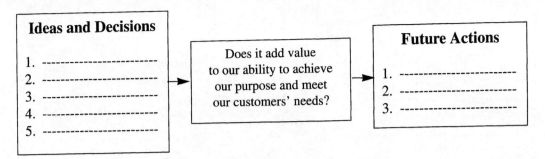

Figure 12-1 Constancy of purpose drives decisions.

Customer-contact and customer-support workers can use the purpose statement to help guide decisions in the absence of supervision. When faced with a problem that must be solved quickly, they can choose the course of action that best meets the stated purpose. In effect, the purpose statement lets management tell its employees what they would have them do if they were available to give advice.

The purpose must also be stated in **operational terms**. This means that customer-contact employees and their co-workers must be able to understand and *act* on the purpose. "We want to give good service" is not a good purpose statement. Its meaning is vague, and it is not really a basis for action. "We want to get satisfied clients by delivering a high-quality product in a timely, cost-effective, and responsive manner," is more specific and operational. If the purpose is not stated in operational terms, there is no way that it can be used as a standard for either management or its employees to help guide decisions.

"Constancy of purpose" means that management is consistent in the messages it sends to both internal and external customers. Once a company states its purpose, it must stick to it. It's one thing to say that "efficient delivery" of a particular service product is important. But if management then turns around and requires employees, and perhaps even external customers themselves, to fill out complex and seemingly useless forms and paperwork, there is no constancy of purpose. The stated purpose must be credible and everyone in the company must work to stay consistent with it in order for service to excel consistently.

2. Cease reliance on inspection.   The fact that the production and consumption of hospitality and tourism service products occur virtually simultaneously makes it impossible for managers to inspect each product. Yet many service managers are increasingly worried about "quality control" and "100 percent inspection." They seem to feel that unless each employee and each activity is closely monitored, there will be no consistency. If anything, the inherent lack of control over service encounters makes them even more uneasy, thus increasing their desire to have some visibility into what is going on. In some hospitality and tourism companies, virtually all customer-contact work is reviewed by a "quality control" person before anything is sent to an external customer (Figure 12-2).

Ironically, the companies that engage in these kinds of procedures often reduce the very quality they are seeking to improve. They borrow many ideas from the manufactur-

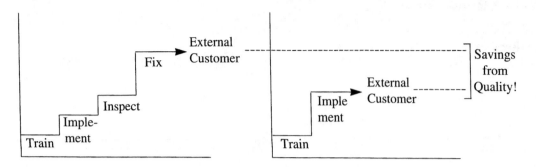

Figure 12-2   Cease reliance on inspection.

ing industry of the 1960–1970s and before—ideas that the most successful manufacturing companies have abandoned.

Not only is 100 percent inspection impossible to actually achieve, but any effort to try is counterproductive. The effort spent on inspection—reviewing paperwork or other material of importance, for example—does not contribute to the delivery of a product or a service. It does, however, contribute to overhead.

It is an obvious fact that it is much cheaper to do something right the first time than it is to go back and try to fix it the second time (or third or fourth or ...). This is the basic premise behind the success of Japanese manufacturing and marketing. It works the same way in service industries. Rather than wasting precious resources by designating "inspectors" or "quality control employees," good service companies dedicate their resources to teaching their employees how to do things right the first time. They give their employees the tools and knowledge they need to do their job. In addition, they encourage employees to feel proud about the importance of their work to external customers—whether the employee is in a customer-contact or a customer-support position.

Companies that rely on their workers to get it right the first time also avoid the "I thought he said/I thought she did . . ." syndrome. This is the situation that inevitably occurs when workers lower their own standards of performance because they expect the inspector to be able to catch any mistakes they make. And the inspectors, being human, are never able to catch all the mistakes. Besides, they believe that the work is supposed to be correct anyway.

Since most workers derive internal satisfaction from a job well done, it doesn't take much to encourage them to do well the first time (anyone who can't be encouraged should be terminated, or preferably never selected in the first place). Ceasing reliance on inspection for quality not only saves money but actually increases the quality, provided that the other six elements are included.

3. Remove barriers.   Managers have the responsibility to establish ways for their employees to get the job done. Paradoxically, it is often their own systems that serve as the greatest hindrance to their employees' work. More often than not, an ineffective workplace is the result of systematic roadblocks that impede worker progress, not the result of incapable or unwilling workers. In fact, Dr. Deming holds that 94 percent of all problems in worker achievement are actually the fault of something in the system itself, not in the person.

Given the opportunity to make recommendations that will be heard, most employees are more than willing to comment constructively on how job tasks can be made more effective and more efficient. To eliminate roadblocks, companies must examine each task to determine whether it is necessary to meet customers' needs. If not, they should eliminate it—even when "that's the way we've always done it."

Later in this chapter we examine some specific techniques for removing barriers. In essence, the approach is to identify and eliminate unnecessary tasks while trying to reduce the time and money spent on worthwhile tasks. At the same time, companies try to find and create new tasks that may add value to the customers' experience. This applies just as much to internal suppliers and their customers as it does to customer-contact employees and external customers.

4. Practice leadership.   There's an old saying, "If it ain't broke, don't fix it." Unfortunately, this may no longer be good enough for success. While a company is busy doing business as usual, someone else is probably thinking of a better way.

The environment and customers change continuously; so must companies and employees. The new saying should be, "Just because it ain't broke doesn't mean it can't be done better." If companies don't make their own products obsolete, someone else will. This takes leadership and a visionary drive for a better tomorrow.

Unfortunately, most of the hospitality and tourism industry today suffers from the syndrome of being overmanaged and underled. Some people have argued that there is not a lot of difference between management and leadership or that they are more interdependent than not. In fact, up until the 1980s, almost all major management texts taught that leadership was one of the major functions of management (along with planning, budgeting, direction, and control).

Today, there is a much better understanding of the difference between management and leadership. Warren Bennis, a well-respected theorist and author on the subject, put it best when he observed: "Managers are people who do things right, and leaders are people who do the right thing."

There is nothing wrong with strong management in a company. In fact, it is necessary for success. The business world is full of examples of people with visionary leadership whose companies failed because no one exercised the management discipline to keep everything operating smoothly and profitably. The management function of doing things right makes sure that people are working together toward a common goal. But if the goal is not the right one to work toward, it takes a leader to decide to change course.

The hospitality and tourism industry is exceedingly complex. There is rarely enough information for anyone to make a fully informed decision. The result is often an overly cautious approach in which companies make sure that they are doing their job right without really knowing whether they are doing the right job. To satisfy their customers, however, they must both do things right and do the right things. They must proactively seek out information from their customers—both external and internal—to identify what the right things to do are. Then, executive management can communicate the appropriate vision as discussed in Chapter 6. This will give the leadership initiative which the organization's managers can use as goals and objectives.

5. Educate and train, reeducate and train.   Education and training (E&T) is a priority in all companies that have achieved service excellence. Just as organizations must invest money in their physical facilities and the tangible parts of their product, so must they invest time and money in their human resources. Service providers—customer-contact or support—cannot possibly do their jobs without adequate education and training. While education and training can be quite expensive, the price of ignorance is much higher. As discussed in Part 1, the lack of adequate and appropriate education and training in both the public and private sectors is a major reason that the quality of service in America has such a poor reputation. It is perhaps the most neglected part of the industry today.

A good education and training program is not a "hit or miss" series of unrelated opportunities. Rather, it is a comprehensive **human resources development** plan that gives employees the opportunity to expand their capabilities and grow into newer and better jobs. At the same time, it provides company management with the opportunity to evaluate continually employees' capabilities which it uses to update and refine its E&T program.

E&T comes in any forms. Although formal degree programs and corporate seminars are very effective, they are not the only way to gain skills applicable to today's job or to help employees qualify for tomorrow's. Asking questions of a supervisor, reading the **trade press** in a particular segment, or reading the morning newspaper can all be effective E&T tools. Education and training also need not be as expensive as customized training classes. Local community colleges or vocational schools often offer highly applicable classes at a fraction of the fee for a one-day seminar. There are also a number of mass-marketed one- and two-day seminars on subjects of interest that can be priced as low as $60. E&T is an investment. It will return several times the cost incurred if done properly.

Education and training must be an ongoing process. The sooner it starts, the better—and it can never end. Disney is famous for starting its orientation and training before they even select employees. All prospective employees go through a training session to teach them what Disney is all about. Then, if the prospective employees think Disney is for them, they are interviewed and a hiring decision is made. If they are selected, they go through a week of general Disney education and training before breaking up into specific job responsibilities. Depending on the job, different types and amounts of additional E&T are required before the employee begins serving customers, external or internal.

The initial E&T experience should only be the beginning. Unfortunately, too many companies rely almost exclusively on on-the-job training as the only form of E&T past initial orientation. Successful companies, however, tend to have a more comprehensive program of continuing E&T. This is usually a combination of incentives to employees to pursue additional degrees or professional certifications and required **refresher training** classes or seminars. It is very easy to begin to get complacent, less caring, or suffer from "burnout" or other forms of fatigue in jobs with high human contact. Refresher training is a great way for employees to get a little break from the daily grind of dealing with customers while reminding them of the importance of their role and the various tools they have at their disposal to do a better job.

6. Build long-term business relationships.   Just as customer-contact employees cannot possibly do their job without the help of their co-workers, companies cannot accomplish their missions and goals without the assistance of other organizations.

In particular, all companies depend on suppliers. Whether it is food for airplanes or restaurants, business forms, or the amenities at a hotel, no company produces everything it needs internally. Unfortunately, in today's "deal"-oriented society, most companies routinely shop around and change suppliers on the basis of price alone. However, if companies want suppliers to invest in their own long-term quality programs, they need the security of knowing that the company will be there as a customer to continue to purchase their products. Also, if companies have a long-term relationship with a supplier and have a sudden need for urgency or some other requirement, they are much more likely to get special help. Their suppliers know that satisfying the company's needs represents far more than a mere single sale—it protects years of future revenue to them.

Companies should choose suppliers on the basis of the quality of their product and their services as well as the cost. Ideally, they should end up relying on only a single supplier for each thing they need. This saves money and resources in two ways. First, it reduces the overhead necessary to negotiate and oversee contracts. Second, and more important, it reduces the variability in the products used by eliminating the differences that will come naturally from multiple sources. Obviously, the one supplier chosen should be adhering to the same high standards of quality (including following these seven points in their own company), and they need to be able to meet a crisis demand.

The importance of building long-term relationships extends beyond suppliers. It is also very important to build these links with customers. The closer companies are to their customers, the better they can understand their needs and adapt their services to meet any changes. Also, from a purely business standpoint, it is much cheaper to service existing customers than it is to recruit new ones. In most service companies, the existing customer base is where the real profits are made. The marketing effort to attract new customers is used to grow the business or to replace lost customers. In good companies, the latter is usually limited to people who have died, moved, or no longer need the company's services—not customers who have been driven to the competition through mistreatment or neglect.

The importance of building long-term business relationships can actually extend to competition as well. If a catastrophe strikes, or even in periods when companies are overloaded, they may depend on their competition to help bail them out. This is routine in segments such as the airline and hotel industry, where overbooking is a necessary and common practice. Every so often, fewer people "no-show" than expected, and passengers may have to be "bumped" or "walked" to another carrier or hotel. Also, no one knows when a fire or other disaster may hit, and companies may be dependent on others to help them meet their customers' needs.

Companies may also band together with their competitors to form alliances to work on areas of mutual interest. The two most common forms of this are marketing alliances and coalitions to address government regulatory or legislative initiatives. In both cases, working closely with competitors can be mutually beneficial.

7. Take positive action.   The last point for achieving service excellence is perhaps the most important. Although it may sound the easiest to do, it is often the most neglected.

All of the theory and logic of the first six points are absolutely useless if people do not take action to change their operations for the better. This may sound trivial, but it is surprising how many people believe in implementing a new approach but never get around to doing anything about it. They get too bogged down in the mire of daily details, or they rationalize why it wasn't such a good idea after all.

Taking positive action implies a proactive approach to continual implementation of newer and better ideas. Everyone in the company must ask themselves, "What do our customers—both external and internal—need?" "How have we empowered suppliers—both external and internal—to meet these needs?" "Is there something more we can do?"

Everybody must be put to work to implement these changes. Service quality is not just the responsibility of the CEO or just the responsibility of the customer-contact employees who deal with external customers. It is the direct responsibility of each and every person in the company. Everyone must be given the training and on-going coaching to provide service excellence. Service is not a passive activity; achieving service excellence requires active and aggressive means.

SERVICE PRACTICES: HOW TO GET IMPROVEMENT

There are many different tools and techniques that companies can use in the pursuit of improved quality. Numerous books and articles have been written about them. There are many different classes and other educational opportunities to learn about them as well. The very nature of "continuous" improvement implies that the only thing that is constant is change. No one can possibly improve things without changing how they are done.

Despite the vast range of specific options at the disposal of every service company for approaching change, all of these boil down to three basic sources: management-driven change, employee involvement, and customer feedback. Each of these approaches is appropriate for different circumstances, and there is no single "right way." In fact, the most successful companies at continually improving their service products use all three approaches. They look at each situation and choose the proper one.

1. Management driven change.   Everyone is familiar with stories about how the boss comes in one morning and announces, "Things will be different starting today." Although management-driven changes are most likely to be resisted by employees, they are not necessarily bad. In fact, good service companies often make use of the management-driven change process—they just limit its use to when it is appropriate.

There are many reasons that management will decide to implement a change. In the first place, it is their responsibility to make sure that the business is profitable. If they see a problem and feel they know what is needed to correct it, they will use their formal power to require the change. In most cases, employees will comply and there will not be a problem. Ultimately, for any change to be effective, it must be supported by management.

There are also a number of reasons why management-driven changes are necessary. Often, management has much quicker and better access to the information necessary to make a decision for change. CEOs can quickly and easily get senior members of their staff from a variety of functions to meet together to discuss change. Similarly, middle managers can call together their varied personnel to provide information to make a decision on a departmental basis very quickly. Also, management is the only place that has authority to pay for outside consultants who may be brought in to recommend appropriate changes. Management is much more in touch with "the big picture" than are individual customer-contact employees.

There are a myriad of situations in which management-driven change is the best approach. If a crisis needs a quick resolution there may not be the time required to involve employees or customers. Managers may be left to use their own intuition about what will be acceptable. Or management may be required to decide between conflicting opinions from different departments or individuals as to what should be done. Management may insist on change when some parts of the company are resistant to a perceived change in customer needs or market conditions.

Also, some decisions are almost exclusively the domain of managers. Much of the planning and goal-setting activities necessary to communicate the company's purpose must be driven down the organization by management (of course, most employee-oriented managers will solicit and listen to employee input). And ultimately, any decisions on change that come from employee involvement or customer feedback must be communicated throughout the company by management. If the company does not support the change (through modifications to its reward and incentive system, for example), it is actually encouraging resistance to that change.

Unfortunately, many managers in business today abuse their prerogative to drive change. They treat employees more like pieces of a machine who should do as they are told rather than as individuals who have their own dreams and desires and who need to be coached and nurtured. Successful organizations, however, need employees who are motivated by much more than fear, and modern service managers will turn to their employees and their customers to contribute to the continuous improvement process.

2. Employee involvement.   One of the best sources any company has for ideas on what to change and how to do it to improve service quality is the employees who give that service—whether they are servicing internal or external customers. Companies that have a continuous improvement culture want employee involvement for a number of reasons. It gives them input from the customer-contact perspective and raises morale at the same time.

Employee involvement can take many different forms. The two most popular are employee opinion surveys and suggestion systems. **Employee opinion surveys** are usually part of a project to assess organizational effectiveness and are given out at one time to a large (sometimes all) portion of the company. They usually ask questions about employee's feelings regarding their own job, their management, and their perceptions about how customers are treated. The survey may ask whether they agree or disagree with particular statements such as "My job gives me a sense of importance," "My supervisor cares about my ideas," or "We are able to resolve most customers' problems in a

So far, we have one suggestion for a raise for Peggy, one suggestion for a raise for Carol, and one suggestion for a raise for Pete. Perhaps I should explain this concept again. . . . (© Derek Barnes. Reproduced by permission.)

timely and efficient manner." Good surveys also give some space for employees to make comments about what they like and don't like and what ideas for positive changes they may have.

Suggestion systems usually are more passive than employee opinion surveys. They allow employees to make suggestions or comments when they feel like it, but they do not actively solicit opinions the way a survey does. They are much more open in the range of things they can get since they allow employees to comment on anything—not just the limited questions of a survey. However, because they do not solicit the information, they only get ideas from people who are aggressive enough or annoyed enough to make a suggestion.

A good suggestion system allows employees to choose whether or not they wish to be anonymous. It also provides a way for employees to be informed of whether or not their suggestions were implemented, and why or why not. In many instances, they provide for recognition, sometimes including rewards of cash or other prizes, for those who submit suggestions that result in monetary savings or substantial quality improvements. They also provide a reporting to management of the number and nature of suggestions. This allows management to see if there are any trends that merit a closer look.

Another method for soliciting employee involvement is the formation of teams to look at either a specific problem or a general area of work. The concept of a "team approach" is central to continuous improvement. The objective is to achieve **synergy**— the situation where the whole is greater than the sum of the parts. In other words, members of a smoothly functioning team feed off each other and can accomplish far more together than the sum of each of them working alone.

When a team is formed to look at a particular problem, it is often called a **process improvement team**. The process improvement team draws members from a variety of jobs—both customer-contact and customer-support—to look at the problem together and try to decide how the tasks can be done better. When teams are established to address the question of how things can be done better in a more general sense, they are often referred to as **quality circles**. Quality circles (QCs) are groups of employees, typically from the same work area or similar jobs, who meet on a regular basis to address work-related problems. The forum is fairly wide open, although all proposals are reviewed by management before anything new is implemented.

QCs became somewhat in vogue in the 1980s as stories of their success in Japanese companies were reported in the United States. They can be very useful in getting employees involved in actively seeking improvement means. By allowing QCs to set their own agenda, they give management the opportunity to get thoughtful input from the employees' perspective. They are also useful in enriching employees' job experience since they can become involved in much more than their limited day-to-day responsibilities.

In forming teams to help with continuous improvement, management may choose to appoint someone to act as a facilitator. This may be an external consultant brought in for a fresh perspective, or it may be internal employees who are trained in the dynamics of group interaction and problem solving. Facilitators act as a sort of third-party neutral observer who help spark the conversation and keep it focused on the issues at hand. They may also be expected to report their interpretations of the group's activities to management.

A final way for employee involvement to occur is employees' own personal initiative. This involves deciding to address the need for a particular change directly with a supervisor or a higher manager. Obviously, this can be risky to employees' good standing with their bosses. In some organizations, this kind of activity is encouraged with an **open-door policy**. The idea is that any manager's door is always open for employees to come in and lodge a complaint or make a constructive criticism without fear of reprisal. In some organizations, this is a sincere statement that holds almost universally true and is a very effective tool for management. In others, however, it is more lip service than reality and people who try to avail themselves of the opportunity end up regretting it. Obviously, in the latter case, it rarely works.

3. Customer feedback.   The third and final approach for change comes from customers themselves. These can be external or internal customers, although external customers often have much more leverage than internal customers for creating change. As with employee involvement, customer feedback can take a variety of forms.

In its most raw form, customer feedback comes from letters of praise or complaint. If a particular situation has occurred, it may generate a change on its own. More likely, change will occur only if a trend is seen over a large number of letters. Since, as discussed in Chapter 8, only a small percentage of people who are particularly satisfied or dissatisfied bother to write about it, companies who want customer feedback to help identify what to change and how to change it should implement more formal approaches.

One such approach is to use customer feedback surveys (also discussed in Chapter 8). Another is to utilize customer focus groups. These are either groups of valued regular customers or a cross section of the demographics of the customer base who are given some incentive to meet with a company and discuss what they like and don't like, what they would change and how they would change it. The company usually employs a facilitator to guide the meeting. Customer focus groups can be very expensive, so they are usually conducted around major issues of enhancement or new product development. They can be very effective at identifying problems that no one in the company even knew existed, and they can be useful in keeping a company up-to-date on the changing needs of their customers. Companies only see what the customer wants today; these groups can help predict what those needs will be tomorrow. They can also help see what the competition is doing since customers (or prospective customers) are in a much better position to observe that.

A final, and very powerful, way in which customer feedback can drive changes is the nature of the marketplace itself. Since most hospitality and tourism companies are "for-profit" enterprises, any shift in market conditions can force a company to change. These can be shifts in market share, in the competition's product or in the economic situation of customers or society as a whole. They may even be shifts in government or industry regulation as customers or competitors find ways to get government to force particular changes or standards.

SUMMARY

There is no single "right way" to practice internal service. Many different researchers and writers have proposed many different programs for quality internal service. Despite the variety, virtually all successful programs incorporate seven basic characteristics:

1. They create a constancy of purpose.
2. They cease a reliance on inspection, opting instead to educate and train people to get it right the first time.
3. They identify and remove barriers to effective employee productivity.
4. They practice leadership—not just management.
5. They emphasize education and training and reeducation and training.
6. They build long-term business relationships with their suppliers and their customers.
7. They take positive action to install these changes rather than merely pay lip service.

Changes can come from above (management driven), below (employee involvement), and outside (customer feedback). Each method or source is appropriate for some things and inappropriate for others. However, companies that strive for continuous improvement seek out all three sources in an effort to identify opportunities for beneficial change.

QUESTIONS FOR REVIEW

1. List seven characteristics of a successful quality plan.
2. What is meant by "stating a purpose in operational terms"? Give an example.

3. What is the term for a cohesive set of education, training, and personal growth programs for employees?
4. What are three basic sources for ideas for change?
5. What are two types of employee involvement systems? What are the differences between the two?
6. What is an open-door policy?

QUESTIONS FOR DISCUSSION

1. How can a company "cease reliance on inspections" without losing quality control?
2. Is there a real difference between management and leadership? If so, what?
3. Do open-door policies really work? Why or why not?

PART 5

APPLICATION OF SERVICE PRINCIPLES IN HOSPITALITY AND TOURISM

Now that we have discussed both the theory behind service and the practical aspects of delivering it, it is useful to examine the application of these principles to some of the specific business segments within the tourism and hospitality industry. While it is impossible to investigate every conceivable segment, we will look at five important ones: (1) hotels, (2) restaurants, (3) airlines, (4) cruise operators, and (5) travel agencies.

Before we begin that look, however, it is useful to understand where these segments exist in relation to each other and where they exist in relation to service industries as a whole. By classifying services and understanding how to categorize them, we gain insight into the similarities and differences between the various sectors of the industry. Although no two businesses are exactly alike, we can use the understanding we gain from this exercise to better understand the role of customer-contact employees in all facets of hospitality and tourism.

In Chapter 13 we examine a number of ways to classify service organizations. In Chapters 14 to 18 we then take a specific look at these five major segments of the hospitality and tourism field. They examine the basic service approach for each and demonstrate how many of the principles learned in Chapters 1 to 12 are put into action in the real world.

It should be noted that these examples do not cover the entire scope of the hospitality and tourism field. To do so would take far too much time and space. We have not covered car rental companies, attractions and theme parks, the national park system, or school and institutional food services, for example. The principles of service in action in these other segments are, however, very similar to what we cover in the discussion of the five segments in Chapters 14 through 18. We have also covered only "typical" examples within each segment. There are so many different companies, each offering their own unique approach, that it is impossible to cover every scenario. Rather, we study some general and typical scenarios that are indicative of how companies can and do behave in each major segment.

13

CLASSIFYING SERVICE ORGANIZATIONS

OBJECTIVES

After reading this chapter, you should:

Understand the variety of ways in which we can classify service companies to better understand how those companies work.

Be able to describe the type of service that specific companies offer.

Understand the implications to customer-contact employees of the various ways in which service companies operate.

KEY TERMS

labor intensity	membership relationship
customer interaction	amenity
and service customization	telemarketing
tangible service	frequent-buyer club
intangible service	preferred-buyer program
continuous service	fluctuation of demand
discrete service	branch location

There are many different ways to attempt to classify services. Currently, there is not any agreement on what the best classification scheme is. Rather, due to the complex nature of service functions, different classification approaches are better for different applications.

There is not likely to be any single scheme that will be universally best. Therefore, it is best to have an understanding of a variety of approaches.

One of the best, relatively uncomplicated approaches is presented by Roger W. Schmenner in an article in *Sloan Management Review*. He identifies two specific elements that can be used to create a matrix of service companies. These criteria are labor intensity and customer interaction and service customization (Figure 13-1). **Labor intensity** is the "ratio of the labor cost incurred to the value of the plant and equipment." A high degree of labor intensity involves relatively little plant and equipment and a correspondingly large amount of worker time, effort, and cost. This is very typical of professional services. A low-labor-intensity business, on the other hand, involves a large amount of capital equipment and facilities in comparison to its level of worker-related costs.

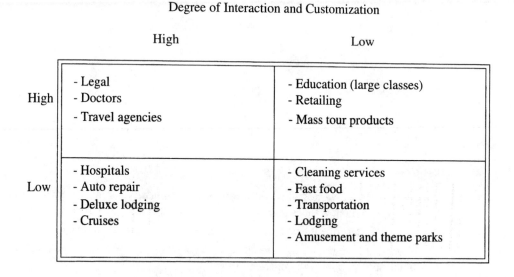

Degree of Interaction and Customization

Figure 13-1   Simple model for analysis.

It is important to remember that the measure of labor intensity in this model is a ratio. It is not a strict measure of the amount of worker-related costs. If only the amount of worker-related expense was combined, airline transportation would be very labor intensive. After all, pilots are highly paid, there are flight attendants, gate agents, phone reservation agents, a large sales force, and a tremendous number of ground crew and maintenance personnel. However, when considering the ratio of labor costs to equipment and facilities, airlines are in fact relatively low in labor intensity. This is due to the fact that so much more money is devoted to the airplanes, airport and maintenance facilities, and ground equipment. Although this ratio is nowhere nearly as low as a utility service, it is still drastically lower than something like a travel agency.

Customer interaction and service customization is a little less simple a concept to define clearly. Schmenner says it "combines two similar, yet distinct, concepts: (1) the degree to which the consumer interacts with the service process, and (2) the degree to which the service is customized for the consumer." In services with high levels of interaction, customers can intervene at almost any step in the service process to make or change a request or to ask that something be added or deleted. In a service with high customization, the company, through its customer-contact employees, tries to meet each person's particular needs. Physicians and nurses (not often thought of as customer-contact workers) fit into this category. They are the customer-contact workers in the medical service industry. They work to provide a full range of services designed to meet each individual "customer's" needs.

The restaurant industry provides an excellent example of a variety of levels of customer interaction within the same basic segment—food and beverage services. At one end of the spectrum, there are fast food restaurants like McDonald's. The customer's interaction is brief, and there is little in the way of customization. The service can still meet customer's basic expectations, but everyone is treated the same. In an effort to provide a higher degree of customization, some fast food restaurants, such as Wendy's and Burger King, evolved a system that allows the customer to have a greater degree of involvement.

Above that, there are cafeterias and buffets that provide a wide selection of choice and meet a variety of specific customer needs, thus increasing the degree of customization. However, the amount of interaction is still very limited. Next in line are restaurants, such as a buffet court, that add limited waiter service. Finally, there are full-service restaurants with complete waiter service that allow customers a full range of options to create the meal of their choice. It should be noted that even here, there is a wide range of approaches with respect to customization. Some restaurants, such as T.G.I. Fridays, offer a wide variety that can meet any need. Others, particularly very fancy ones, may have a surprisingly limited menu.

These definitions can be used to create a matrix that classifies all service organizations (Figure 13-2). Each element has its own challenges to customer-contact employees. In those businesses characterized by a low degree of labor intensity, such as an airline, the challenge often is keeping up with the fast pace of change in the technology and capital equipment that the companies depend on. Customer-contact employees also may have the problem of dealing with peak demand cycles since low-labor-intensity companies often try to keep their personnel numbers to the minimum required. In those businesses characterized by a high degree of labor intensity, such as a travel agency, the challenge is to become fully trained on the wide variety of knowledge needed. Customer-contact employees must also deal with management's interest in ensuring that some degree of consistency is followed between how they and their co-workers handle customers.

Companies that have a low-degree of customer interaction and customization, such as a fast food restaurant, also create unique challenges for customer-contact employees. They must be prepared to deal with fairly rigid sets of standard operating procedures that must be followed. They must also find a way to make their services more "warm." In other words, they want customers to feel that they have gotten personalized service even though the same basic service is given to a large number of people in a short period of time. In these circumstances, customer-contact employees must pay particular attention to the physical surroundings (cleanliness, conformity with others in the chain, etc.) since

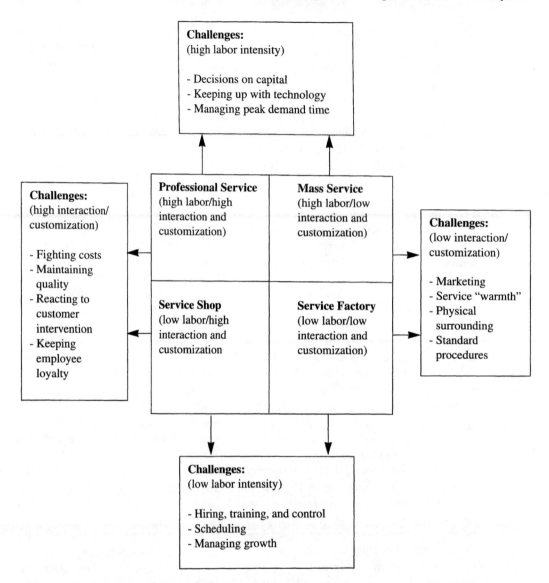

Figure 13-2   Challenges for service companies.

the shorter the time spent interacting with customers, the more the physical surroundings are likely to drive customers' impressions.

On the other hand, in companies with a high degree of customer interaction and customization such as cruise lines and high-quality restaurants, customer-contact employees often have to be concerned with how they react to customers' intervention in the delivery process. Although they may need their intervention at times, they may react adversely when customers intervene at an inopportune time. Obviously, since they are paying for the service, customers usually have the right to intervene when they feel it necessary. Customer-contact employees must use all their communications skills covered in Chapter 8 to both control these interventions and react professionally. Another problem to be concerned with is the maintenance of consistent quality. In these companies, customers depend on customer-contact employees' skills and performance for the quality of their product, so employees cannot afford to be lax on anything. This can be a particular problem when customers request things that customer-contact employees think they know well. If customer-contact employees are not careful, they will suffer from the old adage, "Familiarity breeds contempt."

Another well-known theorist, Christopher Lovelock, has created a more complicated and complete model. In it, he looks at five different aspects of the service product:

- The nature of the service product
- The type of relationship the service organization has with its customers
- The amount of room for customization and judgment on the part of customer-contact employees
- The nature of the demand and supply for the service
- The way the service is delivered

1. The nature of the service product.   Lovelock suggests a two-by-two matrix that completely describes the nature of the product (Figure 13-3). On one side, services are categorized as those that are tangible and those that are intangible. **Tangible** actions give recipients something they can hold onto, such as a meal, or do something to them physically, such as transport them or their goods from one place to another or give them lodging for the night. Intangible services deal more with their frame of mind or their intangible assets. Examples of this are providing advice and assistance or managing money and resources.

Who or What Is Directed Recipient of Service?

		People	Things
Nature of the Service Product	Tangible	- Transportation - Lodging - Restaurants and catering	- Freight shipping - Cleaning services
	Intangible	- Education - Broadcasting - Travel agencies - Tours and cruises - Amusement and theme parks	- Banking - Insurance - Legal

Figure 13-3   Nature of the product.

On the other side, services are split into those that affect people and those that affect things. Some services may seem to spill over into more than one category (airlines may affect a traveler's intangible state of mind and travel agencies' advice may help move people), but the core service is usually confined to a single quadrant. Interestingly, as discussed earlier, the peripheral services may be the ultimate source of satisfaction or dissatisfaction. Since these peripheral services often fall in a different quadrant from that of the core service, it is not surprising that the service company is not as well equipped to perform—it is not the core service where management pays the most attention.

Once these distinctions are made, we can better understand what the role of customer-contact employees is for companies that fall into each quadrant. This is because these categories help answer the questions:

a. Does the customer need to be physically present:
   (1) Throughout delivery of the service?
   (2) Only to start or end the service?
   (3) Not at all?
b. Does the customer need to be mentally present:
   (1) In person?
   (2) Across physical distances (mail, phone, etc.)?
c. How is the service recipient "modified" by the service?

The more customers need to be physically in contact, the more important the personal aspects of the service transaction become. They can even exceed the importance of the service product itself. On the other hand, when recipients are far away, the focus is more likely to be on the product than on the delivery. Unfortunately, this situation is also more likely to result in miscommunications—thus placing a premium on accuracy and feedback.

Understanding the way in which customers are affected by services helps customer-contact employees better understand their customer's expectations. This is particularly important with intangible products. When customers leave a travel agency, they may have the tangible product of an airline ticket in hand. But the real way they have been affected is much more intangible—they have gotten the information needed to enable themselves to go from one point to another. One customer may have this need to take a vacation while another needs to go home for a funeral. Even though both get the same ticket, they really have met very different needs. They may even view them as different "products." Customer-contact employees need to be aware of this to provide the appropriate type of guidance.

By their very nature, almost all the segments of the hospitality and tourism industry affect people, not things. Whether it is food or travel, the services provided give people an experience. The industry, however, covers the entire range from tangible to intangible. Airlines and car rental companies physically affect the people themselves, and restaurants give them a tangible product. Travel agencies, on the other hand, give the intangible product of advice. Although they give the tangible product of a ticket or a voucher, this merely documents their intangible products. Tour operators and amusement or theme parks also give an intangible product—"fun" or "a vacation experience." Although they may physically affect the customer just as an airline, their core product is much more intangible.

2. The type of relationship. While the first categorization scheme focuses on customers themselves, Lovelock's second deals with the relationship between customers and the company. To understand where each sector of our industry fits in this scheme, two questions must be answered:

a. Does the service company deliver its services to customers in a **continuous** fashion, or is each transaction a **discrete** occurrence?

b. Do customers enter into a formal, "membership" relationship, or is there no relationship at all.

In almost all cases, consumers of manufactured goods make discrete purchases (i.e., they buy individual "things" at individual times). In the service sector, this is not necessarily so. There are many examples of continuous delivery of service (Figure 13-4).

Nature of the Customer–Organization Relationship

	"Membership"	No Formal Relationship
Continuous Delivery	- Banking - Education - Insurance	- Broadcasting
Discrete Transactions	- Season passes - Frequent-user programs - "Affiliations"	- Freight shipping - Legal - Cleaning - Transportation - Lodging - Tours and cruises - Amusement and theme parks - Restaurants and catering - Travel agencies

Figure 13-4 Type of relationship.

A second important part of identifying the relationship between customers and companies is whether or not there is any formal **membership relationship** between them. "Membership" implies some form of long-term mutually beneficial relationship that allows the organization to get a large portion, if not all, of the customers' business. This can require formal exchanges of paperwork, such as an account number from a bank or a phone number from the telephone company. Or it can be the result of a mutual relationship, such as those developed with family doctors, dentists, or veterinarians.

The implications of this matrix are broad. Where service is rendered over a continuous period of time, pricing structures usually include periodic charges. Monthly account service charges from banks and periodic policy charges for insurance are excellent examples. This makes pricing and accounting much simpler than when individual transactions need to be tracked. There is much less chance of error on a monthly cable television bill than on a restaurant charge or complicated travel bill. Since almost all hospitality and tourism services are discrete transactions, the ability to accurately track and report on billing is a critical component of the customer's perception of the quality of services.

Payment on the basis of discrete transactions also forces companies to determine how much to charge for each individual service and which services should be "free." Restaurants, for example, often accept a lower profit margin on their core service—meal food—and make it up with a large markup on a peripheral service—beverages. They also must decide whether to give a service such as water for free, or whether to make a nominal charge. Travel agencies often are faced with deciding exactly how much customized work they can do for a prospective client before they have to charge additional for these specialized and time-consuming services.

All of the large hospitality and tourism companies are faced with similar issues. Hotels must decide how many **amenities**, or "free" services, to offer as they seek a marketing edge. This is particularly true in cities where competition is tight for business travelers. Airlines are constantly evaluating and reevaluating their charges and service mix (see Chapter 16 for a detailed discussion).

The biggest advantage to those service organizations that have a membership relationship with their customers is that they know who their customers are. They also usually have a pretty good idea of which services, and how much of them, each customer is using. This allows them to conduct very highly targeted marketing programs—either through direct mail or telephone solicitation, which is also known as **telemarketing**. One of the most difficult things for businesses to do is to attract new customers, and many studies have shown that repeat business accounts for as much as 80 percent or more of the profitable business that a company does. This should not be surprising since the cost of getting and servicing a new customer is much higher than the cost of servicing an existing one. Knowing who their customers are, a membership company can more easily increase their highly profitable repeat business, and they can determine the demographics and needs of their existing customer base to better target advertising and promotion for attracting new customers.

By their very nature, most hospitality and tourism companies do not require membership relationships and deal in discrete transactions. However, they need repeat business and are often willing to pay a premium to people to enter willingly into a membership relationship. Through **frequent-buyer clubs** and other **preferred-buyer programs**, these companies offer free or reduced-price services to those customers who continue to do business with them. In many cases, this peripheral program is the only thing that can distinguish one company from another and convince customers that there is a value in brand loyalty for these services.

3. Customization and judgment.
Lovelock's third way to break the service sector up into different categories concentrates on the customer-contact employees themselves (Figure 13-5). Because customers are involved in the production of any service product, there is always a degree of customization. However, in some cases, the degree of customization is very low. In other cases, it can be quite high. This is neither good nor bad. In some cases, increased customization is good for the customer; in other cases it is

Customization

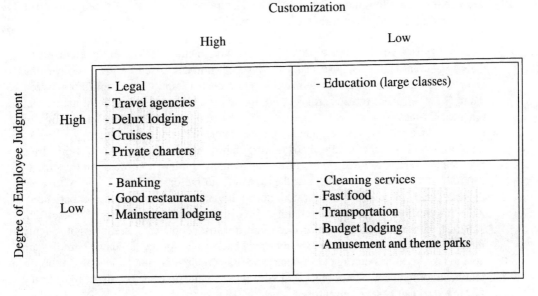

Figure 13-5   Customization and judgment.

unnecessary (speed, price and consistency may be more important). As the Third Law of Service says, "Eliminate the need for service and customers will perceive that they have received good service." At the same time, different sectors of the industry tend to allow their customer-contact employees differing degrees of latitude in exercising their own judgment to meet individual customer needs. Again this is neither good nor bad, although companies that give their employees little room for judgment need to be careful that they don't send the inadvertent message that the employees are not really important.

In many service companies both of these factors are low. Airlines, budget lodging, and fast food restaurants are all good examples of cases where the range of customization is low and customer-contact employees are very constrained in what they are allowed to do. Customers can choose from a range of flights or a specific menu, but they can't easily get something made just for them. And while customer-contact employees have some latitude to serve these customers, they can't violate company policies that dictate specifically what can and cannot be done for most instances. Airline employees are also subject to strict security and safety rules.

In mainstream hotels and restaurants, there is much more room for customization. Customers can easily make special requests for no-smoking rooms, king-sized beds, and so on. Or they can ask for a substitution of one menu item for another. Still, however, customer-contact employees are given limited latitude for making judgments on their own. At best, they may have reasonably quick access to a supervisor who will decide whether or not something can be done out of the ordinary.

Travel agencies, deluxe hotels and resorts, and cruise lines are all examples of hospitality and tourism companies that give a high degree of customization and generally allow their customer-contact employees a wide range of latitude in exercising judgment on how to meet their customers' needs. In these companies, customer-contact employees have come to expect all kinds of strange requests from customers. And most managers in these companies allow their customer-contact employees to do what it takes to meet these—within the bounds of legalities and reasonable cost.

4. Nature of the demand. The first three methods cover all the elements of the service transaction. They arrange each type of company based on the customer, the company (in the form of the customer-contact employee), and the relationship between them. However, these three approaches are limited because they are static in nature—in other words they look at the business of service as a "snapshot in time." In reality, of course, service provision is dynamic in nature—that is, it changes over time.

Lovelock's fourth method for distinguishing the differences and similarities between the various service sectors takes this dynamicism into consideration by looking carefully at the peaks and valleys of the demand and the organization's ability to meet those demands (Figure 13-6). Almost all hospitality and tourism companies experience a wide **fluctuation of demand** over time. This is a natural outgrowth of the fact that American culture has a variety of cycles of need. Most people eat three meals at roughly three different agreed-upon times. Many travel back home for the holidays. Families are able to take vacations during the summer while the children are not in school. All hospitality and tourism companies must deal with these fluctuations especially in light of the fact that they can't "save" inventory.

Demand Fluctuations over Time

	Wide	Narrow
Peak Demands Can Usually Be Met	- Utilities - Fast food - Amusement and theme parks - Mainstream restaurants	- Insurance - Legal - Broadcasting - Cleaning services
Peak Demands Regularly Exceed Capacity	- Transportation - Tours and cruises - Fine restaurants - Travel agencies - Lodging	Services similar to above but company has insufficient capacity for their base level of business

Figure 13-6 Nature of the demand.

For some, it is not much of a problem. Fast food and mainstream restaurants can schedule workers on swing shifts, and amusement or theme parks and other family entertainment establishments can hire temporary summer help. If demand still exceeds capacity, most customers are willing to accept additional waiting time. Some companies actually turn this waiting time into part of the entertainment experience. Restaurants can offer popcorn, chips or appetizers while people wait for their food or even while they wait for a table.

For most others, however, this is a significant challenge. Airlines and high-quality restaurants are limited by the physical capacity of their space. Airlines and travel agencies cannot continually hire and let go highly trained customer-contact personnel to match the fluctuations of market demand exactly. Obviously, the decisions on how to handle these troubles are management's responsibility, but their decisions affect customer-contact employees in a number of ways. These employees run the reservations systems that give priority on a first-come, first-served basis, and they have to handle customer complaints when the services customers want are not available. They also have to be up on all the off-peak specials that marketing departments devise to encourage customers to buy in off-peak periods. They may be limited by management as to when they can take vacations so that the office is not left undermanned. And most important, they will have to deal with the stress that will come during peak times (review Chapter 9 for a discussion of stress management techniques).

Whew! If this lunch crowd gets any bigger, we might have to draft the party at table four to bus tables! (© Derek Barnes. Reproduced by permission.)

5. Method of service delivery.   The fifth and final way that Lovelock suggests to categorize service companies is by their method of service delivery (Figure 13-7). On the one hand, services can be categorized as being available at a single site or

Number of Locations

	Single Site	Multiple Sites
Customer Goes to Service Organization	- Restaurants - Most travel agencies - Theatres	- Fast food - Transportation - Most lodging - Tours and cruises
Organization Comes to Customer	- Lawn care - Pest control	- Emergency repairs
Transactions at Arm's Length (Electronic)	- Direct mail - Telemarketing - Corporate travel	Not relevant

Figure 13-7   Method of service delivery.

multiple sites. On the other, they can be categorized as (1) companies where the customer goes to the service organization, (2) companies where the service organization comes to the customer, and (3) companies where customers transact apart from each other through mail or electronic communication. Most hospitality and tourism companies fall into the first category, few fall into the second, and many operate at least part of the time in the third. This category is the largest growing, particularly as increases in communication technology make it easier to conduct business without ever meeting face to face.

Presumably, the convenience of a service is reduced when customers have to go on their own to get the service. Many companies expand to multiple sites to make it easier. This is second part of the matrix. All the large-scale companies in hospitality and tourism operate from multiple sites—the airlines, hotel chains, car rental companies, restaurant chains, tour operators, and cruise lines. Travel agencies, which depend on people who live or work within 5 miles of them for most of their business, sometimes open up multiple **branch locations**. Other agencies choose to operate out of a single location. Similarly, many small business restaurants operate from one site.

Many hospitality and tourism services (or portions of the total service) can be performed at arm's length. The most obvious is the reservation process. When customers use electronic media to conduct business, it becomes largely irrelevant whether the company has a single or multiple sites. Since there is more room for error or misunderstanding when customer-contact employees do not communicate face to face, their job of delivering quality service can be more difficult, as discussed in Chapter 8.

SUMMARY

Although classifying service companies can be very difficult, it teaches much about how these companies provide services to their customers and how customer-contact employees do their jobs. It is useful to compare hospitality and tourism companies to each other and to service companies outside the industry.

There are many different ways to categorize and compare service companies. One of the most insightful, yet simple methods is to examine the labor intensity and the degree of customer interaction or service customization. Such an analysis gives much insight into how individual companies and their customer-contact employees must deal with change, capital equipment purchases, meeting peak cycle demand, adhering to standard operating procedures, and reacting to customer intervention in the service delivery process.

Another way to analyze service companies in general, and hospitality and tourism companies specifically, looks at the aspects of the service process in a more detailed manner. These aspects include:

1. The nature of the service product
2. The type of relationship the service organization has with its customers
3. The amount of room for customization and judgment on the part of customer-contact employees
4. The nature of the demand and supply for the service
5. The way the service is delivered

QUESTIONS FOR REVIEW

1. List six different characteristics of service companies that can be used to analyze them.
2. List three challenges for a professional service company; a mass service company; a service shop; and a service factory.
3. How do the challenges from question 2 affect customer-contact employees?
4. Give three examples of membership relationships.

QUESTIONS FOR DISCUSSION

1. What is the benefit of analyzing service companies in general? Hospitality and tourism companies specifically?
2. When should service companies allow customer-contact employees to exercise judgment? When should they discourage it?
3. How is the use of electronic means for service delivery affecting customer-contact jobs?

14

HOTELS

OBJECTIVES

After reading this chapter, you should:

Know the core service for the hotel industry.

Understand the hotel industry from a historical perspective.

Understand the service strengths and weaknesses of the hotel industry.

Understand the service delivery system for hotels.

Understand how customer-contact employees interact with customers in the hotel industry.

KEY TERMS

check-in

accommodation service

amenities

telecommunications

checkout

bell service

restaurants and bars

guest activities

OVERVIEW

Obviously, the core service for hotels is lodging. However, a wide variety of style and types of peripheral services is offered throughout the industry.

The history of the hotel industry is as rich as the history of civilization itself. From the moment that cities and towns began to spring up, the need for lodging for travelers was obvious. More often than not, accommodations were available for a charge from villagers with space to share or from a local monastery or other religious dwelling (usually with a donation expected if one could afford it). In fact, most major religious figures (Confucius, Jesus, Mohammed, etc.) were known for their travels, and many stories have built up around how they traveled and where they stayed. Travel and lodging also figures prominently in the history of business—it is impossible for merchants to exchange trade without hospitality and travel.

More relevant to the concerns of customer-contact employees, the first hotels of the modern world were inns at critical points of stagecoach lines. With the advent of railroad, hotels developed near central-city railroad stations in large cities throughout most of the world. Since then, the hotel industry has been modifying its marketing plans and its product continually to meet the changing needs of customers.

As rail travel increased in popularity and scope, the relationship between lodging and transportation began to be exploited. Henry Flagler, developer of the Florida East Coast Railroad, invested heavily in the development of resorts in Miami Beach. He did this to provide a market for his rail services, and the first wave of winter tourism to the Miami Beach area was promoted to fill both railway seats and hotel rooms. By the 1930s, the rich routinely spent their winters in Miami, and other resorts for the wealthy (Greenbrier in Virginia and Asbury Park in New Jersey, for example) sprang up near major railway connections.

Shortly after World War II, a Memphis businessman and his family took a trip to Washington, D.C. that would change the face of the hospitality industry forever. This man, Kemmons Wilson, traveled by car and was absolutely appalled by the lack of facilities for family travelers. The roadside cabins and tourist courts of that time were, with few exceptions, poor in quality. They usually consisted of only a bedroom, a bathroom, and a parking space outside the door. Standards were inconsistent, and dissatisfaction was the norm. In large cities the rates were often excessively high given the lack of quality in the product. Wilson decide to do something about this, and he founded Holiday Inns—the world's largest hotel chain in terms of number of rooms.

Holiday Inn was the first to start a process of market segmentation. They recognized that the family travel market had specific needs uniquely different from those of other travelers and that they were a large segment just waiting for someone to meet those needs. Holiday Inns began their appeal to this segment with free parking, swimming pools and no charge for children sharing a room with parents. They were also one of the first to use franchising as a way of growing quickly. Franchises were expected to meet strict operational standards and pass periodic, unscheduled inspections.

Gradually, through the 1960s and 1970s, the distinctions among hotels, motels and resorts faded. Previously, hotels were commercial in nature, offering just rooms and restaurants. They were usually located in cities. Motels were located near well-traveled highways and provided free parking and a swimming pool. Resorts emphasized facilities

Sorry, honey, I didn't realize the pictures in the brochure were actual size.
(© Derek Barnes. Reproduced by permission.)

for rest and relaxation: pools, golf, shuffleboard, and water sports. Eventually, hotels came to offer many similar facilities to resorts, and motels began to compete for business travelers. In fact, the term "motel," which stands for "motor hotel," has largely fallen into disuse.

Ironically, the 1980s saw a trend back toward segmentation. Large hotel chains began to realize that the gradual loss of distinction also led to customers losing any perception of product identity or brand loyalty. Single chains have created new brand names for business travel, longer-stay, vacation, and other market segments. The growth of the "all-suite hotel," with kitchens and/or living room areas, has forced some hotel chains to develop an all-suite line of hotels and has allowed newer chains to enter the market.

At the same time, the hotel industry has been hit with overcapacity from a building spree during the 1980s. Coupled with the reduced demand during the recession of the early 1990s, this has made for a highly competitive marketplace. It also has forced all hoteliers to examine more closely the relationship between service and profitability. The successful chains are those that have been able to emphasize their core services and distinguish the value of their service from others.

UNIQUE PROBLEMS

The principal problem facing hotels this decade is concern about overall profitability. The 1980s witnessed a tremendous increase in capacity without a commensurate increase in demand. It seemed as though every major hotel chain decided that a new hotel was needed in each location. The result was that some destinations that may have actually needed a new hotel or two had three, five, or even ten new ones built or renovated.

It may seem as though profitability is more a concern for management than it is for customer-contact employees. Unfortunately, the reality is that management often looks at the cost of customer-contact labor when it implements austere cost control measures. Hotels, in particular, are often forced to do this since their other major costs—real estate, building, utilities, and debt—are largely fixed. The result is that staffing levels may not be sufficient to offer efficient service, particularly at peak times.

Other aspects of the hotel business affect the companies' ability to attract sufficient numbers of customers to support profitable, yet service-oriented operations. Hotels are obviously fixed in their location (unlike a cruise ship, which can always be moved to a different set of ports in reaction to market changes). They rely on the business base and transportation infrastructure of the area in which they reside. If the growth of room capacity in an area is not matched by a growth in transportation capacity, all the hotels may be in financial danger.

Another often overlooked problem is that some hotels' profitability is as much related to the changing real estate and finance market as it is to customer revenue. Often, senior managers may be more skilled in real estate and banking than they are in hotel operation. Since building a culture around quality service starts at the top, these companies put their customer-contact workers at a distinct disadvantage.

While there are many problems in today's hotel industry, this should not discourage anyone from pursuing opportunities there. Many hotels and hotel chains are famous for their service quality, and hotels offer a wide range of customer-contact jobs. Hotels have been, and always will be, a critical part of the hospitality and tourism industry that is in high demand. Furthermore, as the travel industry continues to grow, the overcapacity problem will slowly settle out. Although some hotels are perilously close to the rocky shores, the future of the industry as a whole is solid.

SERVICE DELIVERY SYSTEMS

There are two different ways that customers can enter the service delivery system of most hotels. They can either show up at the hotel and check-in if a room is available, or they can reserve a room in advance. To reserve a room in advance, they can call the hotel directly, call the hotel chain's toll-free number (if they have one), or call or visit their travel agent. Agents themselves may call the hotel directly, call a toll-free number, or use their computer reservation system (see Chapter 18). This reservations process may leave the customer with a predisposition toward satisfaction or dissatisfaction with the overall hotel product.

Reservations are usually a completely separate service process from on-site hotel operations. Toll-free reservation systems are remote from the location, and on-site reservations operators may not work other customer-contact jobs. For those working as reservation agents, the hotel operations staff is as much a customer (internal, of course) as the people they are making reservations for (the external customer). What they do may make it easier or harder for their co-workers in customer-contact operations to succeed.

Conversely, those who are working operations at the hotel must rely on reservations agents to deliver the product they need. Even if they discover a mistake, it is a good idea to correct the problem without laying blame elsewhere. Customers are generally more interested in getting a problem solved than in knowing who made the mistake, and publicly laying blame violates the principle of teamwork.

Within a hotel, there is usually a great deal of job segmentation (Figure 14-1). Front desk personnel do not usually work bell service, and vice versa. Similarly, the restaurant staff, cleaning staff, and maintenance personnel all work separate, independently defined jobs. Customers are thus passed from one "department" to another to meet their needs. In optimal situations, this can be very efficient and effective. However, when customers encounter a problem, customer-contact employees need to be careful that they don't appear to be passing the buck as they send customers from one place to another. If the problem is complicated, customer-contact employees are much better off searching themselves for the right person to help and then have them contact the customer rather than expecting the customer to do all the "legwork."

All hotels, no matter what segment of the market they are serving, provide four basic on-site services. The first customers encounter is **check-in**. At check-in, they receive their room key, leave a credit card or cash deposit, and get information on hotel services. Their main expectations are for accuracy and efficiency. Often, customers at check-in have come some distance by air travel or car. They are likely to be tired and somewhat stressed out. The last thing they want is a long wait or a lost reservation. Most hotels use this opportunity to verify address, phone number, checkout date, room rate, and any other important information. This helps make checkout and billing more accurate later.

With the increasing availability of sophisticated computer-based data systems, many hotels are creating and maintaining large databases of frequent guest profiles. This puts all the normal requests (smoking versus nonsmoking, credit card numbers, frequent-user club numbers, etc.) at the fingertips of customer-contact employees, thus allowing them to give more personalized service in a faster manner.

Accommodation service includes everything related to the rooms in which customers stay. The most important aspect, of course, is overall cleanliness and decor. All the furniture should be in good repair, and the "feel" of the room should convey a sense of security and comfort. Another aspect of the accommodation services is **amenities**. These are the "little things" that are provided: soap, shampoo, shoe cleaners, and so on. Some hotels offer shavers and anything else customers may need if their luggage is lost or they forgot something. Others even put television sets and phones in some of their bathrooms. The level and range of amenities is naturally related to the price and image of the hotel.

The third service, **telecommunications**, has two parts: the phone and operator service in the room and the communications technology of the hotel. The former includes the quality and timeliness of message taking and whether or not the hotel offers wake-up calls (in many cases, hotels are taking advantage of new technology to automate these services and thus reduce the cost of human labor and descrease the chance for errors). Telecommunications also covers the charges that hotels add for use of in-room phones or other telecommunication devices. The latter is particularly important in business hotels since business travelers often need access to a fax machine, express mail services, and copiers.

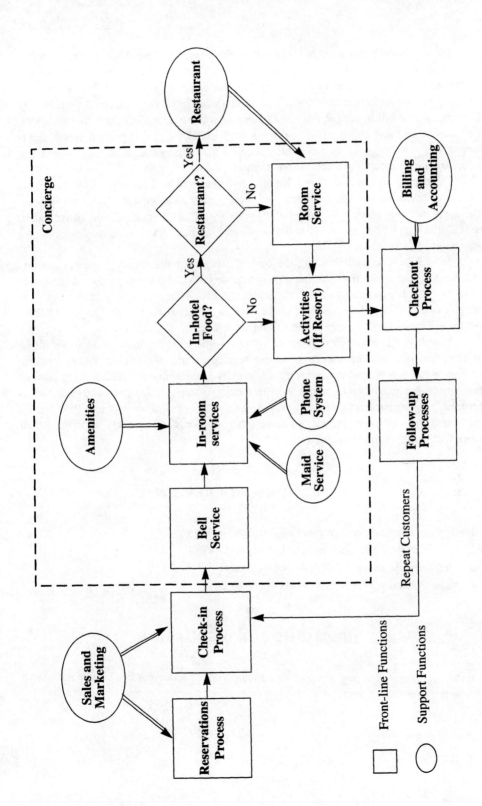

Figure 14-1 Hotel service process.

The last chance that most hotels get to make a lasting impression is during **check-out**. All customers want is an accurate bill and quick service; the last thing they want is to wait on a long line. Some hotels, using the Third Law of Service to their advantage, have largely eliminated the need for checkout service. They have replaced it by either (1) dropping off the bill under the door before guests wake up, thus allowing them to check it at their leisure and call the front desk for quick checkout, or (2) programming the in-room television sets to act as a computer monitor that allows the guest to self-check-out — an excellent example of a self-help computer system.

Depending on the type of hotel, many companies offer three other important services. Almost all but the budget hotels and motels offer **bell service**. These are the customer-contact employees who will assist guests with their luggage, escort them to their rooms, and explain any of the other amenities and facilities that guests may want to take advantage of.

Most hotels, again excluding the budget category, have one or more **restaurants and bars**. These range from poolside or beachside bars and eateries to coffee-shop style to fancy upscale restaurants to any variety of thematic restaurants. Restaurant staffs are usually completely independent from the rest of the hotel staff (see Chapter 15 for a complete discussion of service in the restaurant segment).

Resort hotels also offer **guest activities**. Some of these may be included in the price of the room package, and others may require additional payment. Guest activities include water sports, children's programs, nightly entertainment, and anything else the hotel offers for guests' enjoyment while they stay. At a resort, the guest activities staff is probably more capable of generating satisfaction than is any other segment (this doesn't mean that they are more important, since other segments can quickly undermine their work with dissatisfying performance).

QUESTIONS FOR REVIEW

1. Give an example of the segmentation of the hotel industry.
2. What three challenges does the hotel industry face today?
3. What four basic on-site services do hotels provide?
4. Name four customer-contact positions in a hotel.

QUESTIONS FOR DISCUSSION

1. What are some of the opportunities for customer-contact employees in a hotel to make favorable impressions on their customers?

15

RESTAURANTS

OBJECTIVES

After reading this chapter, you should:

Know the core service for the restaurant industry.

Understand the restaurant industry from a historical perspective.

Understand the service strengths and weaknesses of the restaurant industry.

Understand the service delivery system for restaurants.

Understand how customer-contact employees interact with customers in the restaurant industry.

KEY TERMS

full-service restaurant

specialty restaurant

OVERVIEW

Restaurants' core service appeals to the most basic of customers' needs, the physiological requirement for food and water. But while restaurants' core service is food preparation, people usually choose to "eat out" to meet other needs: socialization, ego, and so on. In meeting these needs, the numbers and types of restaurants cover a very broad range of service operations—from simple yet efficient fast food to the most luxurious five-star establishments.

Restaurants are only part of the much larger food and beverage service industry. Restaurants are the biggest and most visible portion. The National Restaurant Association (NRA) reports that they account for about 69 percent of all food purchased away from home. The remaining 31 percent is sold through a variety of other food service operations—hospital, school, and other institutional operations, club and company dining rooms, and airline catering, for example. The market for restaurants is almost the entire American society. The NRA reports that over 97 percent of all Americans eat out with some frequency (up from 85 percent in 1960).

The history of food service is almost as long and rich as the history of food. Trying to recount the details of this past is far too lengthy to be worthwhile. However, one incident in 1954 changed the face of the food service industry forever. That was the year in which Ray Kroc visited the small milkshake and burger operation run by Mac and Dick McDonald. He licensed their name and product, and the rest, as they say, is history. Kroc ushered in two major new trends: (1) the "less is better" approach of limited menus coupled with the convenience of "fast food," and (2) the power of franchising in the food service industry.

McDonald's was not the first, nor was it the only, restaurant to offer a limited menu. But its overwhelming success seemed to capture the attention of business managers everywhere and the imagination of other entrepreneurs. McDonald's has capitalized on the continuing trend in America toward the need for increased convenience and increased speed while maintaining a consistent product. By limiting its menu, Kroc was able to set up a "service factory" where little about the quality of the product was left to chance. He kept only those items that could be made by machinery that required little skilled operation, little time to prepare, and could be kept warm for at least a few minutes without substantial loss of quality. In this way, food from any McDonald's anywhere in the nation tastes the same, is delivered quickly, and managers do not need to hire and train highly skilled restaurant workers. As time has gone by, a variety of other businesses have marketed a wider variety of choice in an effort to compete, but McDonald's continues to weather the storm by consistently offering, fast, low-price, but limited food.

Kroc also released the power of franchising to create the largest chain of restaurants in the world. Many others have followed in his footsteps to the point that large chains of restaurants have slowly put many small, independent owners out of business. The marketing and pricing advantages of these chains are numerous, and in many places it is difficult for the independent to compete. The franchise approach is no longer limited to fast food. It has also been used effectively for family dining, seafood, steakhouse, and buffet court–style restaurants.

The restaurant industry can be split into two major categories: full service and specialty. The service delivery systems of the two vary in a number of ways. Traditional **full-service restaurants** offer a menu with a wide variety of choices. Most of them also produce this food from scratch (i.e., they don't have precooked packaged products that just need reheating or the addition of minimal ingredients). While there are a few chains of full-service restaurants, the vast majority are independently owned and operated. The decor is conducive to multicourse meals (soup, salad, and dessert as well as the main course). Full-service restaurants range from the neighborhood "mom and pop" operation (usually family run) to the very expensive "haute cuisine" operations often found in densely populated areas. Full-service restaurants offer a range of services that make for "a total dining experience" as opposed to merely "eating food."

Specialty restaurants encompass all the other restaurants, so it is difficult to make a neat definition. The one thing they all share is that they simplify the food service delivery system seen in a full-service restaurant with a particular eye toward reducing the cost. The primary way to achieve this reduction is to limit the number of labor hours (and skill levels required). Specialty restaurants do this through combinations of use of pre-processed foods or ingredients, increased use of machinery, decreased menu options, customer self-service, and reduction in the scope of peripheral products and services. These types of restaurants include fast food, family restaurants (often called coffee shops), and pizza parlors. By reducing the menu and automating the food preparation process, they reduce the skill levels required from employees; and by requiring customers to come to the counter, pick up their own food, and bus their own tables, they reduce the number of employees as well.

Competition among specialty restaurants can be quite fierce. Many restaurant operations revolve around a single theme in an effort to distinguish themselves from the competition. Frequent themes are cars, trains, and geographical locations, but they can be quite bizarre (e.g., a restaurant in a former mausoleum with the theme "Thomas Powell's Funeral Parlor — We'll dig you later"). They capitalize on the socialization and entertainment needs of customers while limiting the menu choices. Money spent on decor is in effect a marketing cost offset by repeat business. The difficulty is that theme fads come and go quickly, and it can be very expensive to reoutfit an entire restaurant.

Another growing segment of the specialty segment is that of ethnic restaurants. Travelers and diners are increasingly looking for a wider variety of opportunities. They want to try Chinese, Mexican, Indian, and Thai food. And Chinese no longer means just "wonton soup and chow mein." Diners are trying Szechuan, Hunan, and Mandarin foods in addition to the Cantonese classics. The ethnic market has even segmented with the advent of fast food Chinese and the growth of fast food Mexican chains.

UNIQUE PROBLEMS

The entire restaurant industry is faced with a number of problems unique within the hospitality industry. For one thing, there is a large amount of government intrusion, particularly given the fact that the vast majority of restaurants are small businesses. Most of this comes in the form of state or local health regulations and liquor laws. While the need for these rules is self-evident, it is still a burden that the small business owner must endure and customer-contact employees must be aware of. Other problems affect the profitability of the industry. For independent owners, there is the pressure from growing chains; and for the chains, there is the pressure of competition and changing customer desires. And for all, there are pressures to reduce loss from employee turnover, absenteeism, and spoilage.

One problem that particularly stresses the service delivery system are the peaks and valleys of demand in food service. There is a natural three-meal cycle, and the cost of "dark" time can be prohibitive. In response to this, many restauranteurs develop incentives for customers to come in during off-peak hours. They give "early bird" discounts, offer happy-hour specials, have separate lunch versus dinner pricing, or offer midweek specials. They may also try to synchronize employee staffing to these peaks by having some work "swing shifts": combinations of two 4-hour shifts offset by a 2- or 3-hour break period. Increasingly, they resort to the use of part-time staff, particularly older people, who do not need (or want) to work a full 8-hour shift.

SERVICE DELIVERY SYSTEMS

As Figure 15-1 shows, the service delivery systems of a restaurant vary greatly depending on the kind of restaurant operation being run. In comparing a full-service restaurant with a fast food operation, one can see and understand these differences clearly.

The fast food restaurant has simplified the process to the bare minimum necessary for delivering food. Customers who enter this process do not have the same expectations as those entering a full-service restaurant. In fact, they really only want "eating," which is distinctly different from the "dining" experience that a patron of a full-service restaurant expects. This is another excellent example of the dynamic nature of individual needs since the same person who chooses to purchase the total dining experience at one time will often forgo that for the speed and low cost of a quick meal another time.

Everything in a fast food delivery system is designed for quickness, efficiency, and low cost. Very little is left to chance. Outside influences are limited to the sales and marketing message (which is consistent and controlled across the nation) and the kitchen (where technology and limited menus ensure consistency). Wherever possible, labor-intensive activities are kept to a minimum by getting customers to order their food, come to pick it up, seat themselves, and bus their own tables as part of exiting.

In contrast, full-service restaurants have a much more involved service delivery system. From the moment customers enter a full-service restaurant, things are different. Not only is the environment markedly different, but so too are the service delivery processes. Customers wait for personalized seating services. They can usually express a preference for smoking or nonsmoking, tables in the middle or the corner. If they frequent the place and have a favorite waiter, they can so request. Often, in fact, they have made reservations ahead of time to ensure that there is space waiting for them.

Once seated, patrons can leisurely peruse the menu. They can choose from a wide variety of drinks, appetizers, soups, salads, and full meals. They have many more options for handling the bill—paying by credit card or cash. All the while, their needs are attended to by the waiter (and in luxury restaurants, the busboy and maître d'). Here service rituals are critical since the main motivators for customers are social and ego needs. For example, at a fine restaurant, it can be catastrophic to commit an error of protocol such as removing a plate from the wrong side or not allowing the head of the table to sample the wine before pouring it. Such errors undermine the credibility of the establishment no matter how tasty the food. Similarly, service cannot be as mechanical as it is in a fast food restaurant. Given the money these customers are paying and their motivations, efficient but mechanical service is not sufficient (in some situations, too much efficiency may even be inappropriate). Rather, these customers want to be treated as honored guests, with all the deference and personal attention that they expect.

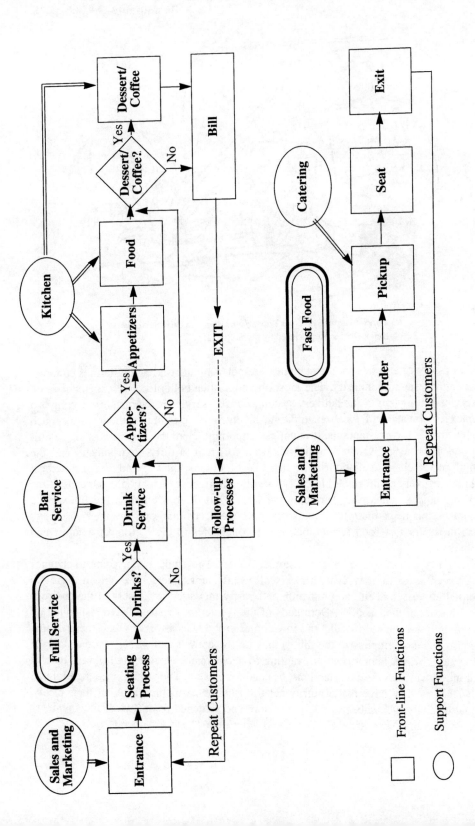

Figure 15-1 Restaurant service processes.

Nice presentation. Exquisite. Bravo. Is my dinner in there somewhere?
(© Derek Barnes. Reproduced by permission.)

Full-service and fast food restaurants are not without striking similarities common to the entire restaurant industry. The most obvious is that both place a great emphasis on the service-setting part of the delivery system. For full-service restaurants, the setting is a complex combination of location, lighting, layout, and furniture. Although it is much simpler for fast food restaurants, it is no less important. Here the emphasis is on cleanliness and consistency. Customers do not want to eat in a dirty environment, and the strength of the chain affiliation is the fact that customers know exactly what to expect (and thus feel very comfortable) in every location throughout the nation. Both ends of the spectrum must also take very seriously the service rituals they employ. For full-service restaurants, this helps them meet the social and ego needs that motivate their customers to use them; for fast food restaurants, it too contributes to the feeling of comfort and familiarity.

Both types of restaurants are customer-driven. They must either adapt to changes in customer needs or they cease to exist. Recently, consumers have shown a greatly increased interest in health and nutrition and vastly increased awareness of the environmental impact of their actions. Both ends of the restaurant spectrum have responded by developing low-calorie, low-salt, and low-cholesterol dishes as part of their menu. Some have also begun to emphasize the things they do to be environmentally conscious. Even McDonald's, which is notorious in wanting to avoid major changes and is very careful about introducing new menu selections, has had to respond. They introduced the McLean sandwich, and they have made nutritional information available on all of their meals. They also finally succumbed to public pressure and switched from Styrofoam containers to paper, joining Burger King, Hardee's, and other major fast food operators.

Obviously, fast food restaurants and full-service restaurants represent opposite ends of the entire spectrum of restaurant operations. There are many restaurants—ethnic, family, pizza shops, and so on—that fall somewhere in the middle. They draw on elements of both to find the right mix for their market and their customers' needs.

QUESTIONS FOR REVIEW

1. What is the difference between full-service and specialty restaurants?
2. What three challenges does the restaurant industry face today?
3. What are the biggest differences between the service delivery systems of fast-food restaurants and full-service restaurants?
4. Name three customer-contact positions in a restaurant.

QUESTIONS FOR DISCUSSION

1. Can fast food restaurants give good service? Why or why not?
2. What are some of the opportunities for customer-contact employees in a restaurant to make favorable impressions on customers?

16

AIR TRANSPORTATION

OBJECTIVES

After reading this chapter, you should:

Know the core service for the air transportation industry.

Understand the air transportation industry from a historical perspective.

Understand the service strengths and weaknesses of the air transportation industry.

Understand the service delivery system for air transportation companies.

Understand how customer-contact employees interact with customers in the air transportation industry.

KEY TERMS

excursion fare	in-flight services
curbside check-in	hub-and-spoke system
security screening	frequent-flyer club
boarding process	airport club

OVERVIEW

The core service for air transportation is getting people from one place to another. Within the industry, there is some degree of segmentation, ranging from commuters to international carriers, and including a few niche market carriers.

The business and service history of the airline industry reflects the history of service companies in the United States better than any other segment of the hospitality and tourism industry. The airline industry began as technology allowed businesses to do things that they previously could not do—no matter what the need of the customer. It was therefore natural that early airlines were product oriented. Each increase in technical capability—increased speed, size, and ceiling—was automatically advantageous to customers.

Through the 1950s and 1960s, airlines continued to be product oriented. Almost all advertising and marketing described the features of airplanes: size, speed, comfort, and safety. There was little recognition that different people travel for different reasons. Although jets first became available in the late 1950s, they were not in widespread use until the early 1960s. Jet transport aircraft vastly increased the capacity or supply of available airplane seats. They carried more people per flight than the propeller technology of the day, and they could travel nearly twice as far per day.

Thus it wasn't until this supply began to exceed demand that customer-oriented marketing even began to be needed. The first efforts at customer-oriented marketing addressed the difference between business travelers and vacation travelers. Airlines recognized that vacation travelers are much more discretionary with their money, so they established special **excursion fares** whose requirements made it unlikely that business travelers would be able to use them.

Then in 1979, the entire face of the airline industry changed practically overnight. With passage of the Airlines Deregulation Act of 1979, domestic skies in the United States were virtually completely deregulated. Numerous new airlines have appeared and disappeared, through merger and bankruptcy. Some, such as Eastern and Pan-American Airlines, were among the original pioneering airlines of the 1930s. Customer-oriented marketing, chiefly by way of special fares, exploded to the point where some flights have more types of fares than the number of seats on the airplane.

However, despite the increased competition of the 1980s, the air transport companies themselves remained product oriented. Continued advances in the technology of the craft and in the sophistication of pricing and marketing strategies were not met by increased service capabilities. If anything, in the customers' eyes, the perception of the quality of service has lowered.

The challenge for the airline industry in the 1990s is clear. To be successful, airlines will have to continue their fine record of safety and product improvement *while delivering a level of service that is* ***at least acceptable*** *in quality in the eyes of customers.* This means that customer-contact employees must meet or exceed customer expectations.

UNIQUE PROBLEMS

As an industry, airlines probably have the biggest set of problems with respect to service of all hospitality and tourism companies. They certainly have the poorest reputation in the eyes of the general public.

In a general sense, the airlines have the toughest job. Given the nature of their product, there are many more ways for them to generate dissatisfaction than there is to generate satisfaction. Customers spend a relatively short time with the airline, and customer-contact employees must perform a large number of tasks with an equally large number of people in this short period of time. Many of these tasks are required by government regulations as well as safety and security standards. Customer-contact employees often have little flexibility for creative problem solving, and even the environment (the cramped inside of a coach cabin) is not conducive to a positive atmosphere. Added to this are some problems beyond the control of the company (weather, air traffic control delays, etc.) that nevertheless will cause some customers to be angry with the airline.

Another problem for airlines is the sheer magnitude of the number of people they must process through an airport in a given day. If all the people came to the airport early, had similar luggage and were experienced travelers who understood how everything worked, it would not be much of a problem. The reality is that customers have their own needs and come to the airport in a variety of moods for a variety of reasons. They may need handicapped access and help, special meals (kosher, vegetarian, low-salt, etc.) and have special baggage requests (firearms, fragile, oversized, etc.). They may be in a great mood as they embark on the vacation of their lifetime, or they may be depressed as they travel on an emergency basis to a funeral. They may be experienced business travelers who don't like being told what they already know, or they may be a family with kids who have never been on a plane before. Each needs immediate personal attention.

All that most customers expect from an airline is a "hassle-free" trip from one point to another. This kind of expectation puts a premium on the hygiene factors while virtually eliminating the "satisfiers." In other words, it is very easy for airline customer-contact employees to do something that causes dissatisfaction, but it is almost impossible to generate the kind of satisfaction that makes customers feel really good about the air-

Success at last! An airline meal with portions so small they can't be seen with the naked eye! (© Derek Barnes. Reproduced by permission.)

line. The best that an airline employee can usually do is leave the impression that the airline "at least didn't mess things up."

The airline industry also has suffered major profit problems. In 1991 alone, three major airlines ceased operations. Two of them, Eastern and Pan-American, were among the pioneers of early aviation. At one point, over 25 percent of all air traffic in the domestic United States was being flown by carriers operating under bankruptcy protection. Just as with hotels, the airline companies tend to look toward employee-related costs to target for reduction since they must continue to fund their airplane and airport facility costs. This results on pressure for customer-contact employees to continue to do more with less. The tensions also grow because many airline employees are unionized and relations between unions and management at some of the major carriers are chronically strained.

On the plus side, the airline industry's reputation for poor service is probably not deserved. Airlines today carry more passengers more miles at a lower cost than ever before. Flights are more frequent and more convenient than ever. Fewer bags are lost, and overall safety has never been better (although many are concerned about the lack of improvement in the air traffic control system over the past decade). The problem that airlines are plagued with is that these increased capabilities have caused the traveling public to increase their expectations—and it is not always humanly possible to meet these raised expectations.

SERVICE DELIVERY SYSTEMS

The service delivery system for air transportation is one of the simplest looking in flow-chart form in all of the hospitality and tourism industry (Figure 16-1). This should not be surprising given the large number of customers that must go through the process in a short period of time. The airlines could not possibly get the job done if the delivery system was too complex. For the average customer, this is no problem; however, as discussed earlier, it can cause difficulties when customers need special attention.

About 85 percent of an airline company's customers make their reservations and purchase their tickets from a travel agent. The remaining 15 percent purchase them from an airline reservation phone center, an airline city ticket office (CTO), or at the airport. Therefore, most customers do not directly encounter airline personnel until their arrival at the airport.

The first process at the airport is usually check-in. Passengers wait in line inside an airport terminal to check in, receive seat assignments and boarding passes (unless their travel agent was able to do it for them ahead of time), check their baggage, and learn from which gate their flight leaves. Alternatively, most airports offer **curbside check-in**, where passengers can check their luggage right where they are dropped off from their car or a parking shuttle.

The next step that passengers take is to clear **security screening**. This customer-contact function is actually accomplished by employees who are contracted by the airport, not the airline. If customers do not have baggage to check or they have checked in their baggage curbside, they can clear security first and then check in at the gate.

The **boarding process** is itself deceivingly complex. In a span of 15 to 20 minutes, one to three gate agents are responsible for loading anywhere from a few to a few

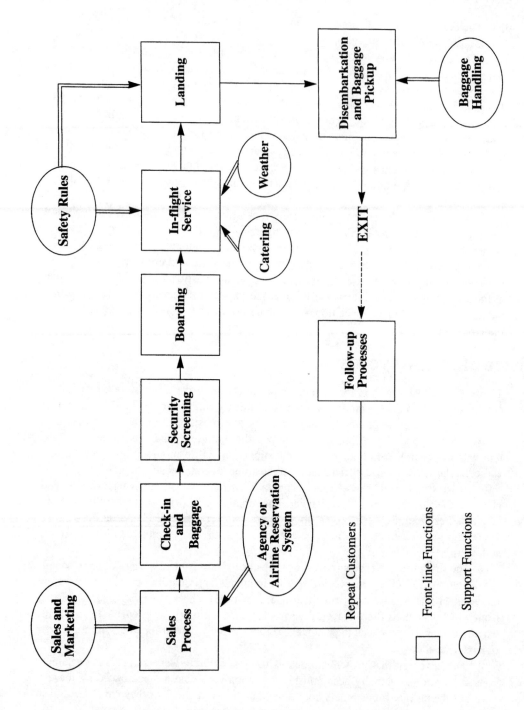

Figure 16-1 Air transportation service process.

hundred people onto an airplane. They have to field questions, take tickets and check them versus the manifest, and handle oversized carry-on luggage—all the while dealing with new customers arriving at the gate close to departure time. If the plane is late, they must deal with irate customers, and if the plane is overbooked, they have to deal with bumping passengers. In an effort to get people onto the plane smoothly, they attempt to board the plane from the rear forward. However, first-class passengers and those needing extra time are usually allowed to board first, and many people ignore the request to board only when their row number is called. Although these customers are rather inconsiderate, it usually is not worth it for the gate agents to confront them.

In-flight service is the exclusive domain of the flight crew composed of flight attendants and the cockpit crew. The latter's direct contact with customers is generally limited to a few minutes of information on the plane's public address system and a "Thank you for flying with us" as customers depart. While the safety and security of all those aboard ultimately rest in their hands, customers generally overlook this as a direct part of the service they get. In fact, some customers will be dissatisfied if their schedules are delayed due to a flight delay or cancellation—even if the delay or cancellation is purely for their own safety. Airlines do not generate satisfied customers merely by getting them to their destination safely.

Satisfying customers while in flight then falls into the hands of the flight attendants. These people are highly trained in the operation of all on-board equipment, particularly safety-related devices. On some airlines, however, they may not get equal training in meeting customer needs. While their primary purpose for being on the airplane is the safety and security of the passengers, they generate satisfaction or dissatisfaction with their secondary functions. These functions include serving drinks and meals and helping to make the flight as comfortable as possible.

In-flight service expectations vary depending on the class of service purchased. Coach-class passengers on domestic flights rarely expect more than an edible meal and a polite response to an occasional request. First-class passengers, however, expect more than just a bigger seat. They get coat-hanging service, better food on better kitchenware, and free drinks. They are much more likely to have special requests, need the in-flight phone, or otherwise require more care. At the same time, some of these passengers may want to be left alone, so the flight attendant in this section must be adept at reading these different desires. Otherwise, they may annoy customers by being too willing to offer to do something for them.

The only remaining steps of the airline service delivery system are the landing procedure, disembarkation, and baggage pickup. Again, there are many more opportunities to give passengers cause for dissatisfaction than satisfaction—some of which may not be within the airline's control. An airplane may have to wait for air traffic control to give them landing authority or they may have to wait on the ground before they get to the gate, either of which easily annoys passengers who do not want to stay in the cramped surroundings of an airplane while they can look out the window and see where they are supposed to be. Many times at overcrowded airports, the latter turns a good thing into a bad one. Planes that arrive early may have to wait on the tarmac for another plane to leave the gate before they can pull in. Imagine how the passengers feel when first they are told they'll be arriving early for a change, and then they have to wait 15 minutes (or more) for a gate.

With today's **hub-and-spoke system**, many more passengers fly on connecting planes instead of nonstop. The airlines could not possibly operate as many flights to as many places as they do without this system, but it places an additional burden on customers. As they come off the plane, they may be stressed if their connection is tight. They have to find out where it is, when it is leaving, and how to get there quickly. Some airlines have customer service representatives meet incoming planes to assist personally with connection information. Sometimes they can even communicate this information to the plane while it is in the air so that the flight crew can relay it to passengers. Inevitably, of course, some people miss connections. Customer-contact employees must deal with these very stressed (and sometimes angry) customers.

Just because customers have reached their final destination doesn't mean that their needs have been completely met. They still need to find their way to baggage claim and pick up their luggage. Customer-contact employees are there to handle complaints about lost or damaged luggage and to assist with moving the luggage to cars or courtesy vans. This entire process is dependent on the behind-the-scenes work of baggage handlers. A half-hour wait for luggage can easily ruin the positive impressions built over a multihour flight, just as a quick luggage pickup can make up for some discomfort during the flight.

Airlines depend heavily on frequent travelers (repeat business), particularly from customers paying business fares. To attract these people, they offer a variety of peripheral services. The most popular are the **frequent-flyer clubs**, which award points for travel taken on that airline. These points can be used for future free travel, upgrades to first class and sometimes even merchandise. The airlines may also offer special bonuses for specific flights, for flying first class, or for flying more than a certain amount each year.

Airlines also operate **airport clubs**. These are membership-only lounges where the busy traveler can relax at a private bar, watch television, or get some work done. They are usually staffed by reservations agents who can provide private check-in reservations for future travel. The clubs are often equipped with full office capabilities, including faxes, computers, and telephones. Members can even reserve conference rooms if they want to have a meeting right at the airport.

QUESTIONS FOR REVIEW

1. What three challenges does the airline industry face today?
2. What is a hub-and-spoke system? What are the advantages and disadvantages of this system for customers?
3. Name three customer-contact positions in an airline company.

QUESTIONS FOR DISCUSSION

1. Can airlines deliver service that greatly exceeds their customers' expectations? What can customer-contact employees do to achieve this?
2. Why does the airline service delivery system look so simple? Does this mean that delivering the services should be easy? Why or why not?

17

CRUISE LINES

OBJECTIVES

After reading this chapter, you should:

Know the core service for the cruise industry.

Understand the cruise industry from a historical perspective.

Understand the service strengths and weaknesses of the cruise industry.

Understand the service delivery system for cruises.

Understand how customer-contact employees interact with customers in the cruise industry.

KEY TERMS

all-inclusive pricing	hotel service
air/sea package	room steward
meal service	hotel manager
activities	purser
cruise director	

OVERVIEW

The core service for cruise lines is a total vacation experience. It is not merely transportation, lodging, or other parts of the vacation. Cruise lines have built a product around the complete experience, including meals, excursions, activities, children's programs, and anything else that a vacationing adult or family could want.

The steamship and cruise industry provides an interesting contrast in the view of the historical perspective of the various segments of the hospitality and tourism industry. From the beginning of the century until the 1960s, the steamship was a major form of transportation. The growth of our nation can be traced to immigrants traveling in "steerage" class across the North Atlantic. Steamships also had first-class service that was exceedingly elegant, expensive, and available only to the rich. First-class travelers and immigrants never saw each other because the ships did not permit movement between the classes. Shipline marketing, too, was product-oriented through the 1950s.

In the late 1950s, however, an event took place that had grave implications for the steamship market—and nobody noticed. This was the first time that more people crossed the North Atlantic by airplane than by sea. With the introduction of jet airplanes in the early 1960s, it appeared that ship transportation was about to go the way of the "horse and buggy."

However, instead of dying, the cruise industry has thrived—through a total restructuring along customer-oriented lines. Some steamship companies had experimented with cruise vacations, particularly in winter months when transatlantic travel was low. But with the decline of the demand for steamship transportation, cruising was introduced on a year-round basis. Slow speed, which was the major disadvantage for transportation purposes, became an advantage for vacationers looking for a relaxing pace. **All-inclusive pricing** made cruising one of the best values in the vacation market, and the introduction of the **air/sea package** concept made it one of the most hassle-free vacations as well. The ability to move the ship from port to port also gave cruise lines the flexibility to change a product quickly to meet changing customer needs—a distinct advantage over their land-package resort competition.

The 1980s saw great advances in the customer orientation of all major cruise lines. New ships were designed from scratch with an eye toward what customers want from a cruise vacation. The new ships are larger (although a number of new, smaller ships were built for niche markets), quieter, more stable, and have much more open space. The decor ranges from "quiet and elegant" to "nothing but neon," thus offering an ever-growing range of options to the discriminating traveler.

This customer orientation is likely to continue with more new ships on the drawing board than ever before. At the same time, the industry may be on the brink of suffering the same kind of overcapacity that has hurt the hotel industry. New destinations and new demand (still only about 5 percent of the public has ever taken a cruise) may keep pace with the introduction of new berths, but it is likely that service and value will be the key selling points of the next decade.

UNIQUE PROBLEMS

Cruise lines suffer from relatively few problems. Their principal problem is probably lack of exposure. As of 1992, the Cruise Lines International Association reported that only 5 percent of the American traveling public has ever been on a cruise—this despite the fact that cruise lines report satisfaction rates based on passenger surveys ranging from 90 to 98 percent. Obviously, the cruise lines as an industry provide the highest rate of service satisfaction, but ironically they have had problems convincing people who have never used them to give them a try.

Cruise lines have been very profitable based on their high degree of repeat business. To capitalize on this and expected growth of the "first-time cruiser" market, all major lines have added new ships to their fleets. This runs the risk of overcapacity and its attendant problems similar to the problems in the hotel industry. It is clear, however, that the cruise segment enjoys a much brighter business environment in 1993 than that of any other segment in the hospitality and tourism industry.

SERVICE DELIVERY SYSTEMS

Because of the length of time that customers stay in contact with a cruise company, the isolation of a ship at sea, and the broad nature of the different individual service encounters that comprise the total vacation experience, the cruise service delivery system is among the most complex in all of hospitality and tourism (Figure 17-1). As we shall see, the isolation also gives cruise lines a greater ability to immerse customers in their service experiences, thus generating tremendous opportunities to generate the highest rate of satisfaction for an entire segment.

Direct contact with the cruise lines' service delivery system begins with the boarding process. Since virtually all cruise passengers book through travel agencies, customer-contact with reservations and salespeople during the sales process was only indirectly through the agent. The boarding process has some similarities to the airline boarding process except that it is much more complex. Some customers arrive at the pier for processing much like airline passengers arrive at the airport. Others, however, fly in and are met by cruise personnel at the airport. Their bags must be loaded onto trucks and their bodies onto buses for transfer to the port. Once there, they join the same processing line as do customers who got to the port on their own.

The pier-site boarding process shares some similarities as well. Documents are exchanged, people and bags are inspected, and questions can get asked and answered. But just as the cruise vacation product is much more complex than point-to-point transportation, the boarding process is more complex as well. The cruise line will verify room assignments, seating preferences, and any other special requests. Once on board, customers get directed to their room and meet their cabin steward. This is often the only time they see him and it gives him a chance to find out what bed arrangement they may want, and so on. At the same time, customers can review the first day's activities and then go off to participate in other orientation or first-day festivities.

Interestingly enough, in an excellent example of the situational nature of service delivery, cruise customers are much more tolerant of waiting in a long line for boarding the ship than the same people would be for boarding an airplane or checking into a hotel. This is because their expectations and frame of mind are different in the two different situations. For the plane, their principal expectation is a hassle-free trip—and waiting is a hassle. Also, they are anxious because deep down they just don't trust that the plane will not leave without them. Many of them also are thinking about whatever stresses they will face in the next few hours—the discomfort of a cramped plane, the poor food, the business meeting or family gathering at the other end of the trip, and so on. At hotels, most

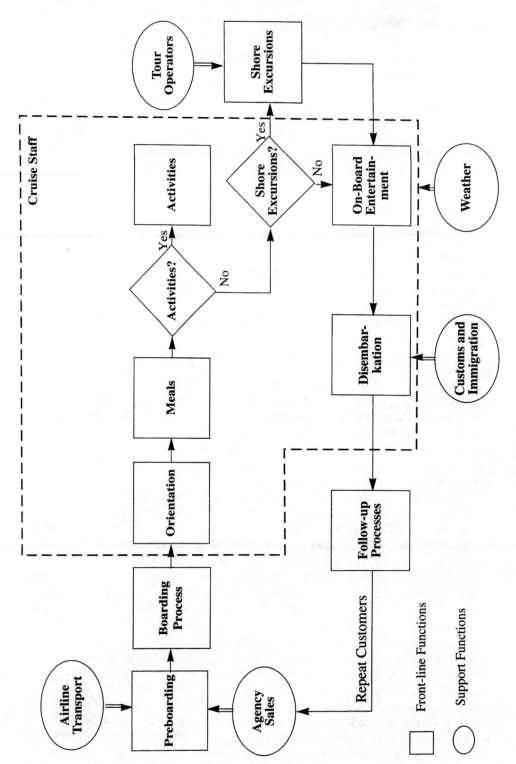

Figure 17-1 Cruise line service process.

I hear the cruise director caught him actually doing work!
(© Derek Barnes. Reproduced by permission.)

people are already tired from their trip and can't wait for the chance to lie down for a few minutes. Cruise passengers' main expectation, however, is fun. The pier often seems a little bit like a carnival atmosphere, and the wait may even give them a chance to meet their first new friends. Although they may not love the idea of waiting, they usually do not feel nearly as stressed. They're looking forward to days of fun and sun.

All cruise ships, as floating resorts, offer three major services. Perhaps the most important is **meal service.** "How is the food?" is often the first question an experienced cruise customer asks a travel agent or friend when evaluating a particular ship. Many of the cruise ships focus on the dining experience in their advertising, and many travel agents note to prospective customers that "all-you-can-eat" dining is included in the package (unlike many land tour options). Its importance is also evident in the fact that most experienced cruise customers consider whether the ship has one seating or two for meals to be perhaps the most important difference between mass-market and deluxe cruise packages.

With either two seatings for each meal or just a single seating, the service delivery system for meals is a complicated and well-orchestrated process on any ship. In the space of a couple of hours, from 100 to 1200 passengers will enjoy gourmet dining. A number of people work together to make this happen. The most critical are the cooks and kitchen staff, the waiters and busboys. The last two are obviously customer-contact workers, and the first two are support staff. With the closeness and camaraderie of a cruise ship, the waiter's job includes building a rapport and relationship with the passengers so that they look forward to seeing him almost as much as the food. For some passengers, the wine stewards can also be important players. All of this is overseen by the dining room captains, who act as maître d's.

Meal service in a ship dining room is a total experience, including food, socialization, and entertainment. On a large mass-market ship, most dinners revolve around a theme. The food, dress, and decor of the dining room and its staff contribute to it. On many nights the dining room staff will entertain with singing and dancing as well. This, of course, would not happen on a ship with a product designed to be very quiet and low key. The food itself is served from a limited menu, but it is surprising how varied it may be. There are low-calorie and low-salt options as well as a number of choices for appetizers, soups, salads, main courses, side dishes, and desserts. The waiters will insist passengers try something new since they can always get something else if they don't like it. If passengers tell their waiter they liked a particular choice, they shouldn't be surprised to see a second helping appear within minutes. Meeting Maslow's need for food and survival is certainly not a problem on a cruise ship.

The dining room is not the only place to get meal service on a cruise ship (although the vast majority of dinners are served there). Most ships have room service (many 24 hours a day). Most offer a buffet breakfast and/or lunch at the lido area (pool area on one of the top decks). They may also have afternoon snacks such as ice cream sundaes, cakes, and cookies. There is also the midnight buffet—the pride of many ships (on the first night some passengers line up early to get photographs of the ice and butter sculptures and other visual food preparations). Some ships follow-up with a 2 A.M. buffet as well.

The second major service that all ships offer is **activities**: both on-ship and off-ship. This service is similar to the activities services that resorts offer. Some of them are performed by cruise personnel and some are contracted out to other suppliers. Obviously, their importance to total customer satisfaction cannot be understated since they represent most of what there is to do during days at sea. In delivering this service, the confines of the ship can help and hurt the process. It may hurt in that the ship presents limited space (they can offer golf driving off the fantail, but they can't offer 18 holes of golf while at sea), but it helps in that customers are a "captive audience." They won't lose them to off-site activities while at sea (at least they hope not).

On-ship activities are run by **cruise directors** and their staff. Simply put, they make sure that people have fun. They'll run the bingo, horse racing, pools games, sports tournaments and anything else that involves organized activities. For people looking for other challenges, most ships have fitness centers. All cruise ships have casinos that may include card games and craps as well as the ubiquitous slot machines. For those interested in more quiet pursuits, there are card rooms, libraries, and other small gathering places. Most off-ship activities are tour excursions which are provided by local suppliers and organized through the activities desks. Some ships offer beach or other theme parties at one or more destinations. These are usually run by the cruise director and staff.

Another major part of activities services is on-ship entertainment. These include shows from professional entertainers (singers, dancers, comedians, jugglers, etc.) and amateur nights (talent shows, cruise staff shows, etc.). It also includes lounge entertainment (piano players, guitarists, and other lounge acts).

Hotel service is the third major service offered on all cruise ships. This includes those services to keep the rooms in order as well as information, cashier and other "front desk" services. On most ships, room services are performed by room stewards who are part of the hotel manager's staff. Information, storage of valuables, cashier and other duties are the responsibility of the purser who reports directly to the captain. The nuances of a ship staff's organizational design is not as important to customers as the functions they serve. What is important is all the functions a hotel staff accomplishes at a hotel or resort must also be done on the ship. These workers are always available to any passenger who needs their services on an "as requested" basis. In other words, when customers need the help, they know where to go to get it. These people work in the background and affect only those customers who require those services.

The final major process of the cruise delivery system is the disembarkation process. This includes orientation and customs and immigration processing all the way through transfers to the airport for those who are flying back home. The orientation part is very important for making sure that all passengers have enough information to make disembarkation as smooth as possible. For example, the head of every household must go through customs and immigration check on board before the ship can be cleared for disembarkation. Anyone who misunderstands what needs to be done can force everyone on board to wait (and now the customers aren't likely to care as little about waiting as they did for the boarding process). Also, since most ships arrive back at their home port early in the morning, luggage for transfer off the ship must be left outside their rooms the night before. Passengers must be reminded to save something to wear. Otherwise, albeit through their own fault, the first morning back starts with a very sour note (and as the service laws say, last impressions are often the best remembered).

QUESTIONS FOR REVIEW

1. Cruises are often marketed as being the most hassle-free vacation. What three characteristics about the product contribute to this perception?
2. What is the biggest difference between the cruise product of today and the steamship product of the 1930s?
3. What two problems face the cruise industry today?
4. Name five basic services that cruises provide.
5. Name five customer-contact positions in a cruise line.

QUESTIONS FOR DISCUSSION

1. Why have cruise lines enjoyed such success through the 1980s and 1990s?
2. What are some of the opportunities for customer-contact employees in a cruise line to make favorable impressions on their customers?

18

TRAVEL AGENCIES

OBJECTIVES

After reading this chapter, you should:

Know the core service for the travel agency industry.

Understand the travel agency industry from a historical perspective.

Understand the service strengths and weaknesses of the travel agency industry.

Understand the service delivery system for travel agencies.

Understand how customer-contact employees interact with customers in the travel agency industry.

KEY TERMS

facilitator

market search

advice

transaction processing

problem resolution

OVERVIEW

Travel agents have a very unique role in the hospitality and tourism industry—one that is quite different from any of those discussed in previous chapters. Travel agents do not actually themselves provide an end service. Rather, they are facilitators for the buying and selling of other companies' services. Insurance brokers, real estate brokers, and employment recruiters are other examples of facilitator services. Facilitators act as sort of "experts for hire."

Facilitators in general, and travel agents specifically, exist in the marketplace for the following four basic reasons.

1. Market search.   Whenever a market has a large number of suppliers, it is practically impossible for the average customer to review the entire range of possibilities available. If, for example, a customer is shopping for a car, there are relatively few alternatives. There are only three American car manufacturers and a dozen or so major foreign ones. Each manufacturer has no more than a dozen or two different basic models.

On the other hand, travel is a different story. There are well over 200 airlines alone. There are dozens of cruise companies with hundreds of ships, hundreds of tour operators, and thousands of hotels. Add to that car rental companies, travel insurance, and a host of possible attractions at any of the thousands of travel destinations. There is no way that the average customer can even begin to wade through this large a volume of product offerings without some assistance. Travel agents, as facilitators, offer this assistance. They spend much of their time becoming familiar with the variety of products and services available. They can then share this knowledge with their customers in a much more efficient manner than the customers could ever do on their own.

This market search function also helps travel suppliers. These suppliers are faced with the difficult marketing challenge of making the public aware of their services. A few (major airlines and cruise lines) can afford large-scale advertising, and many can afford some smaller-scale advertising. However, the travel agency distribution network offers a very low cost and targeted audience to inform. In the United States alone, there are over 30,000 travel agencies. By selling through an agency, a travel supplier gets 30,000 sales locations—much more than they could afford if they had to set up their own offices. As facilitators, travel agencies give suppliers a sort of "public search" just as they give the public a "market search."

2. Advice.   While the market search function may be the most necessary function that travel agents serve, giving advice is probably the most valuable to its customers. Customers look to travel agents not just for efficient access to the market but also for expert opinion on what to do and often on what not to do. Based on their experiences, travel agents can give advice that is useful to customers.

By serving as a "warehouse of information" about what is good and bad about different places and service products, they add "value" to the services that the travel suppliers offer. Furthermore, since the vast majority of travel agent services are free to the public (they make their money from commissions paid by the travel suppliers), this additional value comes free of charge to customers.

The advice function also helps travel suppliers. Since most suppliers are concerned about travelers' satisfaction with their product, it is in their interest to make sure that these travelers have realistic expectations. If travelers expect something very different from what they receive, the First Law of Service says that they are likely to be dissatisfied. Travel agents help direct the appropriate type of customer to the appropriate destination and travel supplier. They also explain to customers what they can expect from the service product.

3. Transaction processing.   A third function that all facilitators perform is the processing of transaction paperwork. For travel agents, this includes ticket generation or review of documents generated by suppliers, deposit and final payment transactions, and the handling of promotional and informational material. This is actually the least skilled part of the job, yet its importance cannot be underestimated. The sale does not actually occur (and agencies cannot make any money) unless this function occurs. Furthermore, because this is where money changes hands, it sometimes can get contentious. Since travel agencies serve only as a holding point for 90 percent of the money, their customer-contact employees must be very careful in handling the money—most of it is not theirs. In fact, travel agency accounting is one of the most complicated accounting procedures around, particularly for small companies.

Again, the transaction processing function serves the interests of both customers and suppliers. It gives both a single place where records are being kept and a single, informed contact who is responsible for ensuring that all the documentation is correct. When dealing with international travel, for example, this can be very important. Something as simple as a slightly misspelled name could result in the traveler's being denied boarding on an airplane or denied entry into a country by customs.

4. Problem resolution.   One of the most important functions of a facilitator is helping to solve problems. Although it is often ignored when academics discuss the reasons why facilitators exist, customers who have any problems with the end services they are supposed to receive learn quickly that the facilitators' ability to solve problems can be very valuable (particularly since this help comes essentially free).

As with the other three functions, facilitators' work in resolving problems serves both the interests of their customers and their suppliers. For customers, the advantages are numerous. When customers have a problem with a supplier, a facilitator such as a travel agency can step in and help solve the problem. They can save customers significant time in chasing down the right people to complain to. They are much more familiar with the standard operating procedures in the industry and can often more effectively state the customer's case. Also, they have the additional clout with a supplier of providing more than a single sale. This clout alone is often the difference between customers getting some concession from the supplier, or not.

For suppliers, the advantages of travel agents performing the role of problem solver may be less obvious, but not less important. Most important, the agents are a third party to the problem who can usually provide a more objective evaluation of customers' problems than can the customers themselves. The agents are usually less emotionally involved and can be a good buffer for the supplier.

More important, facilitators are like a community of ombudsmen for suppliers. They can bring to the attention of suppliers issues and problems of which they were unaware. Since it is in both the supplier's and the facilitator's best interests to have satisfied customers, they can pool their creative resources to think of better ways to do things in the future. In the travel industry, many suppliers institutionalize this concept by creating advisory councils of travel agents to help them fix existing problems, review new products and services, and create new opportunities for the future.

Travel agencies have actually been around since the nineteenth century. Prior to World War II, they were mostly agents for steamship travel. Their customers were leisure travelers who could afford luxury steamship vacations (transatlantic crossings were particularly popular).

The modern style of travel agencies had its beginning after World War II. This is when the majority of airlines made their fares commissionable to agencies. This gave travel agents the ability to earn income on almost all forms of vacation travel. Commissions from air travel slowly became the dominant source of revenue for travelers as jet travel became widespread through the 1960s. A large portion of this revenue came from increased air travel by "VFR" travelers—the acronym for travelers who are "visiting friends and relatives." Jet travel was often able to compete with the automobile for the VFR travelers' choice, and travel agents were there to make the reservations and issue tickets.

The next big change in the travel industry coincided with airline deregulation in 1979. Prior to this time, there were only a handful of travel agencies that specialized in corporate travel. However, about this time, most airlines changed their domestic commission structures, raising the standard commission on most tickets from 7 or 8 percent to 10 percent. This change made the handling of corporate air travel much more profitable. Furthermore, with airlines competing with each other in a deregulated environment, bigger agencies that generated large volumes of travel with individual carriers could often get commission overrides—additional payments based on some measurement of total sales, similar to volume discounts in retail sales.

This resulted in the emergence of approximately six to ten national (even international) "mega-agencies" that regularly compete for most of the largest travel accounts in corporate America. Very few businesses book directly with airlines anymore. At the same time that "the big have gotten bigger," a 1991 survey of all travel agencies indicate that 92 percent of American travel agencies have less than $5 million in volume, relatively unchanged from 1979.

What has happened is that the travel industry is marked by a much bigger difference between the two core segments: the "local, small business" and the "mega." To counter their inherent competitive disadvantage, the smaller agencies have bonded together in record numbers in a variety of consortiums and cooperatives—groups of agencies that negotiate with suppliers together. This often gives the member agencies access to overrides while maintaining their local, independent ownership.

The future of travel agencies is much more difficult to predict. After all, they exist only so long as they provide benefits to both buyers and sellers of travel. It is likely, however, that as travel and travel purchasing become more and more high tech, travel agencies will thrive because they are the sole source of high touch.

UNIQUE PROBLEMS

Travel agencies are faced by a number of problems unique to their operation. Many of these are a function of their operation as facilitators. The principal problem is that while travel agencies may provide four types of services, they are compensated for only one.

They also exist only because they give advantages to both buyer and seller. Ironically, their most useful services are market search, advice, and even problem resolution. Yet they usually receive no income for these specific services—they get paid only when a sale is made and they handle the processing of documents.

As a result, successful travel agents must be skilled in both service and sales skills. Despite this requirement for a wide variety of skills, they are among the lowest-paid workers in the hospitality and tourism industry. Part of this is due to the fact that the standard commission rate in the industry is 10 percent, and not too many businesses can survive on such a low margin. Added to the need for service and sales skills, most travel agents work with sophisticated computer systems and must have detailed knowledge about a wide variety of destinations and all the segments of the industry—hotel, air, cruise, car, and so on. And these days, the rate of change in the industry makes it increasingly difficult to keep pace.

One other difficulty facing all agencies is that they ultimately have no control over customer satisfaction, even though they often take the heat for problems. As facilitators, they rely on the other travel suppliers to provide the actual travel services that their customers are purchasing. However, they are often the easiest target since they are usually much closer to the traveler. Also, when they are forced to be the bearer of bad news, travelers may react and "shoot the messenger."

I'm afraid with a budget like that your only travel options are going by donkey cart or parcel post. (© Derek Barnes. Reproduced by permission.)

Despite all these problems, there are many reasons to pursue a career as a travel agent, owner, or manager. There is little doubt that it can be the most rewarding of all jobs in the hospitality and tourism industry, particularly for customer-contact employees. Travel agents generally have a degree of independence much greater than that for normal customer-contact jobs. They naturally must be given a wide degree of latitude by management in meeting customer needs because the range of those needs is so broad. Also, they can often share in the experience of their customers. In some cases, travel agents can get to take "familiarization" trips. Often referred to as "fam trips," these can be both educational and fun—and similar perks are not usually available to customer-contact employees in other segments of the hospitality and tourism industry.

SERVICE DELIVERY SYSTEMS

Because travel agencies act as facilitators for other companies' services, there is almost no norm for service delivery systems. There are over 30,000 agencies throughout the United States alone, so there is no single model of how agency procedures operate. Each office has its own approach, and each independent owner has different ideas about the best way to do things. There are, however, certain approaches to service that are somewhat universal or are at least espoused by many of the industry's top educators. Travel agencies range across everything from a bank of telephone operators servicing over toll-free phone calls to exclusive, by-appointment-only agencies. With the increase in the number of outside sales agents, there is even a trend toward "house calls" in some areas.

The vast majority of agencies (over 90 percent) are small businesses doing less than $5 million a year in travel. Since the nominal commission is 10 percent, this means that their actual revenues are less than $500,000 per year. Therefore, the common setting is a small office with two to ten customer-contact employees. Most agents do a substantial amount of business both on the telephone and in person.

There are also a number of "mega-agencies." These are large multibranch agencies that often specialize in corporate travel. These agencies employ hundreds, even thousands, of people in many different locations. In each location there may be many agents who each have a small cubicle where they do the vast majority of business over the telephone. Some of these agencies may even have small offices co-located with their larger corporate accounts. In these instances the service settings vary significantly based on the atmosphere and culture of the client company. Agents here must learn to deal with both the customer's immediate setting and the culture and setting of their supervisors who are located at the agency's corporate offices.

The basic service delivery system, however, has many similarities regardless of the type and style of the individual agency (Figure 18-1). Customers enter the process, either in person or by electronic communication, and are routed to an agent. The main concern for customer-contact employees is to limit their waiting period. At industry standard manning levels, agents often have to phone back customers who call in. Some agents also develop appointment procedures to limit the waits for people who come in to conduct business face to face.

Next comes the information, consultation, and sales process. This encompasses the market search and advice functions of being a facilitator. It also is the most likely place for travel agents to generate satisfaction in their customers. Document processing, which includes deposits and payments as well as tickets and vouchers, can be a source of dissatisfaction if mistakes are made. However, customers expect accuracy, so this process focuses on hygiene factors, not satisfiers.

Travel agents usually try to position themselves as "professional consultants," not just order-takers. They want the public to think of them as professionals—similar to real estate brokers, stock brokers, and even doctors or lawyers—not as reservations agents. They usually refer to customers as "clients" to convey this sense of a professional agent–client relationship (although there recently has emerged a trend among some agents to be more aggressive and to use marketing savvy by taking a "retailer–customer" approach, like good department stores or specialty shops). Travel agents usually employ more personal follow-up techniques. Corporate salespeople will visit accounts, and

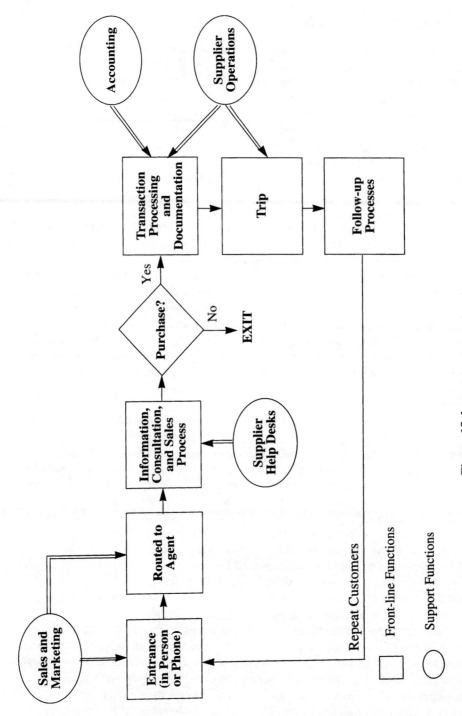

Figure 18-1 Travel agency service process.

leisure agents may send a thank-you card or call clients upon their return from a vacation. All these service techniques are designed to generate satisfaction after the service experience and to engender loyalty. Travel agents depend heavily on repeat clientele for their profitability.

Travel agencies probably have the smallest overhead structure of all the segments of the hospitality and tourism industry, and it shows in the service setting. They have no inventory other than the brochures and other reference material they need for their customers. In fact, there is almost no essential material other than a phone and some stationery. Of course, most travel agencies have some sort of storefront (some corporate-oriented agencies do not), so they need signage and office furniture. Almost all of them have computerized reservation systems (which are leased), and many have copiers, faxes, and so on. But not much else is needed.

QUESTIONS FOR REVIEW

1. Why are travel agents "facilitators"?
2. What four basic services do facilitators provide?
3. What three challenges does the travel agency industry face today?
4. Name three customer-contact positions in a travel agency.

QUESTIONS FOR DISCUSSION

1. Are travel agents just wasteful "middlemen"? Why or why not?
2. What are some opportunities for customer-contact employees in a travel agency to make favorable impressions on their customers?

GLOSSARY

Abilities A person's skills and capabilities.

Accessibility Basic expectation that customers have for quick and easy access to the right customer-contact employee to meet their needs.

Accommodation services All the services related to the room in which customers stay at a hotel or the cabin they have on a cruise ship.

Active watching Making an effort to look around one's surrounding to get as much information from visual sources as possible. These improved observation skills can help employees learn how better to meet customer needs.

Activities (1) In planning a service delivery system, these are the "things" that happen; (2) a term for the organized functions, games, and so on, that many hotel resorts and all cruise ships plan for their guests.

Advice One of the four basic functions of a service company that acts as a facilitator. Customers look to facilitators for expert advice about products, and suppliers look to facilitators for advice about how better to sell their product.

Agricultural age First age of society, when the economy was dependent on agriculture (roughly from the beginning of recorded history through the eighteenth century) and the majority of people worked in agricultural jobs.

Airport clubs Rooms at airports where airlines offer a quiet atmosphere, reading material, and business equipment away from the hustle and bustle of gate areas for passengers who have paid to join their club. These are particularly popular with business travelers.

Air/sea package   Popular cruise product that includes airfare, round-trip transfers between the airport and pier, and the cruise itself.

All-inclusive pricing   Travel product packages that include all meals, entertainment, taxes, and so on, as well as the transportation and lodging. This has worked well for the cruise industry and is increasing in popularity with hotels and tours since it lets customers know exactly how much a trip will cost rather than guessing at how much they'll have to spend on incidentals.

Allocentric   Personality trait that makes customers tend to want to be among the first to do something or try a new experience.

Amenity   Something that facilitates comfort (e.g., the bathroom kits in hotels or refresher kits on overnight airplane flights).

Americans with Disabilities Act (ADA)   Law passed in 1990 that requires all companies in the United States to provide equal access to all customers regardless of their physical or mental disabilities

Attitudes   A person's feelings, emotions, or opinions about a fact.

Attribution theory   Theory of motivation which says that customers will behave based on who they believe deserves credit or blame.

Automated call-routing system   Telephone system that answers the phone and asks the caller to press different buttons based on where they want their call to go.

Automated teller machine (ATM)   Computerized machine at banks that allows customers to deposit and withdraw money, ask for account balances, and pay back loans without interfacing with a customer-contact employee.

Automation   Use of computers and other technologically advanced machines to do work that used to require human labor.

Back office computer system   Computer system used to support a company's service delivery systems that do not need to be used during the service encounter.

Bell service   Term that hotels use for the services of taking luggage up to a customer's room upon check-in and taking it down to the lobby for checkout.

Bias   Impediments to effective communication that can come from preferences or disdain for a particular person or organization.

Boarding process   Procedure used by airlines to get customers and their carry-on luggage on board the aircraft.

Body language   Messages that can be sent by facial expressions, gestures and other body movements

Branch locations   Multiple locations for the same company that are coordinated and controlled out of a single headquarters (this is different from the multiple franchise locations that are independently owned and operated).

Business mission   Statement that clearly communicates the purpose of a company by identifying its customers, the types of goods and/or services it offers, and what distinguishes it from other organizations. A concise business mission statement is one of the three basic components of a sound service strategy.

Business relationship Ongoing association or affiliation between two companies that works to their mutual benefit.

Caveat emptor Translates as "Let the buyer beware." The business approach that puts most of the responsibility in the hands of the buyers to make sure that they are dealt with fairly. The prevailing American philosophy no longer does this, opting instead to put more of the responsibility in the hands of businesses.

Check-in Process that customers go through when they arrive to receive the services of an airline, hotel, tour operator, or cruise line. It includes a verification of reservation and other pertinent information.

Checkout Process that customers go through to leave a hotel, including reconciliation of their bill.

Communication flow Direction in which information travels within an organization: upward (from subordinates to their bosses), downward (from management to subordinates), or lateral (from peer to peer).

Communication model Analytical breakdown of communication into its specific parts: a *message* being transmitted by a *sender*, through a *channel*, to a *receiver*, who gives *feedback* to the sender.

Communications process Analytical breakdown of communication into the specific things that happen for it to occur—the *creation* of an idea that is *encoded* into symbols, *transmitted* to someone who *receives* and *decodes* the symbols, and then acts upon or *uses* that communication.

Communication technology Telephones, telefax machines, and other pieces of equipment that enhance a person's ability to send, retrieve, and process information.

Complementary transactions According to transactional analysis theory, these are interactions where the ego state of the sender gets a response from the desired or expected ego state of the receiver.

Conscious Thinking, reasoning, analytical part of a person that perceives things around them.

Consistency Basic expectation that customers have for being treated by customer-contact employees in the same way (from one customer-contact employee to another or from one day to another).

Constancy of purpose Service strategy that is clearly stated and understood and a business management approach that stays consistent with that strategy.

Consumerism Practice and policy of protecting consumers by making them aware of defective and unsafe products, misleading business practices, and so on.

Consumer sociology Study of society and groups within it, specifically pertaining to their activities and buying patterns as purchasers and users of goods and services.

Continuous improvement Approach of business that strives to improve systems "constantly and forever." Continuous-improvement practices realize that no system can ever be perfect, so management and employees must always seek new ways to do things better.

Continuous service   Service that is delivered constantly with no specific end (e.g., electricity, sewage, etc.).

Core service   Primary service or services that a company provides to its customers (i.e., hotels give lodging, tour operators provide a vacation experience, etc.).

Corrective actions   For each fail point in a service delivery system, these are the plans for recovering from the problem. By training customer-contact employees on how to correct known possible problems, companies can have standard solutions that have been proven to satisfy customers rather than risking the results of a "quick fix" that an employee creates under the stress of the moment.

Courtesy   Basic expectation that customers have for being treated with respect in a professional manner by customer-contact employees.

Crossed transactions   According to transactional analysis theory, these are interactions where the ego state of the sender gets a response from an ego state of the receiver that is different from the one desired or expected.

Cruise director   On a cruise ship, the person responsible for all the passenger-oriented activities on board.

Curbside check-in   Service offered by most airlines at most airports that allows customers to check their luggage with a person at the spot that an auto or bus drops them off.

Customer   Anyone who receives a service or product from someone else in exchange for something.

Customer feedback   Information regarding existing processes and suggestions for changes or improvements that come from customers based on their experiences using the products or services.

Customer flow   How customers are moved through a service delivery system. This includes how they move through a waiting line, pass from one customer-contact employee to another (e.g., from hotel check-in to bell service), and how they are handled in telephone transactions (switchboard operation, voice mail, etc.).

Customer focus   Service philosophy where the customer (whether internal or external) comes first.

Customer-friendly system   Service delivery system that is designed from customers' perspective so that every effort is made to make it as easy as possible for them to use.

Customer-oriented   Management philosophy or organizational culture that is based on the needs and desires of its customers. The tendency is to focus on what customers in the marketplace want and to develop products to meet those needs. Decisions are usually based on customer needs.

Customer participation   One of the characteristic differences between service products and manufactured products. It refers to the fact that for most services, customers must take an active role in the production of the service by communicating their needs, desires, and satisfaction levels to the customer-contact employee.

Customer's point of view   Perceptions and feelings that customers have about specific products and services or the companies that provide them.

Decision point   In planning a service delivery system, the point at which either customers or employees must decide between one or more options.

Demographics   Statistics of a particular human population, particularly with reference to size, density, distribution, and economic status.

Difference in perception   Impediment to effective communication which can come specifically from senders and receivers making different interpretations on the subtleties of a message. These are more likely to occur when senders and receivers come from different cultural, educational, or experiential backgrounds.

DINK   "Dual income, no kids."   A growing percentage of American population falls into this category which is outside the conventional nine life stages.

Direct competition   Competition within the hospitality and tourism industry (e.g., one hotel chain with another, or hotel resort vacations with cruise vacations).

Disclaimer   Written notification that a company or person is not responsible for any loss or damage from a particular product or service.

Discrete services   Services that have a specific start and end to their delivery.

Dissatisfiers   Things that when absent from a service encounter will generate customer satisfaction; however, their presence does not necessarily mean that customers will be satisfied.

Driving values   Set of clearly stated, well-understood corporate principles that can serve as a rallying point for all employees within a company. Stated driving values that are consistent with management decisions and behaviors are one of the three basic components of a sound service strategy.

Ego states   Psychological term for a consistent combination of thought-feelings and related behavior. There are three basic ego states—parent, child, and adult—and individual attitudes and behaviors can be attributed to which state a particular person is in at the time.

Emotional maturity   Degree to which people are able to control their reactions to outside stimuli despite an emotional desire to react differently.

Empathy   Basic expectation that customers have that customer-contact employees will look at things from their perspective and understand their feelings, attitudes, needs, and fears.

Employee involvement   Soliciting or allowing employees to make suggestions for changes or to take part in organized improvement activities.

Employee opinion survey   Organized written and/or verbal questionnaire that solicits information from employees about anything related to how their company functions.

Equity theory   Theory of motivation which says that customers will behave based on how they perceive others to be treated or based on what they perceive to be "fair."

Excursion fare   Discount prices for airline tickets. To qualify, customers must meet certain restrictions

Expectancy theory   Theory of motivation which says that customers will behave based on what they expect to get or how they expect to be treated.

Experience factor   Consideration that must be given to customers' degree of familiarity with a product or their life experience overall.

External customer   Person outside a company who purchases its products and services (e.g., traveler who stays in hotels, vacationer on a cruise, etc.).

Facilitators   Companies such as travel agencies that serve more as a broker of other companies' services rather than providing an end-service of their own.

Fail points   In planning a service delivery system, the place where something can go wrong.

Failure   Lack of success at something. In a customer-contact environment, this often should be viewed as a learning experience on the path to future success rather than as an end itself.

Fax machine   Shortened term for "telefacsimile machine," which is a machine that can send written information from one place to another via normal telephone lines.

Fear of success   Psychological phenomena in which people perform poorly because they are afraid of the potential consequences of success.

Filtering   Impediments to effective communication that can come when a sender intentionally sifts through.

First in, first out   Most common customer flow process in which the first person into the line (queue) is the first person served (e.g., hotel check-in, room service ordering, or a fast-food restaurant line).

First law of service   Satisfaction equals perception minus expectations. Customer satisfaction depends on how much they perceive the service equaled, exceeded, or fell short of their expectations.

Flattening the pyramid   Process of taking a company's management structure and reducing the number of levels between the chief executive and customer-contact employees. The purpose is to close the gap between the two to make the company more responsive.

Fluctuation of demand   Changes in customers' desire or need for products or services over time.

Formal communication   Official communication within an organization—whether verbal direction, written memos or office procedures, letters, and so on—which can be documented and controlled.

Frequent-buyer club   Group of customers that receives added benefits from using a company's products or services multiple times.

Frequent-flyer club   Standard peripheral service that all airlines offer which allows travelers to accrue credit toward future travel, upgrades, or merchandise based on how much they use the service product. Many hotels and other travel companies have instituted similar programs.

Front office computer system   Computer system used to service customers during a service encounter.

Full-service restaurant   Restaurant that offers a menu with a wide variety of selections and produces most food from scratch.

Grapevine   Slang term for how rumors spread throughout an organization.

Guest activities   Individual and group activities offered by resort hotels for the benefit of their customers. Depending on the resort, some are already included in the price of the customer's purchase.

Halo effect   Effect that a positive first impression makes that causes customers to overlook small problems because they are already satisfied with the organization. A poor first impression can have the opposite effect, causing customers to be looking for opportunities to feel dissatisfied.

High touch   System in which customers and customer-contact service providers have a high degree of personal contact.

Hotel manager   Person on a cruise ship who oversees and is responsible for all hotel services.

Hotel service   Part of a cruise ship's operation that is responsible for everything related to cabin and food and beverage service.

Hub-and-spoke system   Transportation system that has evolved for the airline system. Each airline has a few cities ("hubs") around the nation (or world) where it flies into and out of virtually all its destinations (the flights are the "spokes"). Most customers who want to go between two nonhub cities must fly on two different planes that connect through the hub.

Human resources development   Sstrategies, plans, and activities used by companies to educate and train their employees to be able to better meet the skills required in their current job as well as prepare them for their next one.

Imprecise/ambiguous language   Impediments to effective communication that can come from the use of words or sentences which can have more than one meaning or which leave room for receivers to misinterpret senders' desired messages.

Indirect competition   Competition between segments of the hospitality and tourism and other industries (e.g., travel as a discretionary expense competing with remodeling a home).

Industrial age   Second age of society, when the economy was dependent on manufacturing and industry (roughly, the nineteenth century through the late twentieth century) and the majority of people worked in industrial jobs.

In-flight services   Airline peripheral services such as meals, snacks, beverages, unaccompanied minor supervision, and so on.

Informal communication   Communication outside official channels within an organization which is virtually impossible to document or control. Informal communication is usually verbal.

Information age   Third age of society, in which the economy is dependent on information and services rather than manufactured goods (roughly, now through a period unknown) and the majority of people work in service-related jobs.

Intangibility   Something that cannot be touched or held. This is one of the characteristic differences between service products and manufactured products. Service products are "experiential" and intangible, while manufactured products can be touched, felt, and looked at.

Intangible services   Those services that deal more with recipients' frame of mind or act on their intangible assets

Internal customer   Person within a company who depends on the products or services of other people or departments within the company.

Introverted culture   Business environment where employees and management tend to look at things from their own perspective rather than their customers'.

Invisible services   Those services that customers do not see directly but are also a necessary part of the total product (e.g., accounting and billing). These are usually provided by support personnel.

Jargon   Abbreviation and slang used by people who have something in common (similar industry, same company, etc.). Jargon increases the efficiency of communication when both senders and receivers know the terms; however, it can be an impediment to effective communication when senders incorrectly assume that receivers understand the terms.

Job knowledge   Basic expectation customers have that customer-contact employees will know what it is that must be done to meet their needs and that their knowledge base is broad enough to answer routine questions about their company and its services.

Labor intensity   Ratio of labor-related costs to capital costs (costs of the physical plant and equipment).

Last in, first out   Customer flow process in which the last person into the line (queue) is the first person out (e.g., loading a bus for a tour).

Leadership   Act of setting a vision for a company and motivating employees to work together to achieve that vision.

Life stages   Different phases of life that people go through—from single to married to kids to empty nesters, and so on. Customers needs and motivations can change dramatically from one life stage to another.

Management-driven change   Alterations, modifications, or revisions to policies or procedures that result from management directing that the change(s) be made.

Market research   Analysis of what a particular market wants and will pay for as well as an analysis of what a company's competition is doing. Market research is one of the three basic components of a sound service strategy.

Market search　One of the four basic functions of a service company that is a facilitator. The market search function helps customers find the right product for them, and it helps their suppliers get access to customers who will want their product.

Market segmentation　Breaking up of a single large segment into various subsegments for the purpose of focusing a marketing effort. An excellent example is how the hotel industry has segmented to appeal to luxury vacationers (resorts), business travelers, long-term travelers, families, and so on.

Maslow's hierarchy of needs　Theory of motivation which suggests that human beings have five basic categories of needs: physiological, safety, social, ego, and self-actualization. People are not motivated to fill a higher-level need until they have at least minimally met all lower level needs.

Membership relationship　Situation when customers have a formal affiliation with a company or organization in which they "belong" to that company or organization and receive benefits for that membership.

Mentor　Senior person assigned to help a junior employee develop and grow as an employee.

Moment of truth　Interaction between a customer-contact employee and a customer which determines how the customer perceives the service company.

Money management　Planning, budgeting, organizing, and keeping control of one's money to get the most out of it.

Nonverbal communication　Any communication that occurs without the use of written or spoken words.

Nuclear family　Conventional household of American culture with a mother, father, and children all living at home.

Ombudsmen　Person in a company whose job it is to receive complaints about problems with people or services and investigate them.

Open-door policy　Policy that allows employees to feel comfortable going into the office of any of their supervisors or managers to discuss an issue of concern to them.

Operational terms　Stating a purpose or service strategy in a way that employees can understand and act on that statement.

Organizational culture　Basic pattern of attitudes and behaviors about what is right and wrong and how customers should be served, held by most employees within a company.

Overloading　Impediments to effective communication that can come to receivers who are receiving more information than they can handle.

People skills　Combination of communications skills and human behavior knowledge necessary to interact with others in customer-contact jobs.

Perceptions　View that customers have about the quality of service. This is a psychological phenomenon and not necessarily based on objective (or rational) criteria.

Peripherals   Input and output devices that are attached to a computer (i.e., printers, scanners, mouses, display terminals, etc.).

Peripheral services   Services other than core that companies offer their customers to give additional value to their products or to encourage customer loyalty (i.e., amenity kits at hotels, frequent flyer programs, check-cashing privileges, etc.).

Personal attention   Basic expectation that customers have for being treated by customer-contact employees as individuals with unique needs and not as just another name or number that must be dealt with before the shift is over.

Physiological needs   Lowest level of Maslow's hierarchy of needs, which includes the need for such things as food, water, and shelter.

Preferred-buyer program   Programs that identify customers who should get VIP treatment and extra amenities or benefits in exchange for their valued status as frequent users of higher-profit products or services.

Pride   Self-respect and high self-esteem; a joyous or elated feeling resulting from an accomplishment or association with a particular group of people.

Problem resolution   One of the four basic functions of a service company that is a facilitator. If something goes wrong with the end product, customers look to their facilitator for help in fixing the problem or receiving compensation for it.

Process improvement team   Organized group of people brought together to review a specific process at work and to recommend ways to make it work better.

Product-oriented   Management philosophy or organizational culture that is based on the features of the company's product. The tendency is to focus on how to get customers to buy the product, and decisions are based on what is good (or bad) for the company's products.

Professionalism   Dedication and responsibility demonstrated by employees who are held to high technical and ethical standards.

Proficiency   Degree to which employees are able to do their job

Progressive nature of service   Increasing level of expectations over time; the fact that what is satisfactory today may not be tomorrow.

Prosumer   Customer who is both a "pro"-ducer of goods or services and the con-"sumer" of them. The growth of self-help service establishments and advice-givers market to these customers, who either want the fun of doing it themselves, the cost savings of not having to pay for someone else to do it for them, or both.

Protection   One of the two purposes for which political and legal forces exist in the marketplace. Ideally, laws and political actions are meant to protect consumers and businesses from unfair treatment.

Proxemics   Study of territoriality and personal space.

Psychocentric   Personality trait that makes customers tend to want to wait until others have tried something so that they know the experience is within their comfort zone.

Purser　Person on a cruise ship who is responsible for handling passenger inquiries of any sort and helping out with whatever is needed. The purser is very similar to a hotel's concierge.

Quality circle　Group of employees, typically from the same work area or similar jobs, who meet regularly to discuss work-related problems.

Quality plan　Blueprint or strategy for providing high-quality products or services.

Recovery　How a company or a customer-contact employee makes up for mistakes or other problems.

Redress　One of the two purposes for which political and legal forces exist in the marketplace. Ideally, laws and political actions allow consumers or businesses that have been treated unfairly or illegally to recover the damage done by the person or company that did it.

Refresher training　Classes, seminars, and so on, that are given to experienced personnel for the purposes of teaching them new things, reminding them of things they already know and re-invigorating them for their current job.

Room steward　Person on a cruise ship responsible for the cleanliness and upkeep of passenger cabins.

Routing　Impediments to effective communication that can come from how a message gets to a receiver, rather than its contents

Safety needs　Second-lowest level of Maslow's hierarchy of needs, which includes the need for protection against physical dangers, threats, or deprivations.

Sales scale　Balance between the cost of providing a service and the revenue that it will generate.

Satisfiers　Things that when present in a service encounter will generate customer satisfaction; however, their absence does not necessarily mean that customers will be dissatisfied.

Second law of service　First impressions are the most important. Fair or not, customers will "judge a book by its cover."

Security screening　At an airport, the process of checking people and luggage to assure that no explosives, weapons, or other dangerous contraband is allowed on board.

Self-actualization　Highest level of Maslow's hierarchy of needs which includes the need for achieving one's true potential and for feeling at peace with one's own abilities and achievements.

Self-esteem　(1) A person's attitude about his or her own capabilities and self-worth; (2) The second-highest level of Maslow's hierarchy of needs, which includes the need for achievement, status recognition, and prestige.

Self-fulfilling prophecy　Phenomenon in which people visualize either success or failure and subconsciously work toward that end, whether or not it is consciously desired.

Self-help system　Computer system that allows customers to service themselves without the assistance of a customer-contact employee.

Semantics   Impediment to effective communication that may occur when senders and receivers interpret the subtle meaning of words in slightly different ways.

Service   Anything of value, other than physical goods, which one person or organization provides another person or organization in exchange for something.

Service customization   Degree to which services are able to be delivered differently to each customer in relation to their needs and desires.

Service hardware   Physical "stuff" of service delivery systems.

Service-oriented management theory   Management theory that puts customers at the top of the organization chart and thus recognizes the importance of customer-contact employees. It structures companies in a way that empowers these employees to be as responsive as possible to customer needs.

Service setting   Environment in which a service transaction occurs. The service setting often gives customers their first perception about the company.

Service software   Methodologies and procedures used in service delivery systems.

Service strategy   Organizing principle that allows people in a service enterprise to channel their efforts toward benefit-oriented services that make a significant difference in the eyes of their customers.

Simultaneity   Two or more events that happen at the same time. One of the characteristic differences between service products and manufactured products is the simultaneity of the production and consumption of most service products.

Slang   Nonstandard language common to a particular group of people. It can be an impediment to effective communication when senders use it with receivers who are not familiar with it.

Smile training   Service training "programs" that emphasize how customer-contact employees should be "nice" to customers or have "a better attitude" dealing with them in order to provide good service without really addressing the necessary organizational structure and service delivery system design concerns that are necessary to provide a solid foundation for providing service.

Social needs   Middle level of Maslow's hierarchy of needs, which includes the need for friendship, love, affection, and a sense of belonging.

Sociology   Study of the development, structure, and function of human groups and their interactions between themselves and society as a whole.

Span of control   Number of people/departments managers have reporting directly to them.

Specialty restaurant   Any restaurant that is not full service and which uses a combination of limited menus and/or preprocessed food or ingredients. These include fast food, cafeteria, ethnic restaurants, and pizza parlors.

Status/authority barrier   Impediment to effective communication that can be the result of senders and receivers being of a different level of position, status, knowledge, or authority.

Stereotyping   Impediment to effective communication that can come from assuming that everyone within a particular group of people shares a similar set of characteristics.

Structural barrier   Impediment to effective communication that can come from the size, style, and organizational design of a company.

Subconscious   Those thoughts and ideas that exist within a person's mind but are not immediately available to their consciousness.

Suggestion system   Way for employees (or external customers) to provide ideas for changes and improvements in the way their company operates.

Supplier   (1) Anyone who produces work that someone else benefits from; (2) a term for a company that provides services or products to another company; (3) the term travel agencies use to refer to the airlines, hotels, tour operators, cruise lines, and so on, which provide the end service to their customers.

Synergy   Whole effect of a system being greater than the sum of the individual effects of the parts of that system.

System design   Process of planning a service delivery system by identifying what activities must occur, where decision points are, what the timelines and necessary resources allocations will be, where fail points can occur, and what corrective actions ought to be taken.

System focus   Organizational philosophy that focuses on all work as part of one or more processes. Each process uses some form of input, manipulates it, and produces output.

Tangible services   Those services that give recipients a thing or which act physically on themselves or their property

Teamwork   Basic expectation that customers have that customer-contact employees in a given company will work together harmoniously to meet their needs.

Telecommunications services   Telephone-related services in a hotel, including the operator, message taking, and wake-up calls.

Telemarketing   Promotion and sale of products through the use of telephones to contact potential customers.

Telephone transaction   Service encounter that occurs through verbal communication on a telephone only (i.e., no face-to-face encounter).

Third law of service   Service-oriented attitude alone will not assure good service. Hospitality and tourism companies must also organize and staff for customer service, design their systems to be customer friendly, and educate and train their employees in both technical and service skills.

Time management   Planning, budgeting, organizing, and keeping control of one's time in order to be as productive as possible.

Timeline   In planning a service delivery system, this takes the flow of activities and attaches specific time intervals to each in order to plan for appropriate resources.

Timing Impediment to effective communication that can come from when a message is received rather than its contents.

Toll-free number Phone number that allows callers to call long distance and automatically bill the receiving number rather than the caller.

Trade press Newspapers, magazines, and so on, dedicated to a specific industry or industry segment.

Traditional management theory Business management philosophy that places the importance of senior executives at the top and customer-contact employees at the bottom. Executives or managers must make decisions about anything that varies from "standard operating procedures," and customer-contact employees are given little to empower them to handle nonroutine matters during a moment of truth.

Transactional analysis Psychological theory that examines the interactions of human beings based on their current ego states.

Transaction processing One of the four basic functions of a service company that is a facilitator. Paperwork and money passes through the hands of facilitators in the course of bringing their customers and suppliers together for a sale.

Two-factor theory Theory of motivation which suggests that motivators can be split into two categories (1) dissatisfiers are those things whose absence generates dissatisfaction but whose presence may not generate satisfaction, and (2) satisfiers whose absence may not generate dissatisfaction but whose presence will generate satisfaction.

Ulterior transactions According to transactional analysis theory, these are interactions where the ego state of either the sender or the receiver hides the real message in words that appear to be complimentary. This happens most often when people want to couch their intended meaning in a socially acceptable manner.

Visible services Those services that customers see directly in the process of receiving a company's product. By definition, these are delivered by customer-contact employees or an automated service device.

Waiver Statement signed by customers which acknowledges that a company or person is not responsible or liable for a particular problem or loss suffered by that customer.

Walk-in traffic Term for customers who come in person to a hospitality or tourism establishment without a specific reservation.

Work flow How work is routed and controlled in a company. In general, offices are organized based on individual employees being trained either to have generalized capability to handle almost any transaction or to specialize in handling only a few types of transactions.

INDEX